THE UNINTENDED CONSEQUENCES OF SOCIAL ACTION

Also by Raymond Boudon

THE CRISIS IN SOCIOLOGY
THE USES OF STRUCTURALISM
THE LOGIC OF SOCIOLOGICAL EXPLANATION
MATHEMATICAL STRUCTURES OF SOCIAL MOBILITY
EDUCATION, OPPORTUNITY AND SOCIAL INEQUALITY

The Unintended Consequences of Social Action

Raymond Boudon

St. Martin's Press   New York

All rights reserved. For information, write:
St. Martin's Press, Inc., 175 Fifth Avenue, New York, NY 10010
Printed in Hong Kong
First published in the United States of America in 1982

ISBN 0–312–83303–2

Library of Congress Cataloging in Publication Data

Boudon, Raymond.
  The unintended consequences of social action.

  Includes bibliographical references and indexes.
  1. Social action. I. Title.
HM51.B763   1982   361.6′13   81–21372
ISBN 0–312–83303–2   AACR2

Contents

Acknowledgements

The author and publishers wish to thank the following for permission to reprint the author's articles:

International Social Science Council for the article 'Social justice and general interest', published in *Social Science Information*, 14 (3/4) 1975; *Minerva* and with the permission of the co-authors Philippe Cibois and Janina Lagneau, for the article 'Short-cycle higher education and the pitfalls of collective action', vol. xiv, no. 1 (Spring 1976); Transaction Inc., for the article 'The French University since 1968' published in *Comparative Politics*, vol. 10, no. 1, © 1977 by the City University of New York.

1 Introduction: Sociology and Freedom

> *This observation gives me the opportunity to state what I take to be the* main task of the theoretical human sciences. It consists in identifying the non-intentional social repercussions of intentional human actions.
>
> Karl Popper, *Conjectures and Refutations*.

Economists are familiar with perverse effects. In a period of inflation it is in my interest to buy a product that will only be of use to me in the coming month, for I am almost certain that its price will then be higher. In doing this I help to perpetuate inflation. My behaviour has only an infinitesimal influence in this respect, but the logic of the situation dictates that many people should behave just as I do. Together these infinitesimal individual influences generate a social effect.

Effects of this kind, often termed perverse effects or effects of composition, do not only appear in the sphere of economic life. There is no reason, after all, why they should be limited to this sphere. In fact it would not be at all excessive to assert that they are present everywhere in social life and that they represent one of the fundamental causes of social imbalances and of social change.

Many familiar phenomena are the manifestation or the consequence of perverse effects, or again the result of attempts made by the collectivity to eliminate them. Take the queue that forms outside the baker's door on Sunday, after Mass. To account for this phenomenon, we must of course explain why cakes are associated with the Sunday ritual. But we must also explain why a significant number of people are prepared to queue for half an hour and thus undergo a meaningless and psychologically disagreeable wait. In fact these people are *forced* to wait because the rate at which they arrive bears no relation to the rate at which the baker is able to serve them. As a result each person imposes an unwanted wait on the others. Each person on their own intends nothing more than to purchase some cakes, but the convergence of a whole number of such behaviours results in an undesirable *social* consequence: a loss of time imposed by all on each and by each on all, without this loss having been intended by any single person.

Now consider a familiar institution: traffic lights. Why does everyone accept with such a good grace the thousands of minor irritations that having to stop at a red light causes? Because it is clear that, without red lights, traffic would be still more of a problem. Red lights are meant to reduce the perverse effects that would ensue from the juxtaposition of individual journeys which, at any given moment, followed intersecting trajectories. It is important to note that the diminution or the elimination of a perverse effect always implies disagreeable consequences both for individuals and for the collectivity. There is a price to pay for the elimination of a perverse effect: the cost of the lights, the presence of police officers, the irritation felt at the lights. One could certainly imagine less *authoritarian* and less *repressive* solutions. One could envisage a democratic procedure whereby each motorist would undertake with the others to make his journeys – say, over the coming week – according to a time, a speed and a route approved by collective decision. There is no need to dwell on the manifest absurdity of such a solution: this form of organisation would be so ponderous that it would be clearly preferable to give up trying to eliminate the perverse effect produced by the uncoordinated juxtaposition of journeys rather than rid oneself of them at such a prohibitive cost.

A perverse effect is not only maintained because of the prohibitive cost involved in eliminating it. Another basic pattern is that in which the neutralisation of a perverse effect necessarily produces the undesirable neutralisation of collectively and individually desirable effects. This pattern is very common and numerous examples are to be found in this book.

The simple examples just cited bring to mind what Henri Lefebvre, Harold Garfinkel and the *ethnomethodologists* would call the *critique of everyday life*. These authorities automatically confer a theoretical dignity on these examples. Moreover they have the advantage of showing that phenomena of everyday life, however concrete, banal and familiar they may be, call for a relatively abstract, complex and unfamiliar analysis. Without having recourse to the technical orchestration of game theory it is difficult to give a clear account of the abstract structure of the traffic lights or the queue at the door of the baker's. For if the phenomena under discussion are familiar, the same is scarcely true of their structure. This is why their discovery hardly dates back beyond the end of the eighteenth century.

I would stress, at the start, that these remarks lay no claim to originality. It is well known (Merton has pointed it out in a classic text)[1] that the discovery of what we today call perverse effects goes back to Mandeville, Smith, Rousseau and to various other philosophers who can properly be reckoned among the most important precursors of sociology.

But this basic observation of Merton's has remained largely a dead letter. Perverse effects are as rare in modern sociological analysis as they are common in social life. Up to and including Marx, the tradition of Mandeville, Smith and Rousseau was preserved and enriched. For, as Nisbet has opportunely observed, Marx belongs by virtue of both his intellectual orientation and his methodology to the Enlightenment. After Marx however this tradition is interrupted in sociology. Only a few names, apart from that of Merton himself, spring to mind. I could cite Lewis Coser in the United States and Michel Crozier in France as examples. Apart from rare exceptions of this sort, the great majority of sociologists would seem to have made very little of these *contradictions*, as Hegel and Marx would have put it, that perverse effects represent.

It was not by reading manuals or the classics of modern sociology that I came to realise their significance. Merton's text on *creative prediction* struck me on first reading as a dazzling piece of purple prose. But it is only now that I perceive its range and generality. Predictions sometimes have a tendency to come true of themselves, not because those who utter them are able to read God's plans, but because a prediction becomes a social fact the moment it is uttered. If a significant number of people placed in comparable situations come to entertain the same beliefs and utter the same predictions, one may well be witnessing the birth of a perverse effect. In this case it takes the form of an actual realisation of the predictions concerned. During the *Great Depression*, a collective belief in the insolvency of banks, by precipitating simultaneous withdrawals, caused many of them to go bankrupt.

Merton's text convincingly shows that perverse effects play a vital role not only in economic phenomena but also, and in the same way, in phenomena traditionally considered the sociologist's preserve.

In my case it was in the sociology of education that I at first unwittingly and certainly involuntarily came across structures that featured various forms of perverse effect. In *L'Inégalité des Chances*[2] I tried to show that, since the Second World War, the logic of the individual demand for education has produced a mass of collective and individual perverse effects in industrial societies. I mean that the mere juxtaposition of individual actions has produced collective and individual effects that were not necessarily undesirable but in any case had not been included among the actors' explicit objectives. The gains in productivity that probably resulted from the growth in the individual demand for education clearly had nothing at all to do with those individuals' actual objectives. The effect of composition here worked to the advantage of both the collectivity and the individuals who composed it. Unfortunately this same phenomenon produced effects that were negative *individually* and doubtless *collectively* too. The educational investment needed to reach a given level in the scale of socio-professional status is greater for everyone now than it was before. This increase in the cost of social status (to the individual) is certainly only marginally due to the effects of technical progress on the qualifications needed for particular jobs. Apart from this it is the manifestation of a perverse effect, and one that is clearly undesirable both individually and collectively, since it contributes to an unchecked increase in the cost of the educational system for the collectivity. The same increase in the individual demand for education may well have produced another effect by contributing to the increase in wage differentials. Finally it clearly neutralised the positive effects on social mobility that could reasonably have been expected to occur as education became more democratic. This case is therefore fascinating, not only because of the multiplicity of the effects generated but also because of their *multidirectionality*.

Once I had realised their importance in the field it occurred to me to try and draw up an inventory of sociological works in which perverse effects were discussed. It wasn't too hard to find a few: the iron law of oligarchy in Michel's work; the low level of union and political participation typical of the democracies; Tocqueville's paradox (which states that the French Revolution was made possible by the rapid increase in the welfare of all in the preceding period); Durkheim's famous proposition (that an increase in collective welfare may well produce a decrease in individual happiness). The famous Durkheimian theory of *anomie* can be read as an account of the perverse consequences produced by various competitive structures. Many examples of the perverse effect have of course been collected in the field of the sociology of organisations. A mention of Deutsch's paradox[3] should suffice: assume the existence of a very large organisation in which numerous decisions have to be taken. Imagine, moreover, that the validity of these decisions can be unequivocally assessed and that numerous people are in a position to contribute to this assessment. A process of this kind will lead inevitably to a reputation for wisdom being conferred on particular people, even when those who participated (in a school, for instance) decided which options to follow simply by drawing lots.

Thus perverse effects are at work, not only in the familiar phenomena of daily life but in every single sociological domain: political sociology, the sociology of education, theories of stratification, theories of mobility and many others. The critical importance of Merton's article on creative prediction must therefore be admitted.[4] This text dates from 1936 and is so far as I know the first *theoretical* text by a sociologist on the ubiquity of perverse effects in social life and, consequently, on their crucial importance for sociological analysis.

Since the notion of perverse effect is the central theme of the book, it would seem right to clarify some of the terms I will be using here. In the preceding pages I have used the notion of perverse effect in a very wide sense. This included undesired though desirable effects and undesired and undesirable effects. I recognise that the phrase 'perverse effect' fits the second pattern better. I will, however, defend my choice of terms with the help of two arguments. The first appeals to the authority of Goethe. Mephistopheles, in those famous lines that so clearly bear the mark of the political philosophy of the Enlightenment, defines himself as 'a part of that force which always intends evil and always does good' (*Ein Teil von jener Kraft/ die stets das Böse will und stets das Gute schafft*).[5] It is not difficult to accept that, even if it does produce individually and collectively positive effects, the perverse effect is a very apt term with which to describe the spirit of evil. My second argument proceeds as follows. The perverse mechanisms that are most significant socially are those that end up producing *undesirable* effects, those that are in everyday parlance called perverse. By creating unwanted and often unexpected social imbalances, they play a vital role in social change. In other circumstances I will use the phrase 'effect of composition' or 'undesired effect' to designate a perverse effect. Each phrase has its drawbacks. The first is not especially informative and the second suggests that undesired effects are necessarily undesirable. This is not necessarily so. I have sometimes used the phrase 'effect of aggregation' as well. This phrase is perhaps more telling than 'effect of composition' but there is the disadvantage that it borrows a classic concept from normative economics whilst warping its original meaning.

Over and above terminological difficulties, the important thing is to understand the definition of these effects. Let me repeat: it is a question of individual and collective effects that result from the juxtaposition of individual behaviours and yet were not included in the actors' explicit objectives. This definition suggests several different configurations. I have already presented examples of some of these. Individuals may actually attain the objectives they were pursuing but may also have to put up with some unwanted discomfort (the queue in front of the baker's). They may attain both the objective sought after and also reap some unsought benefits (individual profits resulting from rises in productivity that the increased demand for education produces). They may attain their individual objectives but produce collective ills as well (an increase in the going price of social status produced by the increased demand for education), or alternatively they may produce collective advantages that had not been explicitly sought (the 'invisible hand' of Adam Smith). But individuals may also *fail to attain* the objectives they set themselves even though they avail themselves of what are in a way the best means to attain them. A military escalation may thus lead to considerable losses for the antagonists and still end unresolved. Not only may they obtain an individual result other than the desired one, the may also produce both collective advantages and collective disadvantages not cited in their objectives. Finally I must introduce a last and crucial distinction: collective advantages and disadvantages produced at the same time (i.e., those not included among the actors' objectives) may be advantages and disadvantages for some participants but not for all: the greater wage differentials that the increased demand for education may well produce is clearly a bad thing for some and a good thing for others. The same applies in those cases in which only some participants attain their objectives. Structures of competition are the most vivid illustration of this.

The number of possible recombinations of the following criteria does, therefore, define the number of possible configurations:

1. No participant (1a), some participants (1b), all participants (1c) attain their individual objectives;

2. Producing, at the same time, benefits (2a) or problems (2b) or else collective benefits and problems (2c);

3. Each of these applying only to some (3a) or to all the participants (3b).

Numerous illustrations of one or other of these configurations will be presented below.

My aim in this book is to restate the case that Merton in 1936 made for what could be called the paradigm of the perverse effect. There is little point, though, in discoursing on a paradigm in an abstract fashion. If one wants to argue for a paradigm's general pertinence today, the best thing is to present a wide range of examples of it in actual use. This is why I have chosen to tackle my subject by juxtaposing a number of texts, each of which represents an encounter with the paradigm. Two of these texts 'Educational Institutions and Perverse Effects: (1) After 1968; (2) Short-Cycle Higher Education' represent an extension of the treatment given in my *L'Inégalité des Chances*. It is used in phenomena pertaining to the sociology of education and to the politics of education. One text ('The Logic of Relative Frustration') is an attempt to elicit the abstract structure common to both Tocqueville's paradox and to the Durkheimian theory of *anomie*. Another wider-ranging text shows how important perverse effects are in social change ('Perverse Effects and Social Change'). Finally in two general texts I strive to demonstrate the implications of the ubiquity of perverse effects for sociological theory ('Social Determinisms and Individual Freedom') and social philosophy ('Perverse Effects and Social Philosophy: Rawls's Theory of Justice').

For this ubiquity does in fact have immediate consequences for both the paradigms used to analyse the social order (sociological theory) and the normative conceptions that people may have of this order (social philosophy).

In the first case the very notion of perverse effect implies the notion of action. A perverse effect can only occur in an analytic framework in which the sociological subject, *homo sociologicus*, is thought to be moved by the objectives he has in mind and the way he represents their eventual realisation to himself. There is thus a logical contradiction between the perverse effect paradigm and those paradigms in which *homo sociologicus* is always depicted as a creature moved by social forces exterior to him. There is, in other words, a fundamental incompatibility between this paradigm and the contemporary sociological model of a *homo sociologicus* whose actions would have no more reality than that of responses determined by social 'structures'. The image of a 'rational' *homo sociologicus* is not implied in the perverse effect paradigm but the image of an 'intentional' one is.

To sum up: the paradigm necessarily raises questions as to the way actions are represented in sociological theory. As a consequence one is also led to wonder what sort of status the concept of freedom should properly enjoy in sociological theory. I would in the last analysis argue that, if one cannot specify the degree of freedom that social agents, taking structural constraints into account, enjoy in any given situation, one is left with profoundly unsatisfactory sociological theories. There are sociologists who resort to the fiction of the social subject who has no other choice but to submit to the programming that social structure imposes on him, but these positions seem to me to be doomed to sterility. Social structures do sometimes impose compulsory choices on the individual, but if these are not interpreted as extreme cases, one deprives oneself of any credible interpretation of the phenomena (such as social conflicts and social change) that the sociologist makes it his business to analyse. I have tried to tackle these difficult questions in the text 'Social determinations and individual freedom' but I do not claim to have done anything more than assemble the basic constituents for an answer. In any case there is one thing on which, rightly or wrongly, I will stand absolutely firm: the sociologist cannot neglect the question of freedom without exposing himself to serious criticism.

Other immediate consequences of the ubiquity of perverse effects pertain, as I have indicated, to social philosophy, that is to normative representations of the social order. They can be quickly summarised: the ubiquity of perverse effects casts considerable doubt on what I would call cybernetic utopias, or utopias that represent societies as programmed or open to programming.[6] As modern industrial societies grow in complexity they seem to me, contrary to modern belief, to move further away from the ideal (or the nightmare) of general programming rather than drawing closer to it. Possibilities of genetic engineering will perhaps in the near future destroy the quasi-equilibrium between the sexes which, in very broad terms, was assured and could therefore pass as 'natural'. Technical progress, which is an indisputable feature of industrial societies, provides the occasion for new forms of perverse effect to develop. The example of pollution demonstrates this very clearly. The general increase in resources that members of a society have at their disposal, by enlarging their set of options, is another tendency potentially generative of perverse effects. It seems to me therefore that contradictions that do not culminate in a synthesis and chronic conflicts are far more characteristic of industrial societies than the general programming that some wish for and others dread. I have tried to grapple with these fundamental and difficult facts in my critique of Rawls's *The Theory of Justice*, a work that is typical of the programmers' utopias. The great weakness of this theory lies in its underestimation of the importance of perverse effects. Moreover Rawls does not seem to realise that, all else being equal, these effects grow in importance as individual freedom grows (where 'individual freedom' is taken to mean the list of behaviours that an individual may adopt of his own accord, without the at least tacit approval of others).

I would like to make two further points. I gave above an implicit definition of the complex notion of perverse effect according to the meaning I give to this expression in this book. The eighteen different configurations within this typology have a common denominator: the existence of effects that the actors did *not explicitly intend*. The typology indicates that these effects may be positive, negative, or positive and negative at the same time, for some or for all, and that, besides this, the actors (all or some of them) may or may not attain their objectives. I would first of all like to point out that one more criterion must be added to this series: sometimes the observer must ask himself if these perverse effects (to be more precise, if *each* of these perverse effects) were not only unintended (perverse effects are always that by definition) but also whether they were foreseen or unforeseen, that is, foreseeable or unforeseeable. The second case, that of unforeseen perverse effects, corresponds to Merton's *unanticipated consequences*. But perverse effects may, in certain cases, be foreseeable and may be foreseen. One cannot assume that just because they may be foreseen that they definitely will be, even when they are negative for everyone and when they could be avoided. There are numerous applications of this basic proposition below. In other words I propose to consider Merton's unanticipated effects as a particularly important sub-class of *perverse effects*.

I will return to my second point several times in the course of the text. An axiomatic structure organised around the concept of the *homo sociologicus* is employed in several of the analyses hereafter: he is taken to be an intentional actor, endowed with a set of preferences, seeking acceptable ways of realising his objectives, more or less conscious of the degree of control that he has over the elements of the situation in which he finds himself (conscious, in other words, of the structural constraints that limit his possibilities of action), acting in the light of limited information and in a situation of uncertainty. In short the key feature of the concept of *homo sociologicus* used here is *limited rationality*. In taking up Hayek's term once more I take the liberty of insisting on his crucial distinction between limited and absolute rationality. In some but not in all cases this distinction may, for didactic or methodological reasons, be abandoned. But the notion of limited rationality is the only one with any pretensions to realism. I should moreover add that I do not, in what follows, mean either implicitly or explicitly to deny that there are times when this model may be false or inappropriate. There are circumstances in which actors have a set of objectives but at the same time have a consistently false notion of the means available for their realisation. There may be circumstances in which individuals' preferences work against their own best interests. The texts included here are, in part, meant to show that this model does in fact enjoy a wide range of applications. There is, implicit in this assertion, an unequivocal refusal of sociologism, that is, of the doctrine that holds that the social agent's intentions and actions should always be considered as effects and never as causes.

As the reader will have gathered, the present book is not a continuous text but a compilation of essays and articles written at different times and in different contexts. At the risk of some repetition I have kept most of the texts in their original form. Effects of composition and their significance for sociological analysis constitute its *leitmotif*. Variations are then grafted on to this basic theme: no effects of composition without a sociological subject endowed with the capacity for action and intention; the importance of effects of composition for social change; a convergence between the old notions of the dialectic and contradiction (in their acceptable form) and the notion of the unintended consequences of intentional actions that Popper, Hayek and Merton elucidate; contradictions between perverse effects and social order. These variations often depend on examples taken from the sociology of education, of mobility, of stratification, since these are the fields in which I have worked most these last few years. I am well aware that of the assertions presented in the texts assembled here many suffer from a lack of sufficient proof, and that some of the analyses are little more than sketches (this observation applies especially to Chapter 7 on 'Social determinisms and individual freedom' and to Chapter 5 on 'The logic of relative frustration'.) In future publications I hope to develop, in a systematic way, some of the questions for sociological theory that are posed here. But I thought it useful, all the same, to pose them at this intermediate stage.

2 Perverse Effects and Social Change

From its handling of social change it might appear that sociology had come out of the nineteenth century backwards. For some the class struggle is still the dominant factor in an evolutionary process conceived as necessary. For others technological 'progress' leads inevitably to a global social transformation. Development of the means of mass communication, advances in molecular biology, the proliferation of multi-nationals, the intellectuals and holders of knowledge: one or other of these, according to one's preference, is proposed as the bearer of what Hegel had called *Geschichtlichkeit*, historicity.

Localised changes clearly have induced interminable chain reactions. It seems proven that the introduction of the metal plough caused important social changes at the global level. It is true that social conflicts and conflicts between social classes in particular (or, more accurately, between 'organisations' representing social classes more or less directly) have, in some historical conjunctures, caused effects of irradiation extending to whole societies. There are circumstances in which particular categories of social agent may play an especially important role, as students did in the 1960s. These incontestably significant examples do not in themselves however constitute the basis for a general theory of social change.

Besides effects of irradiation and conflicts due to the clashes of interest between social groups, perverse effects constitute an important source for social change. The educational crisis of the 1960s is clearly attributable to this sort of effect: the belief that massive increases in education could only bring benefits was belied by the facts. Equality of educational opportunity did not bring with it equality of social opportunity and whilst naïve theories treat this contradiction as if it were the product of an opposition between a dominant and a dominated class, it is a simple matter to show that this hypothesis does not work and that the contradiction does in fact derive from perverse effects.

States of tension or political crisis are also, as modern political sociology shows, the result of a perverse effect of this sort. I accept that political tensions are sometimes produced by clashes of interests, but I would regard such occurrences as exceptional. Michels, and later Olson, have shown that representative institutions have an oligarchical tendency that often gives rise to political tensions. It is perverse effects that are the cause of this. Rousseau, and more recently, Hotelling, Hirschman, Buchanan, and Tullock have shown how impossible it is to define institutions in a way that that would guarantee that the interests of each were fairly represented. Injustices, inequalities and conflicts are not necessarily produced by domination; the interdependence of social agents, and the impossibility of defining an optimal organisation of that interdependence, may also be held responsible.

Analysis of the educational and political domains thus shows that social crises and social change are often the result, not of the mechanical effect of 'dominant' factors or of conflicts having a zero sum game structure, but of perverse effects generated by the interdependence of social agents.

This text was prepared for the 4th International Congress on 'Mutations: Biology and Society', organised by the René Descartes University (Paris V) (The International Organisation for the Study of Human Development, Paris, February 1977).

> *History is nothing if it is not the activity of men in pursuit of their objectives.*
> Karl Marx, *The Holy Family.*

Sociologists have always been tempted by the Utopian notion of finding the key to social change and therefore of being able to reduce the uncertainty of the future. The nineteenth century is full of attempts to ascertain the supposed laws of history. By demonstrating the contradictory nature of the project, Karl Popper[1] has put paid once and for all to these attempts. Failing to identify the laws of social history, sociologists have also been obsessed with the search for the fundamental *factor* in change. The organisation of the production of goods, the unequal distribution of wealth and of power have been proposed, with greater or lesser success, for this role. Most sociologists are now convinced that the search for historical laws and for the dominant factors in change is a blind alley.

The only effective research generally carried out nowadays involves the identification of typical processes of change in the hope that these patterns will eventually be integrated within a broader theoretical framework. Gabriel Tarde[2] saw in biological processes of contagion a model that offered analogies with processes of social change. We know that some forms of social change have this kind of structure, but not all do. Some have taken technical and scientific innovation to be the main motor of change. Thanks to Lynn White's writings[3] we are now in a better position to appreciate the flood of changes that the invention of the metal ploughshare precipitated, and Henri Mendras' classic study[4] does the same for the introduction of hybrid maize. In these cases an invention, once a particular threshold has been crossed, produces change through a chain of irradiation effects. Although this form of change is quite frequent, it remains a special case. Numerous authors have taken clashes of interest to be the principal cause of change. Some, like Marx, deemed that the conflicts most charged with the potential for change, or as the German philosophers would have put it, with *Geschichtlichkeit*, were conflicts over the ownership of the means of production. Today we tend to think that conflicts over the distribution of power and authority are more important. This tendency marks Alain Touraine's work,[5] and more especially, that of Ralph Dahrendorf.[6] In fact, even in modern industrial societies, conflicts over the distribution of power are not the only ones charged with the potential for social change. Numerous contemporary conflicts involve the boundary dividing public and private domains (consider, for instance, the privatisation of abortion and, in a general sense, the diminishing public control over sexuality, morality and culture). It is therefore impossible to maintain that one particular class of conflicts is the privileged source of social change. One can take this argument further: although social change is often associated with clashes of interest, it does not have to stem from them. The invention of the wheel was probably just as important a source of change as the private ownership of the means of production. In the same way change often stems from a dislocation between customs and institutions and, consequently, from a conflict between institutions and social groups rather than from conflict between opposed social groups. In this case conflict signifies incompatibility not confrontation.

Depending on circumstances, social change may therefore be due to conflicts or oppositions of interest, to dislocations or conflicts (the word 'conflict' here implies the sense of contradiction) between institutions, or to localised changes that generate effects of irradiation. In other words the plurality of processes of change would seem to be irreducible. This being so, it seems necessary to accept the existence (and the irreducibility) of several different forms of social change.

I want here to advance the analysis of social change by isolating one of the basic mechanisms involved, that of the perverse effect. I will therefore assert (to give a brief description of the mechanism) that there is a perverse effect when two (or more) individuals, in pursuing a given objective, generate an *unintended* state of affairs which may be undesirable from the point of view of both or one of them.

A classic example, taken from Jean-Jacques Rousseau's political writings, will serve to illustrate this notion. Re-read the hunting party narrative. This narrative plays a vital part in the second *Discourse* and clearly provides the key to many of the contradictions (in the logical sense of the term) between the *Discourse* and the *Contract*, contradictions whose existence was always vehemently denied by Rousseau. Two 'savages', who are defined as egotistical, hedonistic and rational, decided to change their usual diet of hare and set out on a stag hunt.[7] Although he lives in a state of abundance, the 'savage' is presumed to be incapable of overcoming a stag on his own. The two hunters are presumed to be rational enough to know how to set about achieving their aims, so once these are settled, they take up their positions for the hunt. But the hunting partly fails because Rousseau has attributed to the 'savage' an axiomatic structure which lacks the sentiment of loyalty. The first to see a hare pass therefore abandons his post.

The hunters had set themselves a clear enough objective, they were endowed with rationality, there was no hostility between them and nature had been lavish in the goods it had placed at their disposal, and yet, in spite of all these things, they were still incapable of getting what they wanted. This example shows us a perverse effect of exemplary purity. Rousseau's theorem clearly therefore implies the following corollary: even in perfect conditions cooperation presupposes loyalty. In other words each of the two associates must pledge themselves not to defect. It is clear that the *Social Contract* rests on this prior theorem from the *Discourse*. The first of these works is far from being a eulogy to the state of nature, with the second a kind of hymn of praise to the social order: the second is in fact a logical consequence of the first. So the famous expression 'to force man to be free' is a contradiction not in the logical sense of the word but in the dialectical sense: the structure of interaction implicit in the *Discourse on the Origins of Inequality* means that the two savages can only be sure of attaining the objective that they freely chose to pursue if they accept being forced to realise it. The elimination of perverse effects generated in a state of nature is brought about by the introduction of constraint in cases in which it is hardly realistic to await the appearance of loyalty (as when one is dealing not with two but with a significant number of actors).

It is worth stressing the kinship between these critical moments in the development of Rousseau's political theory and what we today call game theory. This is how I would try to formalise the development of the argument in the *Discourse*: imagine that a hare has, for each actor, a value equivalent to 2 and that half a stag has a value equivalent to 3. Each actor has two possible strategies, a strategy of cooperation and a strategy of defection. The matrix of reward has, therefore, the following structure: if the two actors cooperate, each wins half a stag, but if the second defects and the first cooperates, the first gains no reward at all whilst the second receives a reward to the value of 2. One would therefore imagine that, since Rousseau holds that the state of nature rules out loyalty, each of the two actors will be uncertain of the other's behaviour. This can be rephrased as follows: each will calculate that the other is equally likely to adopt either strategy. Under these conditions Actor No. 2 stands to gain $(3 \times 0.5) + (0 \times 0.5) = 1.5$ if he chooses the cooperative strategy, and Actor No. 1 stands to gain $(3 \times 0.5) + (0 \times 0.5) = 1.5$ if he chooses the cooperative strategy and $(2 \times 0.5) + (2 \times 0.5) = 2$ if he chooses to defect. The same of course applies to the second actor. It is therefore in everybody's interest to defect. But in defecting each is rewarded with less than they might have got by cooperating. This paradox would not of course arise if more divergent values, such as 1 and 4, were attributed to the hare and to the half-a-stag. This analysis therefore shows not that the hunt will necessarily fail but that there are certain conditions under which, whether the actors wish it or no, it will fail. The hunters can very effectively protect themselves against this trap by prohibiting defection, that is, they can guard against the temptation to defect by accepting that this prohibition must necessarily be accompanied by sanctions.

TABLE 2.1 *Rousseau's hunting party*

		ACTOR 2	
		Cooperation	Defection
ACTOR 1	Cooperation	3.3	0.2
	Defection	2.0	2.2

The reader will doubtless have noticed that the structure of interaction in the hunting party of the *Discourse on Inequality* is very close to one of the most familiar game-theory structures, that of the prisoner's dilemma. A classic solution for actors who have fallen into this trap is to accept quite willingly the constraint that obliges them to cooperate. Aside from constraint (which may in different circumstances assume a public or a private form) other resolutions to the prisoner's dilemma do of course exist. Loyalty is one of them, but it does not assume the same form in every situation.

Rousseau's analysis therefore shows that a fundamental social change, namely the institutionalisation of constraint, may result from perverse effects generated in a state of nature, that is, in situations in which each acts according to his own whim.

An Interesting Example of a Perverse Effect, or How Equality May Generate Inequality

Rousseau's example is of a theoretical order. But it is easy to find numerous examples of concrete processes characteristic of industrial societies that do illustrate the relation between a perverse effect and social change.

I want, first of all, to consider in some detail an example borrowed from the sociology of education. This example suggests that the crisis which has marked the educational systems of industrial societies for the last ten years, and which shows no sign of abating, is due to an accumulation of perverse effects that the growth of education, apart from any of its positive effects, has generated.

To analyse the consequences of the considerable rise in school attendance rates typical of most countries in the last few decades is one of the most difficult and controversial tasks imaginable. Everyone knows that sociologists, like politicians, for a long time thought of the development of education as the corner-stone of a basically egalitarian politics. Economists concerned with education still tend to cling to the notion that educational growth leads to a more egalitarian wage structure, and sociologists used to think that increased school attendances would boost social mobility.

I am not concerned to deal with the problem of the overall consequences of the rise in school attendances. As regards the influence of this factor on the allocation of revenues, I would refer the reader to Thurow's works.[8] These show that, if one takes the job structure to be determined, to a limited extent only, by alterations over time in the educational stock, the average extension in the time spent at school leads not to less but to more economic inequality. To be more precise: if one sticks to the distinction between the three classic educational forms (primary, secondary, higher) it is possible to show (1) that the *variance* of the wages tied to each of these three levels tends to decrease; (2) that the average wages tied to the three levels have a tendency to diverge.

The bringing to light of this perverse effect, contradicting as it does the propositions frequently advanced by economists concerned with education, follows on from the clearly reasonable hypothesis that the job structure (or, more accurately, the wage structure) alters more slowly than what I would call the structure of schooling, i.e., the placing of individuals according to their level of schooling.[9]

Thurow's original hypothesis and the conclusions he drew from it concerning the United States have *subsequently* been vindicated by empirical work carried out there. Between 1949 and 1969 there was:

1. *A reduction in educational inequalities.* Thurow used the Gini–Pareto procedure to measure this: let N represent the sum total of years of education shared out among the members of a particular population at a particular time, and n_1, n_2, ... , n_{10} the sum total of years shared out among the least schooled 10 per cent of the population, then the 10 per cent above them, and finally the most schooled 10 per cent. In this way it was established that the share of the total educational stock available to the least schooled 10 per cent increased between 1949 and 1969, whilst the share of the most schooled 10 per cent decreased.

2. *An increase in economic inequalities.* In fact, between 1949 and 1969, the proportion of the total amount of wages that went to the least privileged 10 per cent tended to decrease, whilst the share of the most privileged 10 per cent rose. Thus the growth in school attendances was marked by both a reduction in educational inequalities and by an increase in economic inequalities.[10]

The American statistics also show that from 1949 to 1969 (1) the variance of the wages associated with each of the three educational levels definitely fell; (2) the average wages corresponding to the three levels clearly diverged. These results are quite compatible with those implicit in Thurow's hypothesis.

I want now to consider the influence of expanding school attendance rates on social mobility.

Thurow concludes that the educational system's growth does not of itself cause economic inequalities to diminish, in fact quite the opposite. It is also possible to demonstrate by analogy that it need not entail an increase in mobility, *even if greater equality of opportunity at school is presupposed.*

The part of the sentence italicised calls for some clarification. In 'critical' sociology it is sometimes admitted that the educational system tends not to reduce but rather to reinforce inequalities due to birth, and that there is therefore no reason why a growth in school attendance rates should lead to a democratisation of education. It is true that one can produce statistics referring to particular countries and covering what are preferably very short periods that suggest that inequalities of opportunity with respect to education show no sign of lessening. But if one strives for an overall perspective on the growth of educational inequalities, and if one considers periods of twenty, ten or even fewer years, one cannot fail to note a general diminution in such inequalities. Thurow's demonstration does not take into account the alterations in the demographic structure of the American population between the two periods considered, and in this respect it may be criticised. But the OECD has amassed some impressive statistical documentation that leaves no room for doubt: in industrial societies and particularly in liberal industrial societies *educational inequalities show a constant tendency to diminish.*[11]

We are faced, then, with the following problem: why has a growth, on the one hand, in school attendance rates, and on the other hand, a lessening in the *inequality of educational opportunities* not caused a *lessening in the inequality of social opportunities* or, if one prefers a more scholarly language, an increase in *social mobility?*

In *L'Inégalité des chances*[12] I developed a theory designed to answer this question, a theory that I cannot of course present in detail here. I will present just the broad outlines of the model that derives from it. The model is composed, *roughly speaking*, of three logically linked parts, or if one prefers, three moments.

1. In a first moment it is presumed that the distribution of individuals in a population with regard to their success at school varies in relation to their social class of origin. There is, moreover, a range of decisions available to the members of each social class. This range determines the probability of an individual belonging to a particular social class and enjoying a particular level of success, choosing, at such and such a stage in the academic course, one path or another (for example, entry into long-cycle secondary education as opposed to short-cycle higher education, continuation of studies as opposed to entry into active life etc.) Moreover it is presumed that the stages of the academic course and, more generally, the placing of the points at which alternatives are offered in the course may vary from one educational system to another and may alter with time.

By formalising the above propositions one can produce a model (and I won't go into details here) that makes it possible to predict the educational future of a hypothetical group of pupils. I will suppose three different social classes (upper, middle, lower), and of a group of 100,000 pupils coming to the end of their primary education I will assume that 10,000 belong to the upper class, 30,000 to the middle class and 60,000 to the lower class.

When the above propositions have been formalised and if the right parameters are chosen, one can work out the number of pupils per social class that will reach the various levels defined by the educational system in question.

The results of applying this model to a particularly simple case are given in table 2.2. Six educational levels in all have been distinguished, and columns 1, 3 and 5 give the proportion of individuals in each social class who reach each of the various levels. The three other columns give the proportions as added from the bottom upwards.

It is noticeable that the results given by the model accord structurally with the evidence provided by the educational statistics:

TABLE 2.2   *The Relation between Educational Levels and Social Class*

Educational level	C_1 (upper) (1)	(2)	C_2 (middle) (3)	(4)	C_3 (lower) (5)	(6)
	Social Class					
1. Further studies finished	0.1967	1.0000	0.0340	0.9999	0.0053	1.0000
2. Further studies	0.0905	0.8033	0.0397	0.9659	0.0104	0.9947
3. Secondary studies finished	0.0618	0.7128	0.0357	0.9262	0.0118	0.9843
4. Second secondary cycle	0.1735	0.6510	0.1396	0.8905	0.0653	0.9725
5. First secondary cycle	0.2775	0.4775	0.3609	0.7509	0.3072	0.9072
6. Primary school	0.2000	0.2000	0.3900	0.3900	0.6000	0.6000
Total	1.0000		0.9999		1.0000	

there are significant inequalities between the three social classes up to secondary school, and these become still more pronounced at the level of higher education.

2. With the second moment in the model's construction we pass from statics to dynamics. Some alteration in the range of available decisions is presumed over time. In the simplest case the chances of surviving as far as higher education clearly increase. It is moreover presumed that the smaller the probability to which this increase applies, the more rapid the increase. Thus, suppose that for a given level of educational success, a given age etc., the probability of survival up to a given point of bifurcation is, at a given period, equal to p. I will then suppose that in the following period it is equal to $p + (1 - p)a$, where a is a positive coefficient lower than 1. In parts a, b and c of table 2.3, using the hypotheses and parameters that led to table 2.1, and introducing this dynamic hypothesis as well, I give the main results that can be deduced from the model. The three parts of table 2.3 correspond to the distributions obtained at three consecutive periods. Therefore table 2.1 is taken to refer to the period t_0, and parts a, b and c of table 2.3 to periods t_1, t_2, and t_3 respectively.[13]

These tables give, where it is possible to grasp their diachronic aspect, the educational statistics' structural properties. It is especially noticeable (1) that, from one period to another, the chances of reaching the higher educational levels increase by a coefficient that itself rises as the pupils' social origins fall; (2) but that the additional

TABLE 2.3 *Educational Level as a Function of Social Class in Three Consecutive Periods* t_1, t_2 *and* t_3

Educational level	C_1 (upper)		C_2 (middle)		C_3 (lower)	
a) $t = t_1$						
1. Further studies finished	0.2319	1.0001	0.0491	0.9999	0.0092	1.0001
2. Further studies	0.0947	0.7682	0.0490	0.9508	0.0153	0.9909
3. Secondary studies finished	0.0629	0.6735	0.0418	0.9018	0.0164	0.9756
4. Second secondary cycle	0.1707	0.6106	0.1526	0.8600	0.0832	0.9592
5. First secondary cycle	0.2599	0.4399	0.3564	0.7074	0.3360	0.8760
6. Primary school	0.1800	0.1800	0.3510	0.3510	0.5400	0.5400
Total	1.0001		0.9999		1.0001	
b) $t = t_2$						
1. Further studies finished	0.2689	1.0002	0.0680	1.0000	0.0151	1.0000
2. Further studies	0.0977	0.7313	0.0584	0.09320	0.0215	0.9849
3. Secondary studies finished	0.0631	0.6336	0.0474	0.8736	0.0217	0.0634
4. Second secondary cycle	0.1662	0.5705	0.1629	0.8262	0.1018	0.9417
5. First secondary cycle	0.2423	0.4043	0.3474	0.6633	0.3539	0.8399
6. Primary school	0.1620	0.1620	0.3159	0.3159	0.4860	0.4860
Total	1.0002		1.0000		1.0000	
c) $t = t_3$						
1. Further studies finished	0.3069	1.0001	0.0904	1.0000	0.0233	1.0000
2. Further studies	0.0993	0.6932	0.0676	0.9096	0.0288	0.9767
3. Secondary studies finished	0.0626	0.5939	0.0524	0.8420	0.0277	0.9479
4. Second secondary cycle	0.1604	0.5313	0.1703	0.7896	0.1197	0.9202
5. First secondary cycle	0.2250	0.3709	0.3350	0.6193	0.3629	0.8005
6. Primary school	0.1459	0.1459	0.2843	0.2843	0.4376	0.4376
Total	1.0001		1.0000		1.0000	

number of individuals per 1000 who, from one period to another, reach higher education is much less in the lower class than in the other classes. These two results are consistent with educational statistics.

I do not want to dwell on the first two moments of the model. They are relevant here simply because they make it possible to determine (1) the growth of *class sizes* over time in relation to the different educational levels; (2) the alteration in the *social composition of classes* over time in relation to each educational level.

I want now to tackle the third moment in the process, since it has a direct bearing on the problem that concerns me: that of the effect of the growth in school attendance rates and of the reduction in educational inequalities on social mobility. The first two moments of the model give the distributions characteristic of each group of pupils for the different educational levels. The third moment defines the mechanism that enables individuals who have reached a particular educational level to acquire a particular social status.

What does this suggest? One hypothesis instantly springs to mind: that industrial societies are all, to some degree, *meritocratic*. In other words, all else being equal, those who have had more education tend to acquire a higher social status. This proposition will be given a more precise form below.

A second hypothesis would read as follows: all else being equal, those of higher social origin tend to obtain a higher social status. In particular, numerous surveys suggest that, of several individuals all equally well educated, it is those whose social origin is higher who stand a better chance of acquiring a high social status. In such cases I will talk of a *dominance* effect.

If it was my aim to provide an exhaustive theory of mobility I would have to introduce yet more factors. It is, for instance, well known that individuals who have had exactly the same education will aim for very different sorts of career that seem socially more or less ambitious. Thus young people of a middle social origin, once they have successfully completed their secondary studies, are far less likely than their upper-class contemporaries to head for the prestigious careers of medicine or law.

It is however clear that contextual factors do affect the way mobility works: two apparently similar people (the same kind of social origin, the same educational level, the same time spent at school etc.) will very probably achieve a different social status if they come from different sorts of environment. The OECD has compiled statistics that show clearly that, even when individual characteristics are treated as constant, important regional variations in educational opportunities do occur.

In what follows I will consider the simplest possible case. I will assume that geographical mobility is high enough to render these contextual factors negligible. Since I want to work out how much social mobility is affected by the increase in school attendance rates and the attenuation of educational inequalities, I will also disregard the dominance effect cited above. For the sake of argument, then, we have to deal with a *purely meritocratic structure*. If educational expansion and greater educational equality are ever going to have an effect on social mobility, it would surely be in a society of this kind.

How does one therefore formalise this hypothesis on meritocracy? For the sake of simplicity I will assume that, as before, three kinds of hierarchised social status are distinguished: C_1 (high status), C_2 (middle status) and C_3 (low status). I will assume, moreover, that the social structure is relatively static over time, that is to say, that the distribution of individuals in relation to three kinds of status is approximately constant. In the first two parts of the model it was assumed that a group of pupils reaching the end of primary education would be distributed as follows: 10,000 to C_1, 30,000 to C_2 and 60,000 to C_3. For the sake of simplicity I will take it that this group of pupils has a total of 100,000 social positions to share out, of which 10,000 are at level C_1, 30,000 at level C_2 and 60,000 at level C_3.

It is of course very unrealistic to imagine that all those who finish elementary schooling at the same time will then all be competing with each other for jobs: they will in fact, depending on their qualifications, all enter the job market at different times. It would be easy to complicate this model further by assuming that contemporaries turned up simultaneously on the job market, but the analytic conclusions would not need to be modified in any way.

Translated into other terms, the meritocratic hypothesis assumes that individuals receive their eventual social status through an inegalitarian process favouring the better qualified. So, with the time factor at t_0, 10,000 places are available at C_1, while (cf. table 2.2) $(0.1967 \times 10,000) + (0.0340 \times 30,000) + (0.0053 \times 60,000) = 3,305$ individuals of the original group of pupils reach the highest educational level. It is assumed that a large proportion of these individuals, for example 70 per cent, attain high social positions (C_1). This leaves $10,000 - (3,305 \times 0.70) = 7,686$ positions in C_1 available. It is then assumed that 70 per cent of these positions revert to the individuals who reached the educational level just below the highest one. If one refers back to table 2.2 it is clearly a question of individuals who have not finished their further studies. The successive deduction of candidates from lower and lower levels will continue to effect the number of places available in C_1.

Once that is done the social positions available at C_2 (social statuses of the middle kind) will be accounted for in the same manner: the best-qualified candidates will be accepted first, then those who are slightly less qualified and then those with the most minimal qualifications. The fact that some of these candidates have already been placed in C_1 should of course be taken into account. Again, it will be assumed that the *meritocratic parameter* (as I will call it) is equivalent to 70 per cent.

The mechanism for allocating places is, as we shall see, very simple and there is little point in presenting it at length. It is nevertheless worth pointing out that the number of places available to a particular social level may be less than the number of candidates. Thus, in table 2.2 in the period t_0, the number who have not passed beyond first-cycle elementary education is $(0.2775 \times 10,000) + (0.3609 \times 30,000) + (0.3702 \times 60,000) = 32,035$, a figure that clearly exceeds the number of C_2 places still available when all the better-qualified individuals have been provided for. Let this number be x. I will assume here (for logical reasons that I cannot develop in the framework of this article) that the meritocratic parameter applies to x. The number of C_1 places reverting to individuals who have not passed beyond first-cycle secondary education will therefore be $0.70x$.

The application of the above procedures gives the results presented in table 2.4. This table gives the number of individuals per educational level who acquire each of the three types of social status in the four periods considered. The meritocratic parameter has been presumed to be equal to 70 per cent for all four periods. The only variable is therefore the *distribution of educational levels* among the four groups.

The general rise in educational standards affects the relation between schooling and later acquisition of status in a relatively complex manner. Examination of table 2.4 shows:

1. That the higher educational levels ($S_1 =$ further studies completed; $S_2 =$ further studies not completed) are linked with a stable structure of opportunity;

2. That the structure of opportunity linked with educational level S_3 (secondary studies completed) is initially constant and as advantageous as the one linked to S_1 and S_2. In the last period this structure nevertheless starts to have drastically adverse effects: the individuals who stick at this level find their chances of acquiring the highest social status considerably reduced, whilst in compensation for this their chances of acquiring lower and intermediate social status improve;

3. That the structure of opportunity linked with the lower levels, S_4 (second-cycle secondary education), S_5 (first-cycle secondary education), and S_6 (primary education), deteriorates steadily over time. It is nevertheless noticeable that the higher the educational level, relatively speaking, the quicker this deterioration occurs. Thus,

TABLE 2.4   *Class Sizes and Proportion of Individuals Reaching Each of the Three Social Levels (as a Function of Educational Levels for the Periods t_0 to t_3)*

Educational level		Social status						Total
		C_1		C_2		C_3		
t_0	S_1	2213	(0.7000)	694	(0.2100)	298	(0.0900)	3305
	S_2	1904	(0.7000)	571	(0.2100)	245	(0.0900)	2720
	S_3	1678	(0.7000)	503	(0.2100)	216	(0.0900)	2397
	S_4	2874	(0.0292)	4878	(0.4956)	2090	(0.2124)	9842
	S_5	862	(0.0269)	16345	(0.5102)	14828	(0.4629)	32035
	S_6	369	(0.0074)	7009	(0.1410)	42323	(0.8516)	49701
Total		10000		30000		60000		100000
t_1	S_1	3041	(0.7000)	912	(0.2100)	391	(0.0900)	4344
	S_2	2334	(0.7000)	701	(0.2100)	300	(0.0900)	3335
	S_3	2007	(0.7000)	602	(0.2100)	258	(0.0900)	2867
	S_4	1833	(0.1625)	6611	(0.5862)	2833	(0.2512)	11277
	S_5	550	(0.0164)	14822	(0.4431)	18077	(0.5404)	33449
	S_6	235	(0.0053)	6352	(0.1420)	38141	(0.8527)	44728
Total		10000		30000		60000		100000

TABLE 2.4   Class Sizes and Proportion of Individuals Reaching Each of the Three Social Levels (as a Function of Educational Levels for the Periods t_0 to t_3) continued

Educational level		Social status						Total
		C_1		C_2		C_3		
t_2	S_1	3944	(0.7000)	1184	(0.2100)	507	(0.0900)	5635
	S_2	2813	(0.7000)	844	(0.2100)	362	(0.0900)	4019
	S_3	2348	(0.7000)	705	(0.2100)	302	(0.0900)	3355
	S_4	627	(0.0495)	8421	(0.6653)	3609	(0.2851)	12657
	S_5	188	(0.0055)	13192	(0.3871)	20698	(0.6074)	34078
	S_6	80	(0.0020)	5654	(0.1405)	34522	(0.8576)	40256
Total		10000		30000		60000		100000
t_3	S_1	5025	(0.7000)	1438	(0.2100)	716	(0.0900)	7179
	S_2	3324	(0.7000)	998	(0.2100)	427	(0.0900)	4749
	S_3	1156	(0.2995)	1893	(0.4904)	811	(0.2101)	3860
	S_4	346	(0.0249)	9484	(0.6825)	4065	(0.2926)	13895
	S_5	104	(0.0081)	11331	(0.3325)	22639	(0.6644)	34074
	S_6	45	(0.0012)	4856	(0.1340)	31342	(0.8648)	36243
Total		10000		30000		60000		100000

in the first period, S_4 is linked to a by no means negligible probability (0.2920) of reaching the higher social level C_1. In the fourth period the probability is more than ten times smaller (0.02449). On the other hand the structure of opportunity with which S_5 and, above all, S_6 is linked deteriorates much more slowly.

It would of course be possible to arrive at these results by means of an abstract analysis. I have preferred to use a simulation method (arithmetical analysis of a model) in order to make the demonstration more concrete.[14] It is easy to account intuitively for the phenomena observed: the social structure (the distribution of available social statuses) has been presumed stable over time; the educational structure (the distribution of individuals according to their schooling) has a tendency to warp towards the top, the growth in class sizes varying from one period to another and accelerating at the highest educational levels. It therefore becomes more and more likely that the high-social-status places that are available will be shared out among the most highly qualified individuals. A drastic deterioration in the structure of opportunity linked with the middle educational levels will in time occur, a deterioration whose reverberations are only very slowly felt at the lower levels.

What are the consequences of this model for social mobility? Table 2.3 gives, for each period, the proportion of individuals of a given social origin who achieve a given social status. Table 2.4 gives the proportion of individuals with a given level of schooling who achieve each of the three social statuses. I argued that the eventual status each person achieved was determined by *merit* alone and that *dominance* effects were negligible. To obtain the matrices of inter-generational mobility for each of the four periods, one therefore only has to multiply the matrices of tables 2.3 and 2.4 for each of the four periods, one with another. The result is presented in table 2.5. This table elicits the following observations:

1. It is immediately noticeable that, just as I had foreseen, between the first (t_0) and the last (t_3) periods considered, the structure of mobility alters very little. The probabilities in each of the four tables are almost identical from one period to another. This result can be justified mathematically but appears paradoxical nonetheless. It should therefore be borne in mind that the results of table 2.5 are the consequence of a model that presumes that, between t_0 and t_3, there is at the same time: a) a massive growth in class sizes at the very top of the educational hierarchy; b) a by no means negligible diminution in the inequality of educational opportunity; c) a significant modification in the temporality of the educational structure contrasting with the fixity of the social structure.

Whilst it is tempting to trust one's intuition and conclude that these different factors lead to changes in the structure of mobility,

TABLE 2.5   *Mobility Tables Generated by the Model in the Four Periods t_0 to t_3*

Category of social origin		C_1	C_2	C_3	Total
		Eventual social category			
t_0	C_1	0.3039	0.3290	0.3670	0.9999
	C_2	0.1299	0.3313	0.5387	0.9999
	C_3	0.0510	0.2795	0.6697	1.0002
t_1	C_1	0.3056	0.3226	0.3719	1.0001
	C_2	0.1304	0.3266	0.5428	0.9998
	C_3	0.0505	0.2829	0.6666	1.0000
t_2	C_1	0.3107	0.3174	0.3722	1.0003
	C_2	0.1323	0.3237	0.5440	1.0000
	C_3	0.0488	0.2852	0.6660	1.0000
t_3	C_1	0.3080	0.3198	0.3723	1.0001
	C_2	0.1319	0.3246	0.5435	1.0000
	C_3	0.0494	0.2855	0.6650	0.9999

analysis shows that this just isn't so. The model generates at the same time significant changes in the educational structure and a by no means negligible diminution in the inequality of educational opportunity, but these changes are powerless to modify the structure of mobility.

2. I want now to consider the slight changes in the structure of mobility that occur between t_0 and t_3. Between t_0 and t_2 there is a slight tendency towards increased auto-recruitment within class C_1. During the same period, downwards mobility from C_1 (upper class) to C_3 (lower class) increases, but also only slightly. By contrast, between t_2 and t_3, the auto-recruitment so characteristic of the structure of mobility is both *limited in extent and sporadic*.

Why is this? Without embarking on a mathematical analysis of this phenomenon, it is worth trying to grasp it intuitively. What effects would the structural changes posited by the model between t_0 and t_3 have on the social opportunities of individuals of high social origin? Between these two terminal periods individuals in this category will, on average, reach higher educational levels. Thus, in t_0, out of 10.000 young persons of higher social origin, 1,967 reach the very highest academic levels (completion of further studies); in t_3 they number 2,689 (tables 2.2 and 2.3). More and more people therefore reach the highest educational levels. But, at the same time, the general increase in the demand for education causes the structure of opportunity characteristic of lower and, above all, middle educational levels to deteriorate steadily. A significant number of individuals of higher social origin only reach the middle educational

levels between t_0 and t_3. A sort of *compensatory effect* is therefore
produced: it generates, over time, a stability in the structure of
mobility characteristic of higher-social-class individuals. One could
of course duplicate this analysis for individuals of middle or lower
social origin. It is invariably the complex of compensatory effects
produced by the generalised increase in the demand for education
that generates the almost total stability of the structure of mobility.

3. I want to look again at table 2.4 (what are the chances of
reaching social level C_1 if one reaches educational level S_j?) This table
shows that the structure of opportunity that characterises
educational levels tends to alter over time. Thus the structure linked
to levels S_1 and S_2 stays as it is, whilst the structure linked to levels S_5
and S_6 tends to deteriorate. This result is consistent with Thurow's
conclusions: the relation between social aspirations and educational
levels tends to become more and more marked. It is clear that it is
partly this factor that lies behind the general increase in the demand
for education that characterises industrial societies. However this
increase has triggered off compensatory effects that have caused the
structure of mobility to stay almost unaltered.

The main conclusion that I draw from this analysis is as follows:
there was no reason to expect the considerable increase in the
demand for education that we have witnessed in industrial societies
to produce an increase in social mobility, although it was clearly
accompanied by a reduction in the inequality of educational
opportunity. The preceding model shows in fact that, under a very
wide range of conditions, the upheavals typical of the educational
structure are normally linked with a very stable structure of mobility.
In order to disprove this conclusion one would have to advance some
very unrealistic arguments: one ' would have to grant that
educational inequalities had diminished far more rapidly than they
in fact have, or one would have to posit that social structural
changes, particularly those attributable to technology, had been
extremely rapid (and had kept in step with those typical of the
educational structure).

In my presentation of the model I assumed that social structure
stayed constant over time. This assumption, which has a bearing on
the last point, is clearly excessive. Technological growth may well
modify the socio-professional structure by, for instance, reducing the
number of very repetitive manual jobs. But it is important to note
that the model's conclusions still hold good, even if the social
structure is presumed to alter over time. The following hypothesis
may be advanced: the number of places available at the higher social
level (C_1) increases, while the number available at the lower (C_3)
decreases. But, unless changes in social structure are presumed to
keep pace with changes in educational structure, one can only

conclude that the structure of mobility does indeed remain almost totally stable over time.

I want now to recapitulate: under very diverse conditions, and even when the inequality of educational opportunities also diminishes, educational expansion does not necessarily reduce the inequality of social opportunity, a form of inequality that is at once so specific and so essential (the fact that the son's social status depends on the father's). This result may go some way towards explaining the equally surprising conclusion of Lipset and Bendix's celebrated works on social mobility. When, at the end of the 1950s, these authors set out to compare mobility in different industrial societies, they came to the conclusion that countries that in many respects were very different (in their systems of stratification and in the development of their educational systems) did nevertheless have similar mobility rates.[15] More than ten years later, in an article in *The Public Interest*, Lipset reaffirmed this basic conclusion.[16]

For my conclusion I cannot do better than cite Thurow's: 'In any case, I would argue that our reliance on education as the ultimate public policy for curing all problems, economic and social, is unwarranted at best and in all probability ineffective.' If one accepts Thurow's analysis, educational expansion does not lead to greater economic equality and is no more successful in reducing social immobility. In this respect the main effect of the increase in the demand for education would seem to be the onus it places on the individual to acquire a schooling that just becomes longer and longer whilst social expectations remain unchanged.

Perhaps – and this is the central point to which this analysis leads – these effects, at once unexpected and perverse, are at the root of the crisis in the educational systems of industrial societies. Because they are unexpected they have caused widespread disillusionment with the social and political virtues of education, and because they are perverse they have led people to doubt the ultimate purpose of educational systems and to fear that they will never be able to control them.

Another Example: How People May Well Work against Their Own Best Interests

My second example deals with what could be called the logic of participation. One source of social conflicts, and therefore of social change, lies in the clash of interest between different groups. But the perverse effect may well be more important, for under a very wide range of circumstances it leads a group's members to accept quite passively a situation against their own interests.

Mancur Olson's book, *The Logic of Collective Action*,[17] is concerned with the study of this kind of perverse effect. Olson seeks to advance the heretical proposition that an unstructured group of persons with a common interest, aware of this interest and having the means to realise it, will in fact under a very wide range of different conditions do nothing to promote it. Community of interest, even when quite conscious, is not in itself enough to bring about the shared action that would advance the general interest. The logic of collective action and the logic of individual action are two very different things.

A proposition of this sort would have surprised neither Rousseau nor Marx nor Michels, nor indeed a good number of political philosophers and classical sociologists. Not a single economist would be shocked by it. Olson's theory is in fact an ingenious application to phenomena that are usually considered to be the province of sociology or political science, of results that are well known in the field of economics.

My presentation of Olson's argument will turn around one of his own examples, but I will apply an analytic method considerably simpler than his.

The question is this: is an unstructured group, aware of its own interests and with the necessary resources at its disposal to advance those interests, and whose interests are, moreover, not opposed to those of any other group, going to act to further them, just as an individual in the same circumstances would do? Let me note, first of all, that the minute one rejects the metaphysics implicit in identifying a group with a person, the language used in the above paragraph is necessarily inappropriate: one cannot talk of a group being aware of its own interest any more than one can legitimately use an expression that implies that a group is an entity independent of the persons who compose it, and transcending them. Let me re-phrase Olson's question: assume an imaginary group of people, with a common interest, aware of this interest and with each member able to contribute to the realisation of this interest. Will they in fact work to bring about this common interest?

To fix this in the reader's mind let me take a simple example, one used by Olson himself and with few emotional connotations attached to it. Imagine a group of proprietors wanting to get their tax rate reduced. The group comprises $N = 10$ members. Each member has property to the value of £10 and has to pay £4 in land tax. Suppose too that if they were to start a campaign in their own favour, or if they were to bring pressure to bear on the fiscal authority in one way or another, they would win a tax reduction. To clarify this point I will suppose that if each were to participate in the collective action they would win a 50 per cent tax reduction and that this is a function of the number of participants in the collective action. With n participants the reduction would therefore be worth $5n$ per cent.

With 9 of the group's members participating in the collective action, each of the 10 members will win a 45 per cent reduction in the initial tax of £4; just as if the number of participants amounts to 8, 7, 6,. . . ., 1, 0, the reduction for each of the 10 members will in each case be 40, 35, 30,. . . ., 5, and 0 per cent. Finally it is presumed that participation in the collective action implies certain costs (loss of time, financial stake etc.), that these are measurable, and for the sake of argument fixed at £1 per individual.

Thus if all the members participate they will together win benefits to the total value of £20 (since each of the group's 10 members will see his fiscal contribution fall from £4 to £2) at a total cost of £10 (£1 per person).

If the group could be compared to a person it is clear that the group-person would profit from paying £10 for a benefit worth £20. But a group, even if it is composed of persons with identical interests, is not a person. I want now to consider the arguments that any one member of the group (I will call him Ego) will use. Ego has two possible options: to pay his share or not to do so, i.e., to contribute to the collective action or not to do so. The advantage that he secures from either strategy will of course depend on what the others do. If 9 other members beside Ego were to contribute to the collective action, and if Ego doesn't himself contribute, the tax reduction would be 45 per cent, that is Ego would pay tax to the value of $4 - (0.45 \times 4) = £2.20$. In not contributing to the collective action he therefore gains $£4 - £2.20 = £1.80$. If he does contribute there will be a significantly larger reduction all round: with 10 people paying the tax is reduced by 50 per cent. It therefore falls from £4 to £2 and each person gains £2. Ego then gains, like everyone else, £2 in tax reductions. But given that his participation in the collective action costs him £1, when along with the 9 others he does so, his clear profit will amount to £1. It is therefore clear that, in the eventuality of the 9 others participating in the collective action, it is in Ego's interest not to participate.

Now suppose that there are 8 people, besides Ego, paying (8 participants in the collective action). If Ego does not participate he will benefit from the 40 per cent tax reduction won by the 8 others. His net profit will here be $(4 \times 0.40) = £1.60$. If he does participate in the action each will win a tax reduction of 45 per cent or £1.80. But Ego then has to deduct the amount that his participation cost him: his net profit is therefore £0.80.

If one takes this argument any further it becomes clear that, regardless of the number of members besides Ego who participate, it is in Ego's interests not to. But Ego is by definition identical to the other members of the group, if it is always in his interest to withhold payment then the same must apply to the others. It is thus in everyone's interest to refuse to participate, regardless of the number of people who actually do. So, despite the fact that it would be in everyone's interest if everyone did participate in the collective action, no one in fact does. A single individual would leap at the chance of getting a collective good worth £20 for £10 but it seems that a group would let this bargain slip by.

This disconcerting result is clearly not just a function of the arithmetic peculiar to the example chosen: the arithmetic is simply to facilitate the argument. In fact the paradox derives from the fact that the collective action produces a benefit (a tax reduction) that one had assumed by its very nature would be to the advantage of all the group's members.

One could well object that Olson is being quite unrealistic in supposing that the group's members would behave rationally. To which one can reply that the strictly rational calculus used above in no way presumes that the individuals would in real life have an exact comprehension of the advantages and disadvantages implicit in their actual participation in a collective action, or that they would be capable of analysing the benefits to be reaped from choosing one path rather than another. The same result would be produced by arguments that were more flexible and more realistic *limited rationality*) but they would only complicate the demonstration unduly.

Little more than an adherence to one basic principle is assumed: in many but not in all cases it makes sense to explain individual behaviours in society by presuming that they are basically self-seeking. Olson himself stresses that this premise is often insufficient but that there are many social phenomena that cannot be explained without it. There are therefore many sociologists, among them some of the most eminent, who use it quite explicitly and systematically. But it would be quite superfluous to justify Olson's theory by referring to the authorities who have used it. It can be defended simply in terms of the numerous uses to which it has been put. It explains why taxes are always coercive: although citizens derive long-term benefits from the collective goods that their contributions produce, no one would contribute if they were not forced to, even if everyone was unanimously agreed as to the use to which the tax was put by the authorities. It would also provide one explanation for the relatively painless quality of indirect *vis-à-vis* direct taxation. The former is always included in the price of the particular commodities purchased and, since it is paid each time goods or individual services are bought, the role it plays in financing collective benefits is obscured. Direct taxation, on the other hand, is not linked with the acquisition of individual goods. The distinction between the two kinds of tax evidently has perverse consequences for social justice, given that the fact that taxes on consumption often have a regressive quality.

Olson's theory provides a framework in which another paradox, and one that has stumped traditional political sociology for a long time, may easily be solved. How is it that political parties succeed in recruiting such a modest proportion of all those who vote for them at election time? Olson's answer is simple: a political party can essentially be thought of as a provider of collective benefits. Therefore, if it is accepted that joining a party or working for it as a militant represent costs, in terms of time or money, then Olson's theory applies: each member of the latent group standing to gain something from the collective benefits offered by the party will find it in his interest to let the others pay for these, for as long as the party is incapable of wielding any coercive power over its clientele.

But how is one then to explain the fact a party can nevertheless persuade some people, albeit a tiny minority of the party's electoral support, to join and even to work as a militant? Olson would argue in reply that a party, as a general rule, provides not only collective but also individual benefits. It may offer its members positions of political responsibility within the party and, as it grows more powerful, the chances of being offered electoral positions in local or national political life increase too. Compared with the number of people who vote for it, the number of positions offered by the party is naturally very small. Thus even if there are fewer places available than there are party members laying claim to them (there are more candidates for the *École Polytechnique*, for instance, than places) there are invariably fewer claimants than voters: they are quite happy to benefit from the collective goods provided by the party but see no need to pay the price for them. (Olson does not of course mean to suggest that people never become militants for altruistic reasons. It is simply that if one assumes that there will be more egoists than altruists among a party's militants one stands a better chance of explaining empirical facts of a quite global character which the opposite hypothesis leaves obscure.)

The parallel provision of individual benefits would be a possible loophole to Olson's paradox, and it would account for the power of professional organisations like the American Medical Association. Olson develops his theory in relation to this organisation in an especially brilliant way. He accounts for its power in terms of the quality of the individual benefits that it provides for its members, particularly legal assistance in cases of professional misconduct. Some slightly obscure aspects of union allegiance may also be accounted for in terms of the theory of *selective incentives*, a theory that suggests that it is good policy for any organisation having difficulty expanding to tie individual benefits to the collective ones already provided. For instance how is one to explain the fact that, in spite of the obvious advantages that the union wins for the personnel whose interests it serves, rates of unionisation in countries as different as France and the United States do not on average exceed 20 per cent?

Olson would doubtless argue that while an organisation provides benefits whose promise, like that of wage rises, is realised straight away, it is in no one's interest to meet the price asked for these benefits. This formulation explains why it is that there can be persistently *low* unionisation rates when the efficacy of union activity is itself beyond question. The *overall* rate of unionisation is not itself insignificant, however, and the 20 per cent average observable in France and in the United States may be linked to a very strong *scattering* (in that some branches' membership is close to the maximum whilst others' is close to the minimum).[18] While the provision of collective benefits is the actual *raison d'être* of the unions, one only has to look, Olson argues, at the nature of the *individual* benefits that they are in each case prepared to provide in order to explain these phenomena. If these individual benefits do not stretch further than the different offices available within the union, unionisation rates are likely to be quite moderate. If the union can provide an individual benefit of real value that *everyone* might need, such as legal aid for professional misconduct, a higher unionisation rate is probable. It is for these reasons, among others, that unionisation rates for French students are low. The union provides collective benefits: where a claim for a grant rise is effective the participation of one more student in the struggle is not going to make it much likelier that all students will get a grant. On the other hand a high unionisation rate is likely when a union not only fights for wage rises (collective benefits) but also stands surety against job loss (individual benefit) and guarantees people against industrial accidents.

Olson's theory provides fresh interpretations of many social and political phenomena and it also makes a reinterpretation of some classical authors possible. He offers a very stimulating reading of the theories of social change of Marx and, in passing, of Durkheim. When Marx conceives of the interests of capitalists and proletariat as contradictory, he means that capitalists and proletariat are two latent groups, each composed of people with identical interests, interests that are incompatible with those of the other group. But, Olson objects, the notion that a conflict of interests leads necessarily to class war is inconsistent with a coherent utilitarianism: as latent groups classes are fundamentally incapable of carrying out collective actions destined to further their interests. *Existence of classes*, yes, *class war*, no. But does Olson really assert that Marx was unaware of this problem? His at least unconscious awareness of Olson's paradox is evident in the distinction between class in itself and class for itself, in his endless hesitations about the notion of class consciousness and in the growth of the political organisation of the classes. We should not be surprised by this. Marx was reared on eighteenth-century political philosophy and turn-of-the-eighteenth-century political economy and all of it revolved around the paradoxes implicit in collective action.

Robert Michels' *iron law of oligarchy*[19] is perhaps the most interesting development in the study of social change to have stemmed from Olson's theory. Michels postulates a fairly large number of individuals who are not organised and who have in common an interest in producing a collective benefit. According to Olson's theory there will be a very wide range of conditions under which these individuals will be incapable of producing this benefit. If that is indeed so, the collective *need* created may well tempt an entrepreneur (in the Schumpeterian sense of the term) into setting up an organisation that both *satisfies* and *exploits* this collective need. Coercion or the provision of parallel individual benefits will allow the entrepreneur to capture his potential public. But the existence of the organisation does not in itself guarantee the interests of the individuals it is supposed to represent. Olson's theory implies that, if the organisation's members were to take certain steps or adopt a politics that their constituents disapproved of, they would only be likely to *express* their opposition if they were explicitly consulted: such an expression would correspond to a collective benefit. The theorem therefore shows that an unorganised group is, under a very wide range of conditions, incapable of producing a collective benefit. And the constituents in this example are clearly very *unorganised* in their relations with the organisation (if one disregards those electoral mechanisms – naturally intermittent and often symbolic – by means of which the 'base' exerts some control over the organisation).[20] To put it another way, when the organisation representing the constituents pursues a politics that clearly diverges from their interests, they are in most circumstances incapable of expressing their opposition to what is happening. This latent state of crisis is often 'resolved' by a new entrepreneur turning up and exploiting the 'market' that this discrepancy has created. He will either create a new organisation that is orientated towards the same potential public or he will create an opposition within the old organisation. Olson's theory thus demonstrates that, for a large number of different circumstances, the constituents' interests end up being oligarchically controlled, or at best there is a rivalry between oligarchies.

It was Robert Michels' erudite analysis of the history of the European socialist parties in the nineteenth century and at the beginning of the twentieth century that led him to formulate his *iron law of oligarchy*, but (although Olson does not state this himself)[21] I hold it to be a necessary corollary of the Olsonian theory of collective action. What I want to emphasise is the wide range of consequences that the theory has for the perspective developed here. From the moment that the organs representative of a group's interests begin to assume an oligarchical form, tensions and imbalances occur and these naturally bring social change in their wake.

Olson himself points out that his theory is not universally applicable. There are, after all, cases where the costs of collective action are negligible, non-existent or negative. Participation in a political demonstration may be a pleasure in itself, shattering the boredom of everyday life or giving the actor a feeling of importance. Therefore, amongst the set of situations meriting a utilitarian analysis, only those that effectively imply positive costs may be treated in terms of Olson's theory. There are, moreover, groups to which a utilitarian analysis would clearly be inapplicable. Or if it is applicable it is so only indirectly or at the price of falsifying the notion of interest or utility, a falsification that renders it hollow and tautological. It is therefore clear that charity not only begins at home, it often ends at home. The utilitarian analysis of religious groups nevertheless makes little headway. It is therefore within very precise limits that Olson's theory is useful and applicable.

How Social Ills May Be Attributable to No One and May Be to No One's Advantage

I devoted the two preceding sections to a detailed account of two theories that show how states of crisis, disequilibrium or social 'tension' may result from the appearance of a perverse effect (from an effect that is not sought after by the social actors and does not result from a clash of interests and from the ensuing conflicts). Let me once again emphasise that I do not claim that these effects are the sole cause of social change. There are other processes that lead to social change: once a particular threshold is crossed there are chain irradiation effects that may occur, contradiction (in the zero sum game sense)[22] between the interests of large groups like social classes, institutional obsolescence, war, conquest etc. But the forms of change produced by perverse effects are especially interesting, firstly because they are very common, secondly because they often pass unnoticed, and finally because they are more complex theoretically. The contradiction between opposed interests is not a difficult phenomenon to understand. There are many social conflicts where a gain for one contestant is clearly a loss for another. The contradiction between the different interests involved here assumes the form of a simple logical contradiction (incompatibility of interests) or in game theory idiom, a *zero sum game* (where one person's gains correspond exactly to the other's losses). Perverse effects are a kind of contradiction even more complex than this. In Rousseau's hunting party both partners are losers. Each family unit has a correspondingly greater wish for education than the equivalent family would have had in an earlier period, and this means that each person ends up paying a higher price for their social status. It also means that the democratisation of educational opportunities has hardly any influence on either the inequality of social opportunities (or social mobility) or on fiscal inequalities. As far as the production of collective benefits is concerned, collective action by its very logic engenders oligarchical structures of representation that may well have negative consequences for everyone. All these perverse effects have a *non-zero sum* game structure. It is incidentally worth noting that these structures, which are so crucial to the analysis of social change, are clearly ignored by those who take conflicts between opposed social groups (zero sum games) to be the sole motor of change.

In this last section I want to present, more succinctly than hitherto, some additional examples of perverse effects. I hope that this will lead the reader to appreciate the vast range of contexts in which the concept may be applied.

1. *Hirschman's desertion and protest.* Hirschman's little book *Exit, Voice and Loyalty*[23] grew out of an essentially banal but nevertheless fruitful observation. This observation was fruitful because it contradicted a classic theory: when a firm tries to sell its product above the recognised price, consumers should then, according to the theory of perfect competition, run to other competing firms and thus force the original firm to revert to its original price. It then has to think up some way of reducing its production costs, for instance by improving its administrative organisation or by increasing productivity.

It was in fact while he was researching into the nature of growth that Hirschman came across an empirical example that was in every respect the inverse of this. In a monopoly situation the Nigerian railways fared well. But once they were in competition with road transport, their situation began irreversibly to deteriorate. There is a simple explanation for this chain of events. The emergence of a competitive road transport system didn't deprive the railways of a random fraction of its users. It took away some of the most demanding. Consequently the passage from a monopoly to a competitive situation does not encourage, as the theory would lead one to expect, modernisation of the railways, but tends rather to discourage it.

The first conclusion to be drawn from this case is that the favourable action of the 'invisible hand' does not necessarily imply a competitive situation. It may also arise where there is a monopoly. But – and this is Hirschman's central theme – it then works differently. Where there is competition it works by inducing the consumer to *desert*. If this *desertion* affects consumers at random, and if the firm struck is in a position to react, its effect will then be a beneficial one. If, on the other hand, one of these two conditions is not fulfilled, an unfavourable result (as with the Nigerian railroads) may occur. Where there is a monopoly the invisible hand works not by inducing desertion, which would be unimaginable, but by protest.

Desertion and *protest*[24] are then the two basic forms of reaction to the decline not only of firms but also, as Hirschman's sub-title suggests, of every kind of organisation.

The social sciences are in this respect, Hirschman notes, characterised by an odd division of labour. *Desertion* is the only mechanism that economic theory recognises, while political science considers *protest* alone as worthy of attention. Hirschman argues for a theory that disregards the boundary separating economics from political science. This theory would study the conditions under which desertion and protest appeared and would analyse both the extent of their influence on organisational forms and their efficacy. Instead of studying the effects of desertion on firms and the effects of protest on organisations, why not study the two mechanisms in their complementarity?

Hirschman's critique of Hotelling's famous model contains one of the most brilliant applications of the desertion/protest couple. As is well known, Hotelling[25] had in 1929 suggested that a political system with different parties competing for power was comparable to a situation in which a group of firms sought to share out the market amongst themselves. In the simplest case the model assumes that voters are dispersed along a linear ideological continuum and that they vote for the party adopting a position closest to their own. Figure 2.1 (in which the existence of two parties *A* and *B* is posited) makes it easy to guess what will happen. Take party *A*, for instance. All the voters situated ideologically between *O* and *M* (the midpoint of the segment *AB*) are nearer to *A* than to *B*. By shifting to the left ideologically (towards *O*) *A* would lose a certain number of voters, i.e., those that this shift would bring closer to *B* than to *A*. By shifting to the right *A* would however be able to attract some of *B*'s voters. Similarly, it is only by shifting towards the left that *B* can hope to steal some of his competitor's votes. This suggests that the two parties must in balance have ideological positions that are clearly quite close to each other.

It is not difficult to understand why Hotelling's model has aroused

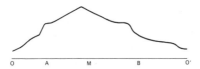

FIGURE 2.1   Fictitious distribution on an ideological continuum

such interest. It explains why the two big American parties are so close to each other ideologically, it explains why revolutionary parties can only win mass support if they trade in their ideals for a moderate reformism, and it explains the common but nevertheless curious phenomenon of two clearly equal parties in a bipolar system sharing the electorate between them.

In the light of the *New Deal* Hotelling's model needed correcting, and it was Downs[26] who pointed this out. To explain the two parties' ideological divergence at this period Downs argues that the captive voter (every voter to the left of *A* or to the right of *B*) may be aware of the distance that separates him ideologically from the party nearest to him and will abstain from voting if this distance exceeds a particular threshold. Downs assumes, contrary to what Hotelling says, that the elasticity (to resort to a term drawn from the language of economics) of the vote in relation to ideological distance is not necessarily zero.

Is it not strange, Hirschman then notes, that as good economists Downs and Hotelling only introduce *desertion* mechanisms into their models? Once the captive voters realise that the ideological distance that separates them from the party closest to them is growing, it is surely reasonable to assume that they will tend to resort to *protest* instead. This hypothesis makes sense of the phenomenon of *over-shooting* that marked the 1964 and 1968 American presidential elections. The concept of *protest* would thus account for a Republican candidate (Goldwater) too far to the right being chosen in 1964, and a Democratic candidate (McGovern) too far to the left being chosen in 1968. Hirschman's interpretation of Michels' iron law of oligarchy also explains the protest/desertion couple quite brilliantly. In a two-party political system, he argues, the ideological distance between the two parties is on average greater than in a system in which there are many parties. But there will be far more captive members in the former system and protest will therefore be more important than desertion. Conversely the more parties there are, the more important desertion (as against protest) becomes. Because of this and because they minimise the role protest plays, multi-party systems strongly favour, as Michels has shown, the emergence of political oligarchies.

But it is important to note, as Hirschman has stressed, that Michels formulated his celebrated iron law of oligarchy on the basis of his experience of multi-party political systems in Western Europe.

These and other observations suggest that institutions or, depending on circumstances, organisations imply by their very structure a particular protest/desertion ratio. Thus if I am dissatisfied with my grocer and if he does not enjoy a monopoly, I am more likely to desert him than to protest. If I am dissatisfied with the party I usually vote for, I will have no problem in deserting it if I can find a rival party that is more congenial; but if I am a militant and belong to a party to which I have only committed myself after serious reflection, I will probably only desert when I have exhausted every possible means of protesting. The protest/desertion ratio therefore varies with the cost of joining an organisation, the cost of leaving it, the presence or absence of organisations providing an alternative product or service, the ease of access enjoyed *vis-à-vis* these competing organisations, and with other variables that Hirschman introduces in the course of presenting his examples.

Loyalty is the third significant notion that figures in the book's title and it is mainly used to account for those situations in which the cost of leaving an organisation goes up or in which protest is itself costly or ineffective. I will then accept unflinchingly some measure of disagreement with the organisation to which I belong and I will remain *loyal* in spite of the distance that separates us. As the cost of leaving goes up, as the cost of protesting becomes prohibitive, and as the efficacy of protest is reduced, so naturally will loyalty tend to get stronger. This is why chauvinism is so rife among those most critical of the society in which they live, and why the decision to emigrate (to desert) is always a dramatic one.

We are clearly a long way from the Nigerian railways, although the original example may be located in very essential detail in industrial societies. Thus the desertion of the leisured classes towards private schooling has brought about an apparently irreversible deterioration in the American public educational system. In the same way competition between the telegraph and telephone systems has deprived the postal services of their best clients and has produced an accelerating deterioration in this public service. But it is the sheer range of examples to which Hirschman applies his concepts of desertion, protest and loyalty that proves the general relevance of his project.

Thus, in spite of the form that his sketch takes, Hirschman's schema hints at an interesting explanation for the 'moroseness' of industrial societies. Using American society as his main example, Hirschman gives only fleeting and faintly defined indications as to the form that this explanation might take. The increasing uniformity of the American urban environment makes desertion less possible, and the growing intensity of protest and of the eloquent denunciations of *suburban* existence also stem from this. Black power is therefore a substitution of protest for desertion the moment that it becomes clear that desertion through mobility is an illusion, or, to take up again a theme developed above, the moment it becomes apparent that a more egalitarian educational system does not automatically produce the social mobility anticipated. The ecology movement began to grow as soon as the more privileged found that they were no longer able to desert the inconveniences of pollution and so began to protest. Consumer defence councils started to attract a serious audience when people in general got richer and durable goods became a more significant part of the family budget: for, if desertion is less costly in the case of perishable goods, protest makes better sense in the case of durable goods. The fight against criminals took on a political meaning when criminality spread to the *suburbs* and the middle classes were no longer able to desert. Hirschman's analysis is in fact endlessly suggestive and one could add to this list the resurgence of regionalisms and particularisms (including age-groups, counter-culture phenomena etc.) The dialectic of the perverse effect provides an account of all these changes: here they are negative perverse effects, frequently but not necessarily produced (cf. Adam Smith's 'invisible hand') by the logic of desertion.

2. *Buchanan and Tullock's conception of organisational costs.* In their book, *The Calculus of Consent*,[27] Buchanan and Tullock reconsider the problem posed by Jean-Jacques Rousseau in the *Social Contract*: what kind of representative organisation would successfully eliminate perverse effects of the prisoner's dilemma sort? Buchanan and Tullock point out that before eliminating a perverse effect one should first of all consider what it will cost. We have known since Rousseau how high these costs may be: to attain civil liberty the savage must surrender his natural liberty. He must, in other words, submit willingly to the constraints and sanctions laid down in the contract. But Buchanan and Tullock's book is interesting because it qualifies Rousseau's propositions: there are cases in which the elimination of a perverse effect can be more disagreeable and costly than the perverse effect itself. Thus, below a certain threshold, it is preferable not to install lights to control traffic. Quite apart from the cost of installing them, pointless waiting at the lights may well be more tiresome than the inconveniences that their absence would cause. Beyond this threshold the situation is naturally reversed. When the traffic is very dense, most drivers have no qualms in accepting the constraint of traffic lights. If this constraint is tiresome it is less so than the inconveniences that its absence would cause. The difficulty here lies in measuring the threshold that determines one

solution being abandoned in favour of another. Actually it is more realistic to substitute the notion of zone of uncertainty for that of threshold: within this zone one cannot say for sure that either solution is preferable.

Organisational problems more complex than those posed by traffic lights could well be considered in much the same way. When a small number, n, of individuals cooperate in the execution of a task, a democratic kind of organisation in while each individual has a fraction $1/n$ of the power to make decisions may prove effective. Provided that the elimination of differences of opinion did not prove too costly (e.g., in terms of time), it would after all minimise the costs of interdependence and share out tasks quite satisfactorily. But as n grows, it is clearly more and more difficult to reach an agreement. If the power to make decisions is shared out unequally and a mechanism of authority thus reinstalled, interdependence will cost less than it does in a 'democratic' organisation. Imagine, for instance, people wanting to adopt the *democratic* solution for the traffic-control problem. This would entail a consensus among motorists, as against the authoritarian solution that is generally adopted (lights). The cost of interdependence would be so prohibitive that the democratic solution would quickly come to seem intolerable.

Each time that an organisational problem occurs, one naturally encounters the above-mentioned difficulty: it is only in extreme cases that one can decide upon the optimum type of organisation. Between these extremes one falls into *zones of uncertainty*. Within these zones it is impossible to determine 'objectively' if one 'solution' is preferable to another. They are therefore necessarily zones of conflict, and they result in the formation of *parties* that strive to impose one solution or another. Joint management is the rallying cry these days of those who think to minimise the costs of interdependence by levelling out the distribution of authority. In their book Buchanan and Tullock show that whilst it does sometimes work like that, it is unreasonable to propose that an egalitarian distribution of authority would always in principle make interdependence less costly. There is an echo here of Rousseau's notion that interdependence may cost more in a natural than in a social state. In modern terms this would be phrased as follows: the relation between the distribution of authority and the cost of interdependence (the intensity of perverse effects) is complex and varies with the examples treated. If, moreover, one accepts that the notion of an optimal allocation of authority has generally, because of the existence of wide *zones of uncertainty*, no meaning, one can only conclude that every problem of social organisation entails conflict *as a matter of course.*

This extended treatment of Buchanan and Tullock's analysis may perhaps be compared with the thesis of the German sociologist Ralf Dahrendorf,[28] a thesis that holds that industrial societies' conflicts are above all conflicts over the distribution of authority. If, as Dahrendorf along with certain others urges, this thesis is taken to mean that the unequal distribution of authority is always arbitrary and illegitimate, since it derives mainly from the balance of forces between social groups, then it is clearly false. But it is also possible to give a more generous interpretation of Dahrendorf's thesis: *except in extreme cases* it is difficult to prove that any one form of organisation and, in particular, any one form of allocation of authority is superior, from the point of view of a society's members, to any other. Problems to do with the allocation of authority are therefore normally (i.e., very frequently) the object of beliefs and conflicts. But this struggle over the allocation of authority should not be taken to confirm people's belief in the unconditional superiority of the egalitarian distribution of authority.

Buchanan and Tullock basically argue that every organisation aims to eliminate the costs that each individual imposes on the other in situations of interdependence. This effectively means that the main function of social organisation is the elimination of perverse effects. But this elimination is never free. It too entails costs that vary with the nature of the perverse effect to be eliminated and with the type of organisation chosen. Unfortunately another proposition must be added to those formulated by Buchanan and Tullock: the determination cannot, except in exceptional cases, be calculated 'objectively'. This solution can therefore only be arrived at in practice through the opposition and confrontation of different viewpoints. In spite of the misleading title of Buchanan and Tullock's book, *The Calculus of Consent*, the Leibnizian ideal, *non disputemus, sed calculemus*, is inappropriate.

3. Last of all I want to touch on Thomas Schelling's works on segregation. These offer another striking example of the relation between perverse effects and social change.[29] The author's main conclusion is that racial or social segregation does not necessarily derive from segregationist attitudes. In other words segregation may be the perverse result of behaviours that are not in themselves segregationist. To bring out this effect of composition Schelling resorts to a simple model in which a chess-board has a set of twenty 10p. and a set of ten 50p. pieces, each set symbolising the individuals belonging to two different social groups (for instance, social classes) or ethnic groups. The thirty pieces are then placed at random on the chess-board. This arrangement may be taken to simulate a set of relations of residential proximity. It is assumed that, although they feel no hostility and have no desire to be segregated from the other

group's members, the members of each group nevertheless feel some embarrassment at finding themselves in a minority. This situation may be simulated by supposing that each piece on the chess-board that finds itself in a minority will keep moving until it is surrounded by at least 50 per cent of pieces of the same category. This equilibrium-point reached, the piece in question is presumed to be 'satisfied' and stops moving (unless its neighbours also move in order to achieve the same sort of balance themselves and the piece finds itself in a minority once more). It is easy to play at this game by moving the pieces on the chess-board and one finds that the equilibrium structure is counter-intuitive. In fact this process produces the most brutal sort of segregation. Far from feeling hostile towards the other group's members, each individual will happily tolerate a situation in which half his neighbours belong to the other group, but a considerable segregative effect does nevertheless occur: the 50p. pieces on the chess-board constitute a sort of submerged ghetto in an environment peopled with 10p. pieces. Thus the desire of each person (not to be in a minority again) generates an effect of composition that is a caricature of individual preferences: I don't feel the slightest hostility towards 50p. pieces but in my capacity as a 10p. piece I feel a very natural desire not to be in the minority. If half my neighbours are the same as I am I will be content. Once expressed this 'natural' desire is bound to produce, in all the individuals concerned, an undesired effect of auto-amplification and the 50p. pieces, like the 10p. pieces, will find themselves back amongst their own kind.

This fable is very significant. It shows how undesirable social states may result from 'natural' individual behaviours undergoing an amplification that no one actually wanted. Apart from any other costs that may arise, the elimination of these perverse effects does clearly imply the interference of external elements in the individual's freedom to act and to make decisions. An undesired and undesirable social state does of course call to be eliminated, but the costs of its elimination may well be considerable. A socially tense situation will probably ensue, factions will form and ideologies run wild. Schelling's fable could be extended. A party, pleading at any price for the elimination of the perverse effect that produces segregation and opting for the elimination or restriction of the coins' freedom of movement, will form, and another party, proclaiming the sacred character of this same freedom, will form too. One can, in short, wager that all this will culminate in a clear-cut ideological confrontation, in conflicts and possibly in social change.

What conclusions can one draw from this survey? I will restrict myself to some propositions that seem to me to be basic. Firstly I would propose that states of social imbalance, of social tension and, consequently, of social change are not necessarily caused by the clash of incompatible interests. They may also be the result of the perverse effects that most structures of interdependence generate. Undesirable social states do not necessarily result from the capacity of a dominant group to impose its whims and interest on 'dominated' groups. A zero sum game of this sort is neither the most characteristic nor the most important structure, although it may on occasion characterise social life. The simultaneous discovery by numerous authors of the importance of zero sum game structures in the analysis of situations of interdependence represents one of modern sociology's most substantial advances in its explanation of social conflicts and social change. Those however who persist in believing in the simplistic opposition between conflict and consensus and who assume that all conflicts have the structure of zero sum games call to mind those doctors in Molière's plays.

Secondly the reader will have seen that situations of imbalance and social tension are in some sense *normal*. Perverse effects are ubiquitous in social life. But one cannot in general expect people to reach a consensus over the relation between their nuisance value and the cost of eliminating them. The example that dealt with the distribution of authority is particularly relevant here and the conclusions to be drawn from it may easily be generalised. Dahrendorf clearly felt this but expressed it badly. An already existing distribution of authority cannot, under a very wide range of conditions, be challenged: it is difficult to give a meaning to the notion of an optimal distribution of authority because, in most cases, it is impossible to work out what it would be. Since every organisational process clearly presupposes the adoption of a defined distribution of authority, the former will normally be the result of conflicts between groups concerned and will bring with it fresh conflicts. As a corollary to this it is worth noting the normal character of the ideological phenomenon. In the absence of an 'objective' solution (any solution that could be unanimously considered optimal) ideologies provide systems of pseudo-objective criteria.

Thirdly, and at a more general level, the above considerations would lead me to rule out analogies borrowed from other disciplines for the analysis of social change. The analogy of epidemiological contagion favoured by Tarde is only applicable in special circumstances. The chemical analogy that Durkheim favoured when he conceived of society as a 'synthesis' is not generally applicable either. Both the biological analogy of the adaptation of supposed social organism to a changing environment and the cybernetic model have still to prove their fruitfulness for sociology. The above analysis shows that the limited value of these analogies is attributable to the difficulty of analysing typical examples of social tensions, social imbalances and social change without taking the individual, with his specific capacities for intentionality, sometimes for rationality and invariably for *action*, as one's logical atom. Given this, physical analogies can only be of limited interest to sociologists. Change in social systems only resembles change in physical systems if one resorts to very far-fetched and heuristically weak analogies.

What of the alleged laws of history that were so popular with nineteenth-century sociologists and still seduce some twentieth-century ones? They can be safely set aside. No absolute spirit watches over human destiny. Certainly statistical regularities and cumulative processes are observable: Sorokin's cultural phases are not totally without foundation;[30] many phenomena assume a logistical or exponential trend over time. But one cannot, because of these regularities, argue in favour of the heuristic value of physical or epidemiological analogies. For once he has ascertained that a phenomenon presents a particular kind of regularity over time, the sociologist has always to explain why it does so, and to explain is necessarily to look for individual action behind the regularities observable at the macro-sociological level.

3 Educational Institutions and Perverse Effects: After 1968

The analysis of the relation between institutions and individual behaviours presents sociology with one of its most critical problems. Institutions never determine behaviours but they do affect individuals' fields of action and of decision-making. As a corollary to this, the analysis of an institutional change's 'effects' invariably entails a study of the modifications in individuals' fields of action and of decision-making that this change introduced.

In the following text I try to apply this procedure to the analysis of institutional changes affecting the French university system after 1968. This is therefore a case-study but I hope that it nevertheless has a general relevance methodologically and that it shows the significance for sociological analysis of the paradigm of methodological individualism used throughout this book.

In analysing an institutional change's effects one can restrict oneself to the study of the convergence or lack of convergence between these effects and the specific objectives that the actors responsible for the change had in mind. This is how I approach the problem in Chapter 4. Here I have attempted a general analysis of the effects, intended and unintended, positive and negative, that were generated by institutional reforms following the 1968 university crisis in France. I have, for instance, tried to show that the various sorts of constraints that the reformer had to cope with did limit the efficacy of measures that were meant to steer the demand of individuals for education and thereby to eliminate some of the undesirable external effects generated by the structure of educational flows. I have also analysed why the mechanisms that were installed with the aim of improving university training and the knowledge produced there were so ineffective. There was actually such a tangle of perverse effects that things took on the aspect of some infernal machine and this largely neutralised the attempts of reformers to revive the French university.

This text was prepared for a special number of the *Journal of*

Comparative Politics on France (1977) and was originally entitled 'The French University Since 1968'.

In the heat of the 1968 events, I proposed an interpretation of the French student crisis.[1] Briefly summarised, my argument focused on two major points. First, I suggested that French university institutions in 1968 seemed not to have adapted themselves to the relatively drastic changes which had taken place in the social composition of their constituency shortly after the beginning of the 1960s. In 1968 the French university remained upper middle class while the public it catered to was increasingly recruited from the lower middle class. Even though the offspring of the upper middle class reached the university level more often than those from the middle and lower classes, the vast majority of students belonged to the middle and lower classes and found themselves in institutions badly adapted to their expectations. On the other hand the increase in the demand for higher education made the social rewards students could expect from their university studies more uncertain: in comparison to his elders, the 'average' student of 1968 found himself disorientated by the university.

I would like to suggest in this article that neither the legislative reform of the French university, accomplished under the pressure of the events of 1968, nor the various changes introduced thereafter have helped resolve the pre-1968 contradictions in the university which the student revolt turned upside down.

The Regulation of Admissions: A Failure

The deterioration of the student condition which preceded the 1968 revolt was largely due to the fact that the university had practically no means of regulating the influx of students whom it was supposed to educate. The quantity and quality of students seeking access to university studies were no longer controlled by the university itself. The baccalauréat (the degree awarded at the end of secondary education) was, and remains in nearly all cases, the sole prerequisite for university admission.[2] This fundamental fact dominated French university life before 1968 and has continued to do so because the quantitative and qualitative make-up of admissions results from an aggregate of individual educational decisions. The sacrosanct principle of free access to the university means that the curtailment of this access cannot be achieved through direct action on the admissions process, but only by means of random incentives.[3] These decisions are made by the central government, not the universities themselves. Prior to 1968, and continuing today, this basic institutional weakness engendered marked individual and collective deficiencies. It has not, however, been corrected. Accordingly the 1968 reformers were bound to fail from the very beginning in their efforts to make the universities autonomous due to this essential point.

An immediate consequence of free access to the university is that the increase in the demand for diplomas has spread from secondary schooling to higher education. In this regard the question of whether France has too many or too few students, on an absolute scale or in comparison to her neighbours – West Germany or Great Britain, for example – has little meaning. But one fact is indisputable: the increase in the demand for university education between 1962 and 1972 has been too rapid to be absorbed by the socio-professional structure. Table 3.1 demonstrates the decrease in the level of professional opportunities available not only to high school graduates but also to those with a university diploma.

TABLE 3.1 *Managerial Opportunities for Secondary and University Graduates (Selected Years, Expressed in Probability Terms)*

| | Degree and Year | | | | | |
| | Baccalauréat | | | University degree | | |
Professional category	1962	1968	1972	1962	1968	1972
Males under 35						
Top managerial posts	30.9	24.1	23.5	61.9	57.8	57.8
Intermediate managerial ranks	39.0	42.1	42.1	25.2	30.2	29.2
Clerical workers	30.1	33.8	34.4	12.9	12.0	13.0
Total	100.0	100.0	100.0	100.0	100.0	100.0
Females under 35						
Top managerial posts	5.4	3.4	2.4	30.6	25.6	22.7
Intermediate managerial ranks	35.3	33.9	30.1	36.7	34.8	35.2
Clerical workers	59.3	62.7	67.5	32.7	39.6	42.1
Total	100.0	100.0	100.0	100.0	100.0	100.0

Source: Data drawn from Lévy-Garboua, 'Les Demandes de l'étudiant ou les contradictions de l'université de masse', *Revue Française de Sociologie*, XVII (Jan.–Mar. 1976) 53–60.

In addition to this deficiency related to socio-professional opportunities there is another deficiency in the educational system itself. The state, in seeking to cope with the rising demand for higher education, has not been able to maintain the level of expenditure per student that was attained in 1970. In 1970, computed in 1975 francs, higher-education expenditures per student reached 8070 francs. Thereafter expenditures decreased regularly until 1975: 7570 in 1971; 7070 in 1972; 6840 in 1973; 6430 in 1974; and 6420 in 1975.

Naturally we cannot claim that the deficiencies highlighted by these figures amount to a prima facie condemnation of the institutions and policies responsible for them. In France, as in numerous other countries, the philosophy of education (typified by the adage 'the more, the better') was justified by the belief that individual shortcomings were necessarily compensated for by the collective benefits resulting from the increase in education. The politicians responsible for French educational policy between 1960 and 1970 vaguely assumed that the rising demand for education would lead to economic growth and increased productivity. In other words rising levels of education would automatically encourage the modernisation and industrialisation of France which was desired, and in great part achieved, by the governors of the Fifth Republic.

The axiom, according to which a rise in the amount of schooling necessarily brings with it collective economic and social benefits, is being increasingly questioned. But is it not readily apparent that the relationship between education and economic growth must depend upon the characteristics of the educational system and upon its relatively high or low adaptability to the economic system? Even if Edward F. Denison's theories on the relationship between educational and economic growth in the United States had been proven[4] it does not necessarily follow that this relationship is automatically relevant to other countries.

In the French case the absence of direct regulation of the demand for education has had inflationary effects of the most classical nature (for example, a decrease in individual returns on the investment in education). But certain sociological trends resulting from the history of the educational system in France have led to a noteworthy consequence: the products of the university system appear largely to be used to reproduce the educational and university system rather than to serve the economic system at large.[5]

It is interesting in this regard to consider the data included in a recent study published by the *Centre d'Études et de Recherches sur les Qualifications*.[6] The two following tables give the branches of economic activity in which a national sample of students distributed according to the types of study completed and the university level attained are employed. Table 3.2 focuses on the male portion of the sample table 3.3 on the female.

Tables 3.2 and 3.3 bring out several important facts. Arts graduates in letters who receive the *licence* or the *maîtrise* (master's) degrees move largely into teaching and research. More surprisingly

Discipline/Degree	Farm and Food industries	Energy and other industries	Transportation, communications, building, public works	Commerce and services	Banking and insurance	Administration	Teaching and research	Other	Total
	%	%	%	%	%	%	%	%	%
Liberal Arts									
First year	1	6	7	12	8	12	51	3	100
Licence	—	5	3	8	4	12	64	4	100
Master's	ε*	2	2	8	3	11	73	1	100
									(N=1339)
Human Sciences									
First year	3	8	4	23	8	14	34	6	100
Licence	—	10	3	31	4	11	31	10	100
Master's	9	7	3	27		12	37	5	100
									(N=211)
Law									
First year	2	12	5	16	22	33	5	5	100
Licence	1	7	4	22	19	32	5	10	100
									(N=792)
Economic Science									
First year	4	22	4	19	25	11	11	4	100
Licence	1	14	4	22	31	20	7	1	100
									(N=667)
Sciences									
First year	4	17	11	12	5	15	35	1	100
Licence	3	16	2	8	2	8	63	ε*	100
Master's	1	27	5	5		8	52	—	100
									(N=1847)

* Less than 0.05.

Source: CEREQ (*Centre d'Études et de Recherches sur les Qualifications*), document no. 26, *L'Accès à la vie professionnelle à la sortie des Universités* (Paris, Jan. 1975).

TABLE 3.3   *Economic Sectors Employing Female Students who Graduated 1969–70, by Discipline and Degrees Earned*

Discipline/Degree	Farm and food industries %	Energy and other industries %	Transportation, communications, building, public works %	Commerce and services %	Banking and insurance %	Administration %	Teaching and research %	Other %	Total %
Liberal Arts									
First year	ε*	7	4	19	3	6	59	2	100
Licence	ε*	4	2	9	2	8	73	2	100
Master's	—	5	1	6	2	6	79	1	100
									(N=2237)
Human Sciences									
First year	—	2	5	17	—	20	51	5	100
Licence	—	2	—	48	5	12	30	2	100
Master's	—	—	—	64	2	6	19	9	100
									(N=295)
Law									
First year	—	12	3	19	5	30	28	3	100
Licence	1	4		14	20	34	17	10	100
									(N=581)
Economic Science									
First year	2	8	—	27	10	17	34	2	100
Licence	—	10	7	9	13	22	39	—	100
									(N=285)
Sciences									
First year	—	10	1	10	3	7	68	1	100
Licence	1	4	3	4	1	2	85	—	100
Master's	ε*	4	1	5	1	4	85	—	100
									(N=1250)

holders of a *licence* or *maitrise* in the sciences are also absorbed to a great extent by the teaching and research professions. If we add to teaching and research administrative services, we see that these three categories absorb a considerable proportion of graduates of arts and science and a somewhat smaller, but still significant, proportion of those in the social sciences. Only graduates in law and economics seem to be moving into the economic system as a whole rather than into the university system or government service.

These figures lead us to doubt that the excessive increase in the demand for higher education since 1960 has contributed optimally to generating collective benefits such as economic growth. This increase was, as we now know, linked to a growing feminisation and democratisation of the student body which in turn partly explains the particularly rapid expansion of the arts and sciences as compared to law studies.[7] In other words overall statistical trends, like feminisation and democratisation of the student body, help to explain the disproportionate growth of disciplines (e.g., the literary and scientific fields and, to a lesser extent, the social sciences) which appear better suited to the needs of the educational system itself than to the economic system. Several additional factors should also be taken into account. First, liberal arts and science faculties have traditionally been regarded as *de facto* professional schools training future teachers just as the schools of medicine and law exist to train doctors and lawyers. Second, the dogma shared by the successive republics, according to which the educational system was supposed to be by its very essence a public service placed directly in the hands of the state, hardly encouraged exchanges between the educational system and the economic system. Whatever the complex reasons for this phenomenon, the recent statistical data we have presented suggest that the exchanges between the university system and the economic system are perhaps not as well developed as one might desire.[8]

As a result of the general increase in the demand for education and the less significant but cumulative impact of demographic growth, the educational system was for many years more or less able to maintain its self-perpetuating function, no doubt to the detriment of its other functions. Today complex factors tend to limit this self-perpetuation.[9] It is not certain that the former Faculties of Arts and Sciences – even renamed, dismembered, and integrated into interdisciplinary units as intended by the 1968 legislature – will interact smoothly with the economic system. The frequent hostility demonstrated by students in the Faculties of Letters and Sciences toward the economic system, the complementary refusal of many teachers to train their students for activities other than teaching, research or criticism are only a few elements of a system which render an opening of the university to the economic world difficult. More important perhaps are the facts that (1) for decades the Faculties of Arts and Sciences have been used primarily to educate teachers; (2) the rise in the demand for education has led to a spectacular expansion of the teaching body; and (3) until now the influx of students in arts and Sciences has been more or less successfully absorbed.[10]

Short-Cycle Higher Education: A Case in Point

Since 1960 public authorities have appeared preoccupied with the problem of controlling enrolments which the institution of open enrolment makes difficult. In spite of the current doctrine, 'the more, the better', public authorities are aware of the inefficiency of unregulated admissions. They are concerned less with the growth of the overall number of students than with the distribution of students among the various disciplines. Unable to control admissions directly, however, they have instead chosen an indirect method of coping with the problem. They created new institutions, intended to modify the structure of unchecked enrolments, that offered students prospects which were made as attractive as possible. The creation of the *Instituts Universitaires de Technologie* (IUT) and the *Maîtrises de sciences et techniques* are two examples of this type of strategy. The IUTs were designed to formalise or, more precisely, to improve the status and expand existing short-cycle and vocational institutions of higher education. Before the creation of the IUTs the system had limited importance and a low visibility. The masters degrees in science and technology, created later, were intended to channel some of the students enrolled in traditional universities towards professionally oriented courses of study. Thus these degrees have three characteristics: (1) they have an immediate professional objective; (2) they are completely integrated into the traditional university; and (3) they fit into a long course of study. Let us keep in mind that the reform measures of the second cycle of university studies, whose implementation was decreed by the secretary of state for universities in 1976, also demonstrated the desire of the authorities to 'professionalise' traditional courses of study in the university.[11] In spite of their relevance it is difficult to assert that these various innovations have to date modified the structure of enrolments. Let us pause a moment to consider the case of the IUTs.[12]

The creation of the IUTs was designed to correct, or at least to help correct, three major characteristics of French higher education: the rapid growth of enrolments, the relatively large proportion of students opting for university careers without clear professional objectives (such as literary studies), and the increasing duration of university studies. (The first two factors are illustrated by table 3.4.) On the third point a rapid historical overview would show that in the last thirty years the duration of university studies has increased from two to four, or even six years or more. Before the Second World War a student who progressed at a normal pace could obtain a *licence* in the majority of fields two years after the *baccalauréat* and the education acquired provided ample qualification for jobs in the executive ranks. Since then however there has been a steady increase in the number of years spent in the university. The introduction of the *Propédeutique* has resulted in stretching the time required to obtain the *licence* to a minimum of three years.[13] The creation of the master's degree in 1967, though not formally lengthening the time necessary to get the *licence*, contributed to the devaluation of this older degree by interposing a new degree above it. Besides, the division of higher education into two-year cycles tends to extend by one year the duration of longer courses of study. In addition several years earlier the law and economics faculties had already extended to four years the time required to obtain the *licence* in those fields.

TABLE 3.4   *Distribution of Students among Disciplines (1967–73)*

Discipline	1967–8	1968–9	1969–70	1970–1	1971–2	1972–3
Sciences	137100	123300	122800	115400	120800	119400
Liberal arts and human sciences	169100	196100	218300	234400	246900	254900
Law and economic sciences	114300	126700	138700	148200	153700	165700
Medicine, pharmacy and dental sciences	80900	118900	128500	135700	142700	158500
University Institutes of Technology	5400	11900	17300	24400	33700	37000
Total	506800	576900	625600	658100	697800	735500

Source: *Tableaux de l'éducation nationale*, 1970 edn, p. 415; 1971 edn, pp. 402–3; 1972 edn, p. 363; 1973 edn, p. 363; 1974 edn, p. 329

The creation of the IUTs was designed to help compensate for shortcomings at the individual and collective levels brought about by these trends. The rationale for their creation rested on the following assumptions: (1) it was hoped that the development of shorter programmes in higher education would help reduce the pressure on the individual demand for higher education; (2) the creation of IUTs would make possible an increase in the geographical dispersion of institutes of higher education, thereby helping to equalise chances of access at this level of the educational system; and (3) these new institutions would permit the creation of new channels leading to professional degrees. It would also be easier to introduce new pedagogical methods there.

The new institutions created since 1965 are characterised by a break with the traditional university model. They are multi- and interdisciplinary in nature, that is to say the students are offered a certain number of major options defined not by traditional academic boundaries but by the needs of the regional or national economy.[14] The course of study lasts two years and, in contrast to the universities, attendance is compulsory. The work is done in small groups. Admission into the IUTs is neither entirely open as in the traditional universities, nor rigorously controlled through competitive examinations, as in the *Grandes Écoles*. The rector of the academy determines the number of students who are to be allowed to enrol in each department and his decision is based upon the recommendation of the admissions board which selects the candidates. The number of applicants accepted varies with each field of specialisation and is not well publicised. But we can estimate that the overall rate of acceptance is not above 50 per cent. The IUT programmes lead to the *Diplôme Universitaire de Technologie* (DUT). On the recommendation of the director the IUT students may pursue their studies either at the university level or in engineering schools.

Did the IUTs live up to what was expected of them when they were created? Tentative answers to this question may be proposed now that they have been functioning for several years. The essential fact to be emphasised here is that the IUTs have not deterred a large number of students from long courses of study. The Fifth Plan for French development forecast that in 1973 the IUTs would enrol 21 per cent of all students. However in 1972 all of technical higher education accounted for a mere 7 per cent of the students enrolled in post-secondary programmes. In actuality the development of the IUTs seems only to have complemented pre-existing channels in technical education. But it has had practically no effect on the growth of enrolments in the universities (see table 3.5).

The Sixth Plan, based on actual trends, reflected far more modest ambitions: the IUTs were henceforth responsible for providing personnel qualified for certain types of socio-economic functions.[15] It is as though no one any longer believed in the indirect effect of the IUTs on easing university enrolment. The Sixth Plan, whose projected figures are far lower than those of the Fifth Plan, proposes the objective of an enrolment of 67,000 to 105,000 students by the end of the plan's term. In reality there were 32,200; 35,400; 39,000; and 41,700 students respectively in the IUTs for the academic years 1971–2 to 1974–5. Even revised downwards the objective of the Sixth

TABLE 3.5   *Growth in Student Enrolments by University Institutions*

Year	Public teacher training	Preparatory classes for *Grandes écoles*	*Grandes écoles*	Sections of high-level technicians	University Institutes of Technology	Total technical education	Universities	Total	Short-cycle education as percentage of post-secondary education
1959	10000*	17600	30000	5700	—	5700	161400	224700	2.5
1960	10900*	18900	32000	7500	—	7500	172400	241700	3.1
1961	13900*	22600	34000	8000	—	8000	173600	252100	3.2
1962	12800*	23600	32000	9400	—	9400	202300	280100	3.4
1963	11100*	24700	33000	12200	—	12200	242700	323700	3.8
1964	12500*	25900	36000	16200	—	16200	273400	364000	4.5
1965	14000*	28000	38000	18700	—	18700	309700	403400	4.6
1966	13700*	28800	42000	25600	—	25600	332500	442600	5.8
1967	13600*	28000	46000	30000	1600	31600	370900	490100	6.4
1968	13800	28100	51000	28700	5400	34100	432000	559000	6.1
1969	14200*	30000*	56000	27600	11900	39500	540000*	679700	5.8
1970	14700	31900	62000	26500	17300	43800	591500	743900	5.9
1971	14500	31200	68000	26800	24400	51200	613200	778100	6.6
1972	18200	32800	80000	30200	37000	67200	698500	896700	7.4
1973	16400	33700	78300	35300	38900	74200	745200	947800	7.3
1974	**	33600	**	39700	41900	81600	718600	**	**
1975	**	**	**	44400	43500	**	767700	**	**

* Estimate.

** Data not available.

Source: *Tableaux de l'éducation nationale*, 1969, 1970, 1972 and 1973 edns.

Plan is far from having been attained. In any event one point seems clear: the corrective effects on the university enrolment flows that had been sought through the creation of the IUTs have proved to be negligible.

For the students, however, the IUTs were not entirely unsatisfactory: scholarships were much more generously granted to IUT students than to those in traditional universities. In 1969–70, 41 per cent of IUT students were recipients of scholarships as opposed to 17 per cent among students enrolled in university programmes.[16] The pedagogical methods in use in the IUTs were seen as more effective and more modern than those used in traditional university teaching. In short the public authorities had accomplished what lay in their power: to attract future students to the IUTs. Moreover the experience of the first years shows that by way of economic compensation IUT graduates receive average incomes comparable to those of students who have completed three, four or five years of university and have received the *licence*. Finally the salaries of IUT graduates are less unpredictable and divergent than those of their counterparts in longer university programmes. Their incomes do not deviate either up or down from the average as much as the incomes of university graduates.[17]

But how do we explain the failure of the larger purpose for which the IUTs were created? Evidently the IUTs allow students to obtain in less time, and thus at lower cost, a degree that gives them a level of social marketability which, on the average, is as favourable as that to which the graduates of longer university programmes can lay claim. The theory that Janina Lagneau, Philippe Cibois, and I have advanced to account for the failure of the IUTs can be summarised as follows: the traditional university retains a considerable advantage over the IUTs in that it can offer, if not a guarantee, at least an expectation of social compensation greater than that of the IUTs. Given the inflationary nature of the demand for higher education the university can offer a small and ever-shrinking majority of its graduates a level of social compensation higher than that of the IUTs, but each prospective university student, taken individually, has no reason to give up the hope that he will be among the lucky ones even if the probability of his actually receiving these greater advantages turns out to be very small when everyone reasons in identical terms.[18]

In short the experience of the IUTs shows that the principle of free access to the university still acts as a heavy liability. This principle has considerably lessened the impact of the many and varied courses of action taken by the authorities in their effort to control enrolments in higher education, both as to quantity and quality. These measures had only very limited effects. The character of enrolments continues to be the product of the aggregate of individual demand for education. As far as this individual demand is concerned, its logic is governed in all likelihood by a principle whose negative potential is evident – that is, that for each individual taken separately it is advantageous to attempt, within the limits of his resources, to obtain the highest level of education possible.

If the indirect regulation of entry into the university was thus made difficult by the principle of free access to the university, is direct regulation possible? An essential point here is that families and individuals can abstractly envisage how the lack of controlled access to longer university programmes engenders both individual and collective problems. But it would be unrealistic to expect support for a measure which might in given individual instances have harmful effects. Thus it is hard to imagine parents' associations campaigning for a restriction of access to the universities. Each individual family with children of university age, or each teenager who has finished high school, can fear that such a measure would be detrimental to his own interests while it benefits everyone else.

The struggle against all attempts to control access to universities seems to be a natural campaign issue of broad appeal for those taking advantage of public educational services, such as parents' organisations. Since within the French system any attempt at fundamental reform of this kind could only be initiated by the central government, opposition to such efforts would normally be not only viable but would also pay off handsomely: it is easier to disarm adversaries, such as elected government officials, who are readily identifiable and who are considered a 'natural' enemy. We can therefore expect political authorities to move in the direction of restriction of access to universities only with the greatest caution. As for the possibility of an initiative coming from 'autonomous' universities themselves, it is difficult to see this as a serious possibility.[19] They are autonomous by the letter of the 1968 law but they also compete with each other for appropriations based on the number of students and faculty in each institution, thereby necessitating the maintenance of their high numbers of teachers and students, as well as of the level of funds they receive.

It would be hard to find a clearer example of a jammed system. Unless a group existed which sought expressly to espouse the 'common interest', it would be difficult to find any interest group or aggregate of social forces directly involved in the system that would derive any advantage from changing that system.

Modernisation of the University

In the preceding pages I discussed the paralysing effect of the principle of free access to the universities on the various measures formulated by the government in order to (1) control enrolments in higher education in quantity and quality (i.e., in their volume and their structure); (2) eliminate deficiencies at the individual and collective levels brought about by a monolithic system which the 1968 law barely touched; and (3) achieve a better congruence between the university system and the economic system. These neutralising effects have been remarkably powerful. The efforts of the authorities have proven futile in effectively combating the perverse influence of certain fundamental structures. In this section I will examine briefly the effects of these structures not on the system of higher education as a whole or on the relationship between the educational and economic systems, but rather on the university itself taken as a sub-system. The 1968 reform law had sought, in General de Gaulle's words, to adapt to the new French society a '*grand corps* which had not been able to reform itself'. This situation, according to the head of state, had led to the 1968 revolt. The Minister of Education, Edgar Faure, with his admirable political dynamism, succeeded in having the legislature enact a law which made the universities *autonomous* (but not responsible since their resources continued to be disbursed by the central authorities on criteria having nothing to do with the universities' internal policies). This law transformed the universities into cooperatively managed institutions – evidence of the spirit of the times. In addition, by granting certain decision-making powers to the students, albeit very limited ones, and by broadening the influence of junior faculty members, it was hoped that the mandarin-like habits considered partly responsible for the 'sclerosis' of the university could be broken.[20]

As we shall see, the law was not without its effects. It contributed, for example, to reducing the dependence of young teachers on their elders and to 'mollifying' (in Giscard's terminology) their tense relationships. It has certainly had still other effects, but it is doubtful that the law succeeded in 'modernising' the universities as was hoped by the 1968 reformers. If I may for a moment open a parenthesis and venture into the fields of sociology and political history, it seems evident that the president of the Republic, General de Gaulle, as well as Faure, had one major objective: the prevention of another outburst of student agitation at the beginning of the school year in October 1968 which might again threaten the state itself. It is equally evident, however, that the president, the minister, and his advisers had more than this political objective in mind. They sought not only to take into account at least the justifiable demands of the students, but also to learn something from the revolt. In other words, with the help of the information provided by its symptoms, a diagnosis of the disease had to be made in order to deal with the causes themselves. The major elements of the diagnosis were autonomy and participation. Certainly everyone agreed that the excessive power of the administrative mandarins over the other factions in the university system and, on the other hand, the power of the state itself over the universities were among the fundamental causes of the revolt. Today we are aware that this was a superficial analysis. It is true that every revolt pits the bottom against the top, but this is insufficient reason to conclude that the causes of the revolt can be found only in the existence of the phenomena of authority. This may be true in certain cases but not necessarily valid in all. It seems that this naïve diagnostic error guided the advisers of the chief of state in 1968. Although the students had attacked the university and the political authorities, one of the essential causes of the revolt had nothing to do with the phenomena of authority or power. The situation of the students in France in 1968 was simply a condition from which escape was impossible and which benefited neither students nor government. Entry into the university offered hope of future benefits which it would be absurd to give up voluntarily. These hopes however could only prove illusory for most students because of the inflationary nature of the demand for higher education. Moreover the enormous and sacrificial investments a student had to make in order to have a chance of receiving these future benefits seemed at times incomprehensible. There were certainly 'programmes' established at the national level, but teachers enjoyed complete freedom in their conduct of them. The kind of treatment a student received depended essentially on his previous academic and social background which was not controlled by the system. Thus before 1968 the average student vaguely felt that entrance to the university would be profitable to him in the long run, but it was difficult for him to identify the nature of these benefits and to understand the link between the efforts the system required of him and these anticipated rewards. After 1968 the student condition remained to a large extent the same and in some instances even worsened. The notion of 'programmes' progressively disappeared. It was no doubt necessary to abandon officially the fiction of the uniformity of university programmes, but this new approach led to a proliferation of '*Unités de valeur*' (UV) which disoriented students far more than the routine courses of study of the previous defunct system. In short the 1968 reforms, based as they were on an erroneous definition of the problem, do not seem to have been related in any way to the causes which led to the revolt. The situation of the French student in 1977 is as contradictory and unappealing as that of the 1968 student.

On this topic we can refer to an interesting study recently

published by Louis Lévy-Garboua,[21] which relies on a poll conducted by the *Centre de Recherche et de Documentation sur la Consummation* (CREDOC) among a sample of university students. Lévy-Garboua's thesis is the following: the expected benefits associated with a university degree are tending to decline in France. Statistics show that this is true for socio-professional status: the probability of holding a high position tends to decrease while the likelihood of ending up in an occupation of lesser status tends to increase. On the other hand public expenditures per student tend to decline. Both points were raised in the first section of this article. What must now be explained is why, in light of the increase of student enrolments, the demand for higher education has not decreased directly in proportion to the decrease in educational investment. I have elsewhere suggested a possible answer to this question: despite the observable decline in the returns on investment in university education there is still a positive correlation between the level of studies attained and, for example, status and income. Even if a student has a strong chance of attaining a level of status or income lower than someone with less education, hopes for higher status and income are still associated with a higher level of education. In spite of the devaluation of diplomas, it is still a judicious choice to attempt to raise one's educational level.

Lévy-Garboua attempts to complete this interpretation with a set of propositions which he terms an eligibility model: students are aware of the devaluation of their investment in attending a university, but they are also conscious of the positive nature of this investment and are therefore not willing to forgo a university education. They seek to strike a balance between the investment they make and the return they can hope to receive by reducing the amount of time and effort involved in the earning of a university degree. Naturally in all fields the university requires that the student spend a certain minimum amount of time on his studies. Beyond this minimum he is free to determine the extra time he wishes to devote to his studies. This quantity, according to Lévy-Garboua's model, decreases in proportion to the returns on education and the utility of the other uses of his time (recreation or outside work, etc.). The following data are interesting in this context for the persuasive argument they bring to this interpretation.

Table 3.6 shows that, with the exception of students from the lowest socio-professional strata, the time devoted to extra-curricular remunerated labour tends to increase over time. Thus in the case of the students from higher strata (upper middle class and liberal professions) not only did the proportion of salaried students increase between 1963–4 and 1973–4 but the proportion of such students who work at least part-time grew spectacularly as well. Generally the

TABLE 3.6 *Student Employment, according to Father's Occupation*

Year	Farmer	Industry/Commerce Businessman	Shopkeeper	Top Managers, Liberal Profession	Middle level Managers	Employees	Service Worker	Others (inactive, undeclared)	Total
	%	%	%	%	%	%	%	%	%
% total student population employed:									
1963–4	39.0	*	*	26.5	32.2	43.0	31.9	25.3	31.4
1973–4 (unmarried students)	19.0	37.9	30.3	30.1	34.2	24.6	33.4	27.0	30.2
All students	22.0	42.8	29.8	31.5	35.4	28.0	37.0	28.6	32.1
% employed students working part-time:									
1963–4	29.1	*	*	7.8	20.5	22.5	37.8	32.4	21.7
1973–4 (unmarried students)	28.0	12.8	27.1	21.9	25.4	22.3	31.6	33.0	25.0
All students	32.2	19.6	27.1	27.6	27.5	31.2	38.6	34.0	29.5

* Data not available.
Source: Lévy-Garboua, 'Les Demandes de l'étudiant ...', op. cit.

growth of salaried employment for the time period under consideration depends directly on the individual's social origins: the greater the increase in the time devoted to paid employment, the higher the social background of the individual. From the additional well-known fact that the upper classes are over-represented and the lower classes under-represented in the university system, we can infer a general increase in the time devoted to paid employment (noted in the last column of table 3.6). The decreasing proportion of salaried employment among students from agricultural and working-class backgrounds is to be viewed in relation to the redistributive impact of public financial aid to students.

Additional data published by Lévy-Garboua must be evaluated against this background of information: they show that there is an inverse relationship between the time devoted to studies and the time devoted to paid employment; the amount spent for recreation remaining constant so long as the period spent working does not exceed a certain point. In other words the time for work is taken first from the time for study and only in case of necessity (when the job takes more than twenty hours per week) from the time allotted to recreation.

The data point to an important conclusion: in the absence of a mechanism that controls enrolments the French university system contributed to the appearance of lower expectations associated with individual investments in higher education. If, as seems to be the case, a decrease in the time devoted to study means a decrease in the quality of education, the system must also lead to a decline in the quality of students and ultimately to greater inefficiency in the university's performance of one of its essential functions – the production and transmission of knowledge.[22]

That the 1968 reforms have not made the university more attractive to students is due mainly to the fact that these reforms took place without a general analysis of the causes leading to the revolt. To paraphrase a famous saying, the degree of participation by the members of an organisation can be observed but not decreed. The 1968 law decreed participation by providing, among other things, for the election of student delegates to various levels of administration of the remodelled university. In reality it decreed participation without correcting any of the factors which prevent the students from developing a sense of identity with the university; without such identification real participation cannot occur.

A simple measure of the degree of student identification with the university provided by the reform itself can be found in the results of annual elections of student delegates to university councils. What is striking in these results is the low rate of electoral participation of the student body and the decline of this participation over time. Only a small minority of students has enough interest to take part in the election of student delegates. Second, there are also the complex relationships between the rate of participation and a group of institutional variables. Thus the IUT students on the average take part in voting much more frequently than their counterparts in other sectors of the university. The reason for this relationship is intuitively obvious and partially borne out by the results of several polls: IUT students are subjected to a relatively constraining regime of study; their university career is rather narrowly predetermined; it can be predicted with relative accuracy. In contrast traditional university students are offered an '*à la carte*' choice between numerous '*unités de valeur*', not always organised into a coherent unit. Furthermore they have inadequate information about the contents of courses. Student decisions therefore are often made on the basis of short-sighted criteria; we observe a rush on the UVs that are reputed to be easily completed and, when the field allows it, on those UVs dealing with fashionable subject matter. The traditional university student cannot have a clear view of the objectives for which the university is training him; the requirements which apply to him are vague; a large margin of choice is left to him in the organisation of studies, but the system often leaves him with the sole alternative of short-term choices. Under these conditions we cannot expect the development of a strong feeling of identity with the institution. Believing that the autonomy, that is to say the capacity for self-determination of the student, has been increased, what we have above all done is to increase the level of *anomie* of the system.

These hypotheses are borne out for the IUT students by a poll showing that they seem to a large extent satisfied with their university situation. They find their studies more attractive than the longer programmes of study in liberal arts and science faculties; the IUTs, they say, offer better training for professional life; teaching is better organised there, etc.[23] To complement these findings several polls, though unfortunately too few, seem to confirm what observation suggests – that students in longer programmes come to the university with specific expectations which change from year to year.[24] The anomic situation which confronts students in the traditional sectors of the university is no doubt responsible for the large amount of self-selection and reorientation which we observe there and for the low degree of student electoral participation.[25]

A comparison of the disciplines within the university concerning the degree of participation shows complex differences which still require further investigation. But we can still realistically explain these differential rates of participation in terms of three factors:

1. *The degree of professionalisation of the discipline.* The more rigorous

structuring of the curriculum and greater precision in the distribution of rewards lead, all things being equal, to greater participation.

2. *The degree of technicality of the discipline.* If a field involves a long technical apprenticeship this leads, all things being equal, to a better structuring of the curriculum and a more discriminating distribution of rewards.

3. *The extent to which a discipline lends itself to politicisation.* Certain disciplines (social sciences, for example) are for intrinsic reasons easily politicised. Others, such as physics or biology, are not intrinsically very politicisable in the sense that their principles must be subject to the ideal of ethical neutrality. However they may lead to politicisation on a secondary level by virtue of their link with visible and salient social problems. This type of discipline can exert – this is at least a valid hypothesis – an influence on the student's selection of his field; such a discipline will thus attract students with strong political sentiments and their political and social preoccupations can be even more vigorously expressed in as much as their academic discipline prepares them to a lesser degree for a cautious analysis of social and political phenomena.[26]

It remains to be seen how these different factors combine to account for the differences in voting rates among various disciplines and, more generally, the idiosyncratic differences in the student condition with respect to field of specialisation. But the principal conclusion we can draw from this brief analysis of the participation of students in university elections is that low rates of participation indicate low levels of student integration into the institution. How can the function of integration be satisfactorily performed in an institution whose ends are vague from the individual as well as from the collective point of view and which renders the student anomic? Since Durkheim we have known that *anomie* and integration are antithetical.

The University, Politics and Intellectuals

The effort of the 1968 reformers to stimulate higher levels of student participation in the universities was naturally linked to their desire to democratise the system. It was necessary first to encourage the admission of students from modest backgrounds and, second, to involve students in the making of decisions concerning them. On the first point the 'natural' logic of the demand for education, in addition to the apparently effective redistributive measures, have contributed to a lowering of the social origins of French university students. On the second point, probably due to a lack of clear objectives during their university careers resulting from the obligations imposed upon them, students have little interest in university governance. Thus the reformers who initiated the mechanisms of participation fostered politicisation at the expense of participation. As soon as nominations for offices were subject to elections, a process of politicisation was inevitable; theoretically this process might have been a constructive one and could have attained a more than symbolic significance. But this was possible only if students felt 'integrated' into university institutions and demonstrated a direct interest in voting. This necessary condition was not met and it was inevitable that political organisations outside the university would benefit most by the process of politicisation which would provide them with a legal foothold there. Each year political groups work to get as many of their members as possible elected to the numerous student delegate offices at various levels of university government. As a result of this and taking into account the general indifference of students, the universities are becoming political states. Because of low voter turnout, a university where group X obtains 60 per cent of student seats in the various student councils will take on the political image of that group. Once this image is well established it will annually attract students who have an affinity for it. Thus we have white, pink and red universities. Guidebooks drawing their inspiration from handy restaurant guides are widely circulated in periodical literature.[27] Ratings are provided in order to help students choose among universities described primarily in political terms. Recently the walls of the *lycées* were littered with posters attempting to estimate the percentage of 'red' teachers in Parisian universities. This information was presented in the form of a white (red) circle with a red (white) portion of the surface corresponding to the percentage of reds (whites).

Politicisation naturally spreads to the faculty. Union organisations can occasionally intervene decisively to further the careers of junior faculty members; these unions enjoy success similar to that of 'voluntary' organisations capable of offering their members collective benefits (their primary function) and some 'selective incentives'[28] such as job security, promotions and legal and social aid services. The traditional presence of union organisations in the university was further encouraged by a structural change in the teaching body. Various factors have contributed to this evolution: an increase in the demand for higher education from 1960 on; a consensus on the necessity of improving teacher–student ratios; the substitution of work in small groups for large lecture courses. These factors have led to a rapid rise in the number of junior faculty (*assistants* and *maître assistants*) in absolute terms as well as in relation to the professorial staff, as table 3.7 shows.

TABLE 3.7   *University Teachers by Rank*

	1956–7		1963–4		1967–8		1971–2	
	N	%	N	%	N	%	N	%
Professors and Associate Professors	3152	56	4903	33	6257	28	9060	27
Assistant Professors and Assistants	2479	44	10195	67	16256	72	24841	73

Source: Raymond Poignant, *L'Enseignement dans les pays du Marché Commun*, Institut Pédagogique National, 1965; *Statistiques des enseignements, tableaux et informations*, Paris, Ministry of National Education.

But university unions also benefited from the 1968 reforms. By officially politicising the university, the reforms paved the way for the emergence of political groups. The formation of these groups reinforced, by a sort of multiplier effect, the unions which are traditionally associated with them.

Politicisation, an outgrowth of this institutional system, not only governs elective offices in university government but often leads to basing decisions on appointments to professorial or more junior positions on political criteria and, only secondarily, on scientific criteria. In most cases this ordering of criteria is disguised. The hidden criteria only surface in special cases when the decisions involve persons whose fame goes beyond the limits of their discipline. In such instances the matter becomes an openly political 'affair' involving people outside the university in question, perhaps even outside the academic world, and leads to articles in the press.

To be sure, hiring procedures for teaching personnel before 1968 were not altogether apolitical. It would be naïve to deny it and foolish to decry these procedures.[29] But the 1968 reforms served, if not to make official, at least to institutionalise and aggravate this practice. It is certainly not an exaggeration to say that, as a consequence of the institutional procedures now in operation, many members of higher educational institutions devote considerable energy to such issues as avoiding or ensuring that a certain party might receive or lose a single post in a given institution. Arguments of a scholarly nature tend to be superseded by arguments of a political nature and, since political criteria cannot be openly admitted in issues of a scientific nature, the 'contradiction' is resolved by an effort to come back to the old distinctions between good and bad science. But good and bad are distinguished in the final analysis according to political criteria. The new university institutions have perhaps facilitated the rebirth of a distinction which we thought had disappeared with the Stalinist era – at least this is a hypothesis worth testing. But the fact remains that in France there exists, or at least we speak of, a politics, economics, sociology, psychology of the Right and of the Left. The 'reality' of these distinctions, to use W. I. Thomas's famous theory, is no doubt confirmed by the politicisation introduced by the institutional structures.

Another perhaps unanticipated but nontheless foreseeable consequence of the reforms was the reduction in the rate of teacher mobility among institutions. Given the importance of unions in the new institutions and the role they play in determining the careers of their members, seniority becomes a major factor in promotion whenever a vacancy occurs in a particular university. Previously promotion usually entailed a move to another university. Today however the question of promotion just as often arises within the context of a single department.

All of these trends are undoubtedly a part of the same alarming syndrome. In many areas French universities are neither professional schools nor bastions of culture and dynamic research. For many students and teachers the way out is withdrawal from the system or innovation, in Merton's sense of these terms. Withdrawal may reflect demoralisation or cynicism toward the university system. Innovation may mean a double life for those who live within the system. Students will study as a hobby, channelling most of their interests elsewhere; teachers will devote themselves to research, literature, library work, thereby minimising the time spent on teaching, or instead will create a network of scientific and professional contacts largely outside of their immediate scientific and professional environment. But the most interesting solution from a sociological perspective is the flight toward the intellectual world of '*tout-Paris*'.

A brief word is necessary on this important point. It seems that the disorganisation of the university has led a large and probably growing number of academics (when their background and field made it possible) to seek the meaning of their research and the source of their social gratification, not in their fragmented professional surroundings, but rather in an environment transcending barriers between fields and bringing together those who share similar backgrounds and identical interests in general problems. I am referring here to the intellectual circles and, more specifically, to Parisian intellectuals. In short it seems that the disorganisation of the universities gave new impetus to Parisian intellectual life. After 1968 many philosophers (in the sense of 'specialists of philosophy') who, before the 1968 university crisis, were known for their erudite work on the history of philosophy began to work in new areas that are closer to what Benda called Byzantine literature than to scientific or philosophical research.[30] This work is characterised by a taste for tenuous and shattering hypotheses, obscurity, the cult of an esoteric and personal style, hasty and premature syntheses, the refusal to use common sense described as an epistemological breakdown or a lack of reasoning, and vaticination. The model that many of these converts try to emulate is probably that of a simplified Heidegger.

The same phenomenon manifested itself among many intellectuals who before 1968 specialised in social sciences and economics. Discarding their econometric models and sociological research which had gained great importance after 1950 and had undoubtedly contributed to a better understanding of French society, economists and sociologists have shifted to 'philosophical' essays and gross, tenuous, premature syntheses.[31] Here the model emulated is Marshall McLuhan's.

Like McLuhan, the *new* sociologist, the *new* economist and the *new* political scientist go beyond their professional circle and seek to appeal to journalists and media critics of intellectual life and the public at large.[32] The anticipated recipient of the product retroactively determines the nature of the product. 'The basic rule is to please and to touch the emotions,' said Racine. This is what the new philosophers are trying to do and in doing this they naturally break with the norms regulating scholarly work. But it is important to point out that whereas the case of McLuhan still seems atypical in the United States it has become a cult in France. A proportion (the size of which is as yet undetermined, but which is certainly significant) of professors as well as students in economics, sociology, political science or in philosophy are looking for models in Reich rather than Piaget, in Myrdal rather than Arrow, in Fourier rather than Max Weber, Tocqueville or Durkheim. In short there is an imbalance in French intellectual output today in the field of the study of man and the social and economic phenomena – an imbalance which does not appear to exist in the United States or in Great Britain, for example – which favours aesthetics, ethics and politics at the expense of traditional scholarly research. This crucial difference, whose social and political consequences can be considerable, is no doubt largely the result of the current state of the French university.

Space does not allow me to deal at great length with these problems here, but it seems clear that one of the consequences of the disorganisation of the French university system and its incapacity in large areas to stimulate scholarly research is that many academics now channel their energies into areas which may have aesthetic, ethical or political value but are without scientific interest. The history of the French university (especially in economics and social sciences) demonstrates, if indeed this was still necessary, that important breakthroughs in knowledge cannot result simply from political or moral design, 'need' or impulse. It is also necessary that the sometimes unpleasant activities involved in the acquisition of knowledge appear desirable and gratifying to those who undertake them. This entails the existence of institutions like professional and scientific associations or universities – institutions which must be organised in a manner which enables them to impose a system of *norms* allowing for the harmonious development of research activities and the distribution of rewards, in the absence of which the system would not operate. In certain essential sectors of research these institutions malfunction to such an extent in France today that talented people are tempted to search for rewards in establishments such as the '*tout-Paris*' intellectual environment[33] which seem to offer more than the university institutions. Naturally reward differentials have a retroactive effect on the nature of the output.

The negative aspects of the picture having thus been described (and I believe that the negative aspects far outweigh the others), it is necessary to look for more encouraging ones. From the teachers' point of view, if it is true that many have been forced to withdraw from the system, others have benefited from certain aspects of the evolution discussed above. The massive quantitative growth of the French university system has necessitated the recruitment of a large number of adjunct personnel (for example, secondary school teachers have been given the opportunity to teach at the university). These adjunct personnel have often benefited materially as well as intellectually from the system's inflationary trends. Similarly the new institutions have provided access to teaching positions for experts and specialists who do not have the required credentials for a teaching job. Again the rigidity of the university hierarchy has certainly decreased as a result of changes brought about by the 'movement' and the 1968 reforms. This increased flexibility comes in part from the institutional reforms which have allowed junior faculty to take part in the decision-making process of the university and in their own departments – the *Unités d'Enseignement et de Recherche* (UER). Perhaps more fundamentally it also comes from the various changes that have substituted pluralism for monism and an oligopolistic structure for a monopolistic one. The increase in the number of Parisian universities resulting from the dismemberment of the former University of Paris and the creation of new universities in the Parisian suburbs have reinforced these trends. But other factors have combined with these institutional changes: the increase in the number of teachers and students has brought about a quantitative growth and diversification of the intellectual output of the university. We have seen that this evolution occurred to the detriment of scholarly work. I will not return to the negative effects of this imbalance. Mention must be made here, however, of a positive consequence of this phenomenon – the demise of oligopolistic cliques, factions and groups which before 1968 were capable of enjoying monopolistic power. Prior to 1968 it was not uncommon to find that a given field was represented by a dominant academic group having more or less direct control over the teaching positions to be filled within that field, often even beyond the institution itself since it controlled the journals and scientific publications of the discipline.

Such situations could and, in many instances did, create intellectually sterile conditions: outside the dominant structure there was no chance of success. It also resulted in relationships of dependence between masters and apprentices. These monopolistic tendencies of the university system were replaced after 1968 by oligopolistic structures. On this point it would be interesting to ask whether the new superstructures followed a change in the infrastructures, to use Marxist terminology. I believe that the answer would be essentially negative. Many senior academics today who were in junior positions at a time when these structures were strongly monopolistic have maintained monopolistic attitudes and behaviour. This seems to partially explain at least the sectarianism of the French academic world. The substitution of oligopolistic structures for monopolistic ones does not seem to have brought about a corresponding shift from dogmatic monism and aggressive clashes to intellectual pluralism, or at least constructive confrontations. This analysis appears to be confirmed by all sorts of converging signs – the frequent mediocrity of discussions in scientific journals (a statement naturally more true for some fields than others), the attempts by certain academics to increase the number of institutions under their control, sectarianism in the tone of scientific discussion, and many other characteristics which it would be interesting to identify systematically.

In short the structures have become more oligopolistic than monopolistic, but the monopolistic 'mentality' (attitudes, values and strategies) still exists. This contradiction can partially be explained by the effects of inertia well known to experts of socialisation. But, on the other hand, we have seen that the overall weakness of the university system prevents the increased number of universities and the other changes which have facilitated the evolution towards pluralistic and oligopolistic situations from creating a real competitive relationship between universities: due to its structure the system has a scarcity of symbolic resources for rewarding those who operate within it. Many of the latter, as we have seen, turn toward another structure, the intellectual '*tout-Paris*'. This again creates monopolistic tendencies within the system; the academician dreams of being the thinker, the guru, the one that *tout-Paris* will talk about for a few months at least. To summarise, the star phenomenon which creates the weakness in the system as a whole tends to give rise to monopolistic situations. But it is a monopoly of prestige, not one that includes control of symbolic and material resources as was the case before 1968. Whereas the old system produced mandarins, the new one produces gurus.

Again these changes have their positive side as well. More precisely they have created collective goods (such as the increase, diversification and liberalisation of intellectual output), as well as individual benefits (such as a better relation between masters and apprentices and the end of the 'closed shop' which came from the monopolistic structure in certain academic disciplines). They also include a collective shortcoming: the devaluation of pure research in certain vulnerable fields.

Turning now from the teachers and the intellectual output of the university to the students, we should balance the negative traits analysed above by attempting to see the positive aspects. (Again my feeling is that the overall balance is more negative than positive.)

We have noted that the over-investment required[34] from students in relation to the social and economic rewards they can, on the average expect to obtain, seemed to have brought about a decrease in the amount of time devoted to study and an increase in the time devoted to paid employment. We remarked that, from this point of view, social origins make little difference, or at least are no longer as important as they once were: students of working- or upper-class backgrounds spend a comparable portion of their time in paid work. It is possible that one of the happiest consequences of this state of affairs for the individual will be a decline in the social marginality of students. One of the most negative characteristics of the pre-1968 system was that students were expected to spend an ever-increasing number of years in the university, at the very time when they were generally older and when the various forms of maturity (psychological, physiological, civil and social) tended to manifest themselves at an earlier age. This contradiction, which I argued[35] was one of the essential causes of the student movements during the 1960s, is partially, obliquely and incompletely resolved by the fact that one consequence of the complex evolution has been to increase considerably the proportion of part-time students, that is those students who are partially 'integrated' into 'society' by their involvement in professional institutions and who remain isolated as a result of the part-time participation in academic structures.

It may also be that the anarchistic pedagogical innovations which have proliferated since 1968, in addition to their destabilising impact, have also had a positive effect in certain cases. In other instances the credit system (*Unités de Valeur*) can also have positive effects by allowing students to combine subjects from very different fields. When the system was first implemented disappointment was inevitable. The reformers did not realise that substituting the new system of credit units for the old degree (*certificat*) system (wherein curricula were rigidly determined and once the field of specialisation had been chosen, the possibility of free choice was very limited) called for considerable expenditures from an organisational point of view. It entailed in particular the buttressing of the adminstrative structures of the universities. Likewise a restaurant which limits its menu choices to one selection is necessarily very different organisationally from a restaurant with a comprehensive menu. This problem was not anticipated and the new system of credit units began inauspiciously. In the future it seems clear that the broadening of choices open to students should have essentially positive effects because on the individual level the '*à la carte*' system contributes on the whole to a better fit between course work and the student's aptitudes and tastes, while on the collective level it can be conducive to a real interdisciplinary approach – exemplified by the fact that everyone today senses that the frontiers separating the social sciences in particular must be seriously re-evaluated if we wish to better understand social phenomena. But how can we hope to achieve a truly interdisciplinary climate if, for example, the sociologist cannot study at least the basics of the economist's language? In the past, interdisciplinary study and output was the result of individual effort and planning. The system of granting credit units encourages such planning and may bring about positive collective benefits.

On the other hand the '*à la carte*' menu system presupposes that customers are able to understand what each '*entrée*' (or course) contains and can make an enlightened decision about the quality of the final product resulting from a succession of distinct choices. It also supposes, naturally, that all courses differ from one another. The quality of each course is more likely to be high if customers are more discriminating.

Other external factors, to use economic terms, in the evolution of the French university since 1968 should be taken into account: the multiple functions of the university, which were perhaps not desired but which resulted from this evolution, may have conferred on the universities the role of 'centres of cultural life' which they did not previously have to the same extent. The success of certain experiments with adult education, the 'third stage of life' university, suggests that the new university has developed a cultural function that the traditional university lacked. A detailed analysis of the cause-effect relationship between the modest phenomena of cultural revival and local traditions which we observe in France and the multifunctional role of the French university today would also be useful. To cite just one example, let us keep in mind the creation of local periodicals, such as the *Heimdal* which is sold in general bookstores in Normandy. *Heimdal*, which has its origins in academia, has the purpose of popularising in the full sense of the word the history of Normandy during the Middle Ages before the province became simply the richest province of the French kingdom.

In 1968 the students were extremely demanding: to use Albert Hirschmann's concept, they used *Voice*.[36] Today it seems that the reaction to decline generally takes the form of the classical mechanism of defection, as economists call it, or of *Exit* (once again Hirschmann's terminology). To be more exact, since defection is impossible and since university studies are necessary because others do it, *Exit* manifests itself in the form of a Mertonian 'retreat'. The phenomena of *Exit* and 'retreat' also affect the behaviour of the faculty. In spite of all this it is possible to credit the French university with certain positive effects, for the most part indirect and unplanned.

Conclusion

The history of the French university during the past decade is complex and instructive not only from the point of view of an analysis of educational institutions, but also from that of sociological theory. The French university rests on an institutional system which engenders several kinds of negative effects, both from a collective and an individual point of view, all of which tend to reinforce one another. (A chart drawn of these effects would no doubt provide an interesting example of systemic analysis.)

Unfortunately the numerous reforms which have followed one another since 1968 in order to correct the system were simultaneously too ideological and legalistic: it is one thing to prescribe participation in the legislative text, but another to make it a reality. It was not clear that the latent meaning of the 1968 revolt was identical to its overt meaning; in other words, that this revolt was essentially against authority.

I acknowledge that my assessment is not particularly optimistic. But my pessimism is heightened by the fact that a majority of the French élites is apparently satisfied with the existing system. The system of the *Grandes Écoles*, which distinguishes France from Germany, is reassuring for those who can send their children there and, to a lesser extent, for the entire population because it provides for the education of the top managers, the highly trained and responsible individuals the country needs. Most intellectuals have placed their interests outside the university even if they occasionally hold a teaching position. Despite the good intentions of the 1968 reformers and their continuous hymns to democracy, the French university system cannot be considered a model. It performs its traditional functions in a mediocre way, both in terms of academic production and as an instrument for the transmission of knowledge. It is not certain that it has contributed optimally to improving the general welfare and it does not provide the public it caters to (students) with a congenial environment. In addition, it remains definitely as élitist as ever – not the least of the harmful effects brought about by its institutional structure.

Of course the balance sheet is not entirely negative. It is possible, as we have seen, that the student is no longer socially on the fringe of society as he once was. Oligopolistic structures are replacing the old monopolistic ones, but this change has not brought about real competition nor cooperation among universities. The new system has liberalised and intensified intellectual life and weakened the archaic effects of the closed patronage system. It has allowed a considerable and rapidly increasing number of people to be consumers of the products offered by the university system. It has opened up elective options to students and thus for the future increased the possibility of interdisciplinary efforts with all the benefits they entail.

But the system is far from functioning optimally in the creation of new knowledge – which is, after all, a traditional goal of the university. This is also true for the individual and collective returns produced by the individual and collective investments that it absorbs.

4 Educational Institutions and Perverse Effects: Short-Cycle Higher Education

The following analysis brings to light a structure of interdependence that is both akin to and distinct from the famous prisoner's-dilemma structure. It is similar to the prisoner's dilemma because if the players play with some awareness as to what is happening they will achieve a worse result (or at best an equivalent result) to the one they would have got by playing in a non-rational way. The juxtaposition of rational strategies will, in other words, engender a worse result than Pareto's equilibrium. It is therefore a question here of a typical perverse effect, but some of the players achieve a satisfactory result and it therefore differs structurally from the prisoner's dilemma. Since each player can hope before the game starts to achieve this satisfactory result himself, it is in no one's interest (at least, prior to the game) to oppose it. In spite of the perverse effects that it engenders, it would be harder to achieve a consensus as to its suppression than in a game with a prisoner's-dilemma structure.

This perverse structure may be theoretically complex but in practical terms it is quite banal. I mean by this that one comes across it every day and that it represents the essence of a whole series of different institutions. It explains why the candidates for the *Grandes Écoles* and those competing for decorations and honorific distinctions are necessarily more numerous than those chosen and it explains why a host of people will make various economic, social and psychological investments as a matter of course, even though they gain nothing from them. It explains why failure and frustration are normal components of social life. In spite of this these perverse effects endure, for, before the game starts, everyone stands to gain from it.

But the model developed here is not only applicable to these banal cases. It can be used to analyse larger-scale political questions. I therefore use it to analyse an institutional innovation in the field of education: the creation of alternatives for short-cycle higher education. I show why the hopes that people had placed in this innovation have been, to some extent, disappointed. More generally

I try to show how fruitful some simple interdependence models prove for the analysis of the effects of institutional changes.

There will of course be those who will raise the by now almost ritual objection to this procedure: is it legitimate to use, as a model for *homo sociologicus*, the model of the rational man that game theory uses? I always respond to this objection as follows: (1) one could, if one wanted to make the exposition and the demonstration even more ponderous, use a model that was less shocking from the realistic point of view (it would be a simple matter to assume that social agents tend on average to follow their own best interests rather than what works against their own best interests); (2) that the model's axioms should be considered as methodological rather than ontological.

The following text is a new version of an article written in collaboration with Janina Lagneau and Philippe Cibois and published as 'L'Enseignment supérieur court et les pièges de l'action collective, *Revue Française de Sociologie*, XVI (1975) 159–88. An English-language version of this text, 'Short-Cycle Higher Education and the Pitfalls of Collective Action', appeared in *Minerva*, XIV (1976) 33–60. I would like to thank Janina Lagneau and Philippe Cibois for giving me their permission to reprint the article in this book.

In the course of the 1960s governments in most European countries and, more generally, in industrial societies, became increasingly aware of the difficulties created by the expansion of traditional higher education. The more optimistic among them looked on the expansion of demand for education as being at least partly responsible for the production of such desirable collective goods as rising productivity or growing social participation. On the other hand it was becoming clear that a not insignificant and probably growing number of students were entering occupations which by their nature and their remuneration – both economic and social – were no different from what they could have entered with markedly fewer years of education than they had actually received.

This situation raised a major political problem. It was undesirable from the point of view of the students, whose social rewards were more and more frequently out of proportion to their investment in education. It was also undesirable for the community as a whole, since in most European countries the educational system is financed not only by those who reap direct private benefits but by the entire community.

Understandably, then, most industrial countries took this opportunity to develop what is known as 'short-cycle higher education'. Here students are offered as an alternative to traditional higher education a new, shorter type of education intended to be sufficiently attractive to drain off some of the growing numbers of students in traditional higher education.

The general impression gained from the early years of this experiment is that it has been a relative failure. The number of students who actually decide to enrol in the new institutions has fallen well below expectations in several countries, including France. What accounts for this? There are two kinds of answer. First, there is the theory of the 'bad bargain': it is true that higher educational institutions offer would-be students a course of study which is less burdensome in terms of individual investment in years of education and renunciation of income, but in exchange for this investment it can only offer remuneration which is greatly inferior to that provided by traditional higher education. Not surprisingly therefore few students fall for the bait. Only those who would have abandoned their studies in the absence of short-cycle institutions are attracted.

The Prisoner's Dilemma

Another possible theory, which we shall explore here, holds that the creation of short-cycle higher educational institutions has, in some cases,[1] resulted in the emergence of a structure in which individuals, by making rational decisions, manage to produce results which are prejudicial both to themselves and to the community. This structure of collective action is both akin to and distinct from the 'prisoner's dilemma', the formulation of which dates back at least to Jean-Jacques Rousseau. It has however come to be known as the prisoner's dilemma on account of the example devised by A. W. Tucker.[2] Two prisoners have committed a crime together. The judge offers them the following opportunities in order to force a confession: each will be sentenced to five years in gaol if both confess, or two years if neither confesses; but if only one prisoner confesses, then that one can be acquitted while the other will be sentenced to ten years. The alternatives are summarised in table 4.1.

TABLE 4.1   *Prisoner's Dilemna*

		Second prisoner	
		Confesses	Does not confess
First prisoner	Confesses	5.5*	0.10
	Does not confess	10.0	2.2

* The first and second figure in each case refer to the number of years in gaol imposed on the first and second prisoner respectively for each strategic combination open to each of them.

Clearly, it would be preferable if the two prisoners were each sentenced to two years' gaol instead of five. But if each plays intelligently, each will be sentenced to five years of imprisonment. Whatever the behaviour of the second – whether he confesses or does not confess – the first will get better treatment if he confesses: five years instead of ten if the second confesses; acquittal instead of two years if the second does not confess. Meanwhile the second prisoner reasons along the same lines, noting that if the first confesses he risks five years in gaol if he, too, confesses, and ten years if he does not confess; if the first prisoner does not confess he – the second prisoner – will be acquitted if he confesses and will be sentenced to two years if he does not confess. In either case he gains by confessing. Consequently both prisoners will find it advisable to confess, whatever the other does, but in doing so they will each be sentenced to five years' gaol, whereas they could have got away with only two years each.

The relative failure of short-cycle higher education may be interpreted as a structure of collective action analogous – although not identical – with the structure of the prisoner's dilemma.

The Failure of Short-Cycle Higher Education in France and Elsewhere[3]

In most European countries short-cycle higher education still only occupies a relatively minor place in the higher educational system as a whole. Despite this it has become a major subject of concern in most of these countries, because the pattern of traditional higher education is thought to produce undesirable results for society and for the individuals concerned.

The three main features of the transformation of higher education in the period since 1945 are the rapid rise in the number of persons receiving higher education, the predominantly literary character of the various courses of study and their considerable duration. In France there has been a very rapid increase in the number of students from 1950 onwards, especially in secondary and higher education. Although it is true to say that technical education also increased considerably, by and large literarty training was predominant (table 4.2). The situation in most other Western European countries is substantially the same.

Of those who passed the examination for the *baccalauréat* in 1970, more than half obtained theirs in philosophy and arts, or in economics and social studies. These courses of study did not prepare students directly for any particular occupation or profession; generally speaking they required additional courses of study at post-

TABLE 4.2   *French Students Receiving Secondary and Higher Education between 1900 and 1972*

	General secondary education	Vocational and technical secondary education	Higher education: public universities	Higher education and *grandes écoles*	Population
1900–1	136869	14107	29901	4308	38962000
1910–11	193357	23582	41190	4128	39605000
1920–1	245808	28010	49931	4908	39210000
1930–1	275966	45790	78674	4109	41835000
1940–1	429927	67863	76485	2807	41000000
1950–1	719822	239825	139503	15972	41647000
1960–1	1637200	605300	214672	73743	45465000
1965–6	2435400	819800	413700	123578	48687000
1967–8	2702900	837800	509898	125735	49650000
1971–2	3612000	919000	704000	139735	50000000

Sources: *Annuaire statistique de la France* (Paris: INSEE, 1966), résumé Rétrospectif; *Annuaire statistique de la France* (Paris: INSEE, 1968); *Ministère de l'Éducation Nationale*, 1971–2.

secondary level. The great majority of students chose to pursue studies in arts and social sciences (table 4.3).

Over the past thirty years the period of study in higher education has increased from two years to four, and sometimes even to six years or more. Before the war a student who did not fall behind in his studies for personal reasons could obtain a first degree in most subjects two years after his *baccalauréat*, and the training thus acquired qualified him for an appointment to an administrative post. Since then the period of studies has lengthened consistently. The introduction of an intermediate year of study at the beginning of the course means that the minimum period of study necessary to obtain a degree in science, for instance, has been increased to three years. The introduction in 1967 of the *maîtrise* – roughly equivalent to the master's degree – while it did not formally lengthen the period of study required for a first degree, nevertheless turned the latter into an inferior degree which was bound to decline in value in the future. The period of study required in order to obtain a first degree in the law and economics faculties has long been four years. The division of university studies into two-year cycles moreover has tended to lengthen the period of long-cycle studies by a year. The same phenomenon has occurred in the engineering colleges, where five years are usually required in order to obtain a diploma.

If we add to this one or two years which have to be repeated, the

Table 4.3 *Distribution of Students According to Subjects Studied in France from 1969 to 1972*

	1967–8	1968–9	1969–70	1970–1	1971–2	1972–3
Natural sciences	137100	123300	122800	115400	120800	119400
Arts and social sciences	169100	196100	218300	234400	246900	254900
Economics and law	114300	126700	138700	148200	153700	165700
Medicine, Pharmacology, and dental surgery	80900	118900	128500	135700	142700	158500
IUTs (technical college)	5400	11900	17300	24400	33700	37000
Total	506800	576900	625600	658100	697800	735500

Sources: *Tableaux de l'Éducation nationale* (Paris: Ministère de l'Éducation Nationale, 1970) p. 415; 1971 edn, pp. 402–3; 1972 edn, pp. 362–3; 1973 edn, p. 363; 1974 edn, p. 329.

great majority of university students need a minimum of five to seven years in order to complete their courses of study. In view of the scarcity of employment in most subjects – though especially in the case of arts and social sciences – a growing proportion of students have either continued their studies beyond the master's degree (another two years of study; at least) or have taken another first degree in order to improve their chances of finding employment. One finds students switching from one faculty to another; sociology graduates round off their training by working for a degree in economics, psychology or political science, for example; graduates in literature, economics, law or political science seek to supplement their qualifications with a degree in the social sciences.[4]

The lengthening of the period of study may partly be explained by the growth in the stock of knowledge to such an extent that it takes more than two or three years to gain a small part of it. But there is a futher, more fundamental, explanation. In all industrial societies, and in France in particular, economic and social remuneration tends to vary positively, on average, with a person's amount of education. Each student therefore seeks to obtain the largest possible amount of education for himself. If everyone pursues the same strategy, this results in a rise in the demand for education; the supply of educated persons increases beyond the demand for particular skills in the labour market. This in turn leads to underemployment, with its attendant devaluation of qualifications, and this gives a further twist to the spiral by again increasing the demand for education.[5]

It was in order to avoid such undesirable consequences that many countries sought to develop new types of short-cycle higher education. The argument has run as follows: short-cycle higher education would help to solve the problem of constantly rising demand by individuals for higher education. In principle this was seen to require a type of institution capable of relieving – at least partially – the quantitative pressure with which universities were having increasing difficulty. In addition it would help to diversify traditional forms of post-secondary studies.

It was further argued that by means of a broader geographical distribution, shorter periods of studies and more practical courses, short-cycle higher education would serve to enhance equality of educational opportunity. It would also, it was argued, allow students to acquire the practical skills and qualifications which universities had been incapable of supplying because their courses were too theoretical, and which secondary education could not supply. Short-cycle higher educational institutions, it was claimed, would be better suited than universities to provide the entire range of courses and the types of teaching for which there would be a demand in consequence of economic and technological change; it was also hoped that these new establishments would encourage innovation in teaching methods and research.

Finally the development of short-cycle higher education was recommended in order to contribute to social justice. In most Western European countries higher education is free; it is financed out of taxation. Since a disproportionately high percentage of students come from families with larger incomes, this has probably meant that the poor have been subsidising the rich, and increasingly so as education has expanded.[6] It may be added that part of this subsidy is wasted when a not insignificant number of students find employment they could have found with less education than they actually received.

Instituts Universitaires de Technologie

The underlying motivation behind the establishment in France of colleges of technology (*Instituts Universitaires de Technologie*: IUTs)[7] corresponds to this analysis. Government documents are clear in asserting that the aim of the IUTs was to introduce a new type of higher education better suited to the requirements of a modern economy, on the one hand, but also to some extent capable of 'replacing' the traditional higher education which is becoming increasingly prolonged.

In 1965 the Committee on Institutes of Higher Technical Training under the chairmanship of the Minister of Education (or the permanent under-secretary of the ministry), made the following observation:

> A major series of reforms aimed at renovating our educational system so as to bring it into line with the aspirations of contemporary youth and the demands of the modern world has now been in progress for the past several years. . . . New technical and supervisory functions are emerging in every area of society, and those who occupy these posts are closely associated with the work of engineers, research workers and senior administrative, financial and commercial executives. . . . The training required for these functions differs both in content and in method from the training provided by the universities or the *Grandes Écoles*. Such interesting attempts as have so far been made to adapt our educational system in this respect can only continue to develop through the creation of a new type of higher education.[8]

The committee which made this observation was unique in its procedures and in its composition – eight academics, two leading industrialists and two trades-unionists. As the permanent under-secretary said:

> Of all the committees which have examined the problems of educational reform, this is probably the only one to base its work on a functional analysis, that is, a discussion of the nature of higher-grade technical supervisory functions, the characteristics they have in common and the shortcomings of our educational system in terms of training requirements in this area.[9]

The committee recommended the following measures: (1) there should be intermediate-level training between the *baccalauréat* and the *Grandes Écoles'* engineering diploma for graduates to be employed in production, research and management posts; (2) the IUTs should offer a small range of very broad specialities, defined to meet the needs of the economy and grouped together in multidisciplinary establishments under the supervision of a national council for advanced training; (3) new teaching methods should be used; (4) a specific common organisation for teaching courses; (5) suitably adapted administrative structures; (6) the training courses leading to the BTS (higher technical certificate) or the *diplôme d'études supérieures techniques* should be integrated into the new arrangements or they should be discontinued.

From the very outset, in 1965, the IUTs were regarded by their sponsors as opposed to the long-cycle higher educational establishments with regard to structure, level of training and teaching methods. The educational level of these institutes lay somewhere between the *baccalauréat* and the diploma of engineering awarded by the *Grandes Écoles*. The new institutions were multidisciplinary in the sense that students were offered a range of specialised subjects which were determined in advance in terms of the needs of the economy – both regional and national. The types of training offered were to prepare students for the secondary and the tertiary sectors of the economic system. Each speciality was to be taught within a department, which is the basic unit of the IUT. Unlike the universities one third of the teaching staff was to consist of persons actively engaged in such fields as industry, management and data-processing. The teaching was to lay heavy emphasis on vocational, and even manual, apprenticeship; to this end courses provided for a great deal of practical work in workshops or laboratories and compulsory practical courses in the second year, alongside the theoretical teaching.

Teaching methods differed from those employed in the long-cycle institutions. In contrast with the practice in universities, attendance at all lectures and practical classes was made compulsory. Work was conducted in small groups and examinations were replaced by continuous assessment. Admission to an IUT was not entirely open, as in the case of universities, nor was admission controlled by performance in a written examination, as in the case of certain higher educational institutions. The regional director of education was to decide upon the number of students permitted to enrol in the first year of each department. Then, on the basis of recommendations made by an admissions board, the rector would select the candidates to be admitted. The admission board was to be made up of both representatives of the IUT and of professional interests; after examining each case the board would select those candidates meeting the requirements of each particular speciality. In principle the *baccalauréat* − an equivalent qualification − was to be required, but 'it is not enough to hold the *baccalauréat* and to wish to be admitted in order to gain admission to an IUT: the *baccalauréat* is neither necessary nor sufficient.'[10]

> The *diplôme universitaire de technologie* (DUT), which is awarded on completion of two years training in an IUT − a maximum of three years is allowed, bearing in mind the possibility of repeating a year − is a professional qualification and not a certificate of aptitude for further studies.[11]

In principle the *diplôme universitaire de technologie* awarded to those who complete the IUT course would lead to middle-level management jobs in the public and private sectors. In certain cases however, and on the director's recommendation and authorisation, graduates might be offered an opportunity to pursue their studies beyond the DUT. According to the statutes, these possibilities are of two types: either 'classical' studies at university, or long-cycle professional training leading to an engineering diploma.

In practice however the situation has been less clear-cut than originally envisaged with regard to access to long-cycle education and to professional opportunities. In the civil service, for example, a good many regulations which ought to open the door to careers for those holding the DUT are in fact still 'under preparation.' Similarly the status of IUT diplomas still awaits recognition in collective agreements,[12] although the law of 16 July 1971, concerning technological education, referred to professional qualifications to be incorporated into collective agreements as from 1 January 1973.

IUT: Success or Failure?

Have IUTs come up to the expectations they aroused at the time of their creation? After several years of operation it is now possible to begin to answer this question.[13] The truth is that the IUTs have not managed to attract a significant number of students away from higher education. The Fifth Development Plan forecast that by 1973 the IUTs alone would be educating 21 per cent of all students. In fact, in 1972, the entire system of technical education accounted for only 7 per cent of all students receiving post-secondary education. One discrepancy between forecast and reality cannot however be assessed in mere decimal points. What has happened in actual fact is that the development of IUTs has simply taken over existing streams of technical education. It has had virtually no effect on the rise in the number of university students (table 4.4).

This quantitative failure has been admitted semi-officially:[14]

It would appear that attempts to establish a short-cycle higher education system in France have been a relative failure. None of the initial objectives has been achieved, above all in the case of the two most important aims, which were to reduce the average length of the period of study and to innovate by developing, alongside the university system, a modern type of education adapted to the demands of the economy, providing the student with both a general education and training for an occupational career.

The education provided by the IUTs and STSs [higher technical colleges] has not yet been developed sufficiently to achieve the objectives fixed for these types of education and thus to satisfy the requirements of Level III.[15]

These types of education do not attract a sufficient number of students. On the basis of observed trends and bearing in mind the magnitude of the requirements of Level III, the Sixth Plan provided for the stabilisation of STS students at a rate of around 10,000 graduates per annum, thus confirming the coexistence of STS and IUT; it also proposed, bearing in mind the number of graduates, that the number of students in the IUTs at the end of the Sixth Plan should be between 67,000 and 105,000.

Although this objective represents a distinct lowering of sights by comparison with the aims of the Fifth Plan, it is still very ambitious, since even if we take the lowest target it assumes that the present number of IUT students – 35,000 in the autumn of 1972 – will multiply by two in the space of three years, whereas extrapolations from the past give us a figure more in the region of 55,000 students in the autumn of 1975.[16]

The failure of attempts to encourage the development of short-cycle higher education is not limited to France alone. Governments have been led to develop short-cycle educational institutions in other

TABLE 4.4 *The Growth of Post-Secondary Education in France, 1959–72 (students in '000s)*

Year	Teacher training (for state system only)	Preparatory classes for Grandes Écoles	Grandes Écoles	Higher technical colleges (STS)	Instituts Universitaires de Technologie (IUT)	Total technical education	Universities	Total	Short-cycle education as % of total
1959	10.0*	17.6	30.0	5.7	—	5.7	161.4	224.7	2.5
1960	10.9*	18.9	32.0	7.5	—	7.5	172.4	241.7	3.1
1961	13.9*	22.6	34.0	8.0	—	8.0	173.6	252.1	3.2
1962	12.8*	23.6	32.0	9.4	—	9.4	202.3	280.1	3.4
1963	11.1*	24.7	33.0	12.2	—	12.2	242.7	323.7	3.8
1964	12.5*	25.9	36.0	16.2	—	16.2	273.4	364.0	4.5
1965	14.0*	28.0	38.0	18.7	—	18.7	309.7	403.4	4.6
1966	13.7*	28.8	42.0	25.6	—	25.6	332.5	442.6	5.8
1967	13.6*	28.0	46.0	30.0	1.6	31.6	370.9	490.1	6.4
1968	13.8	28.1	51.0	28.7	5.4	34.1	432.0	559.0	6.1
1969	14.2*	30.0*	56.0	27.6	11.9	39.5	540.0*	679.7	5.8
1970	14.7	31.9	62.0	26.5	17.3	43.8	591.5	743.9	5.9
1971	14.5	31.2	68.0	26.8	24.4	51.2	613.2	778.1	6.6
1972	18.2	32.8	80.0	30.2	37.0	67.2	698.5	896.7	7.4

* Estimated.

Source: *Tableaux de l'éducation nationale*, 1969, 1970, 1972, 1973, edns; *Ministère de l'Éducation Nationale, Service central des statistiques et sondages*: DT 16 Jan. 1973, document 4367, documents 3177, 3507, 4212, 4314.

TABLE 4.5 *Short-Cycle Higher Education in the Higher Educational Systems in the 1960s*

Country	Short-cycle higher education			Total higher education			Short-cycle higher education as % of total higher education		
	1960–1	1965–6	1969–70	1960–1	1965–6	1969–70	1960–1	1965–6	1969–70
Germany	50201[b]	68833[b]	71986[d]	289211[c]	367684[c]	419000[d]	17.3	18.7	17.2
Belgium	21307	35191	–	51999	89991	–	41.0	39.1	–
Spain	40582	71945	73627	109926	197824	265676	36.9	36.4	27.7
Finland	4122	7226	9145	27955	47662	65616	14.7	15.2	13.9
France	38574[h]	74353[h]	97113	274263	505278	700000[a]	14.1	14.7	13.9
Norway	–	9584	11573[a]	–	28999	38658[a]	–	33.0	30.0
Netherlands	35686	45857	–	85558	124011	–	41.7	37.0	–
Sweden	4476	7032	8122[d]	30981	77623	124161[d]	11.2	9.0	6.5
United Kingdom	142610	223851	292875[g]	286218	431132	500000[a]	49.8	51.9	58.6[a]
Yugoslavia	31662	68650	81074[f]	140574	184923	261203[f]	22.5	37.1	31.0
Canada	30531	47076	67849[e]	175800	326976	427849[e]	17.4	14.4	13.9
United States	453617	845241	1484000[f]	3610007	5570271	7608000[f]	12.6	15.2	19.5
Japan	81858	145458	258680	710019	1085119	1613507	11.5	13.4	16.0

[a] Estimate.
[b] Excluding the *Höhere Fachschulen* for lack of statistical data.
[c] Including the *pädagogische Hochschulen*, which are considered as being of university level.
[d] 1968–9.
[e] 1967–8.
[f] 1970–1.
[g] Northern Ireland has been estimated.
[h] Excluding 'medical sciences' and 'education'.

Sources: 1960–1 and 1965–6: *Development of Higher Education: Statistics on a Country Basis* (Paris: OECD, 1970) 1969–70: national statistics.

countries for very similar reasons. Similarly the failure in France is parallel to that in many other countries. In all, with the exception of the United Kingdom, the United States, Canada and Japan, the number of students in long-cycle higher education rose more rapidly than the numbers in the short-cycle stream between 1965 and 1966 and between 1969 and 1970 (table 4.5).

The most plausible explanation for these differences lies in the fact that in these countries, as in Yugoslavia, graduation from secondary education does not automatically open the door to long-cycle higher education.[17]

Reasons for the Failure: The 'Bad Bargain' Assumption

Is the obvious failure of short-cycle higher education in France, which is apparently characteristic of several other countries, also a consequence of the fact that it offered students a 'bad bargain'? For France at least, this is probably not the most realistic assumption.

Long-cycle studies are obviously more costly to the individual than are short-cycle ones, if only on account of the loss of income resulting from the longer duration of study. Furthermore the French authorities have offered incentives for study at IUTs through the distribution of scholarships; for all IUTs the total number of scholarships awarded in 1969–70 was 7205, or 41 per cent of all students. This is a far larger figure than that of the total number of scholarships offered in all French higher educational establishments, with barely exceeds 17 per cent.[18] It should be noted, however, that the IUT system requires virtually full-time attendance on the part of students, with the result that it is much harder for these students to take paid employment than it is for university students. Only 11.7 per cent of a sample of IUT students stated that they held paid employment. It is relevant to point out in this connection that the social origins of IUT students tend to be lower than those of university students (see table 4.6).

But as the work of L. Lévy-Garboua suggests, average resources available to university students do not vary very markedly according to social origins.[19] It is possible therefore but not by any means certain, that IUT students possess resources roughly equivalent to those available to university students.

IUT students tend to end up with higher salaries on average than do university students who abandon their long-cycle higher education at the end of two years, and their salaries are much the same as those received by university graduates; that is, by students who have spent at least three years in long-cycle higher education. After completion of the IUT course, men received a monthly salary of F. 1450, and women a salary of F1390.

TABLE 4.6   *Parental Occupations of IUT Students (1972) and University Students (1971) in France (%)*

	Farm-labourers, farmers	Industrial-ists, shop-keepers	Professional, senior executives	Middle-level management	Office workers	Workers	Miscel-laneous	Total
University students (1971)*	9.5	14.6	29.5	17.0	9.6	14.5	5.3	100.0 (399007)
IUT students (1972)	12.8	12.6	13.6	14.1	10.7	22.8	13.4	100.0 (29317)

* Excluding IUTs and the Paris Region.

TABLE 4.7 *Monthly Income by Sex and Course of Study Completed*

Graduated in 1966	Men				Women			
Earnings in 1970	Graduates in education	Graduates in humanities	Graduates in law	Graduates in economics	Graduates in education	Graduates in humanities	Graduates in law	Graduates in economics*
Less than F. 1200	14.4	9.0	3.4	0.5	18.1	10.7	4.6	1.6
From 1200 to F. 1400	24.2	9.8	7.4	3.3	33.5	17.4	11.7	6.5
From 1400 to F. 1600	21.3	12.3	15.1	9.3	22.5	20.1	25.0	21.0
From 1600 to F. 1800	13.3	9.0	14.3	5.7	10.8	18.1	20.4	14.5
From 1800 to F. 2000	9.5	10.7	11.8	8.2	6.7	12.8	15.8	14.5
From 2000 to F. 2200	5.4	12.3	10.6	8.0	3.3	8.0	8.2	12.9
From 2200 to F. 2400	3.2	9.0	9.2	8.0	1.5	4.0	4.6	6.5
From 2400 to F. 2600	3.5	4.1	6.2	13.9	0.8	3.4	2.0	11.3
From 2600 to F. 2800	1.7	4.9	4.9	8.0	0.6	0.7	1.5	1.7
From 2800 to F. 3000	0.8	4.9	5.5	8.5	0.4	—	2.0	4.8
From 3000 to F. 3500	1.6	7.4	5.5	11.6	0.9	1.3	2.0	3.2
More than F. 3500	1.1	6.6	6.1	15.2	0.7	3.4	2.0	1.7
Total	100.0	100.0	100.0	100.0	100.0	100.0	100.0	100.0
N=	945	122	595	389	1562	149	196	62
Median earnings (in francs)	1502	1994	1974	2452	1391	1621	1629	1925
Proportion of incomes below F. 1800 (as percentage)	72.2	40.1	40.2	18.8	85.0	66.3	61.7	43.6

* Not significant statistically.
Source: Vrain, P., *Les Débouchés professionnels des étudiants* (Paris: Universitaires de France, 1973).

The median earnings of university graduates in education in 1972 amounted to F. 1502 for men and F. 1391 for women.[20] Median earnings are higher for humanities, law and, above all, for economics graduates. But, of the population surveyed here, about 75 per cent of the women and more than 40 per cent of the men hold a teaching qualification rather than the other, more remunerative types of degree.

The distribution of salaries of the long-cycle graduates is more dispersed than is that for students who have passed through the short-cycle stream (see table 4.8).[21] But where average and median incomes are concerned, these do not seem to differ markedly if one compares university graduates with short-cycle graduates.

TABLE 4.8   *Earnings at Beginning of 1971 of 1969 IUT Graduates Currently Employed*

Salaries (per month)	Men	Women	Men and Women
Less than F. 800	0.7	1.4	0.8
From 800 to F. 1000	2.4	5.1	2.9
From 1000 to F. 1200	7.1	15.5	8.8
From 1200 to F. 1400	25.0	36.5	27.2
From 1400 to F. 1600	28.3	20.2	26.8
From 1600 to F. 1800	13.9	9.7	13.1
From 1800 to F. 2000	12.4	7.6	11.4
Over F. 2000	10.2	4.0	9.0
Total	100.00	100.0	100.0

Source: *Centre d'Études et de Recherches sur les Qualifications*, 'L'accès à la vie professionell à la sortie des Instituts Universitaires de Technologie', Paris, *Documentation française*, dossier no. 7, June 1973.

To conclude, it is fairly certain that a student who chooses the short-cycle course of study incurs costs not higher than those incurred by a student who enters the long-cycle stream up to the level of the first degree. In addition the average income which the latter can expect on graduation does not appear to be markedly higher than the income the former can expect. This second proposition can be applied with virtual certainty to those with teaching degrees, who account for the major proportion of all university graduates. Finally it would appear that there is a greater scattering of earnings among students in long-cycle education.

Up to this point we have dealt with differences between the objective costs and advantages associated with the two types of higher education in France. But it would be equally interesting to find out something about IUT students' subjective assessments of the comparative advantages of short-cycle and long-cycle courses of study.

The IUT students consider their position to be at least equal to that of students in faculties of letters in every respect, except as regards the opportunity of acquiring a well-rounded culture. Similarly, they regard their position as being at least as good as that of students in faculties of science, except as regards 'prestige'. Naturally they consider that on most points their position is inferior to that of students in the *Grandes Écoles*[22] (table 4.9).

It is interesting to observe that, with respect to future earnings, opportunities for employment and careers, attractiveness of studies and a sense of personal fulfilment – that is, both with respect to anticipated material rewards and present non-material rewards – the great majority of IUT students consider their position at least as good as that of students who have chosen long-cycle higher education.[23] The IUT students were asked several questions to elicit their degree of 'satisfaction' with their experience of the IUT. A first group of students, whom we shall call 'satisfied', consisted of those who never wished to attend any institution other than the one in which they were at that time enrolled and who would repeat the experience if they had to. These constituted 49 per cent. A second group consisted of students who originally wanted to attend another type of institution but who found satisfaction in short-cycle higher education and who would now make the same choice if the situation were to arise again. These students may be regarded as 'converts' to short-cycle higher education. There were 16 per cent who were classified as 'converts'.

In contrast to these, certain students originally chose short-cycle higher education but now regretted their choice; if they had to begin all over again they would not do the same thing. These students make up the 'disappointed' group, which was 20 per cent of the total. A fourth group consisted of students who had not wished to go through short-cycle education in the first place, but who nevertheless did so, although they had not been 'converted'. They would not repeat the experience if offered the opportunity to do so. These are called the 'opponents' of the system; 7 per cent of the students fell into this category. There was a class of students who did not reply to the questions. These we classify under the rubric, 'don't know'. There were 8 per cent in this class.[24]

From these observations regarding remuneration and 'satisfaction', it appears that the 'bad bargain assumption' does not really provide a satisfactory explanation for the lack of success of short-cycle higher education among French students. The costs associated with this alternative are certainly not higher, from the individual's viewpoint, than they are for those in the long-cycle stream. In remuneration the two streams appear to be roughly comparable. The great majority of IUT students are satisfied with

TABLE 4.9 *Assessment by Students in IUTs of IUTs and Other Higher Educational Establishments*

Comparison of IUT with respect to:	Universities: Faculties of Letters			Universities: Faculties of Sciences			Grandes Écoles		
	IUT better	IUT same	IUT worse	IUT better	IUT same	IUT worse	IUT better	IUT same	IUT worse
Opportunities for careers	82.5	10.7	6.7	33.7	44.5	21.7	6.1	25.5	68.4
Quality of teaching	52.7	32.8	14.5	24.2	47.4	28.4	4.8	31.3	63.9
Social advancement	49.8	32.6	17.5	19.6	49.4	31.0	6.3	25.0	68.6
Future earnings	47.2	32.6	20.2	12.9	45.4	41.7	3.4	11.3	85.2
Opportunities for employment	79.4	12.8	7.7	41.1	41.1	17.7	9.0	32.8	58.1
Attractiveness of studies	59.0	27.0	13.9	26.9	51.4	21.7	11.1	45.2	43.7
Acquisition of well-rounded culture	20.4	22.6	57.0	23.3	43.8	32.9	8.9	38.6	52.5
Personal fulfilment	32.6	37.2	30.1	25.9	51.5	22.5	16.8	49.6	33.6
General atmosphere	50.6	29.6	19.8	42.3	39.5	18.2	31.4	43.6	25.0
Prestige	36.6	25.1	38.2	6.2	36.1	57.7	2.9	5.5	91.5

Source: P. Cibois, and J. Lagneau, *Bilan de l'enseignement supérieur court: Grande-Bretagne, France, Yougoslavie* (Paris: OECD, 1975)

their choice and consider their present and future remuneration as favourable, if not superior, to that of students engaged in long-cycle higher education. Obviously if we compare the situation of IUT students with that of university students who drop out of the long-cycle before obtaining their first degree, then the balance works out in favour of IUT students. How, then, are we to account for the failure to attract students on the scale anticipated by those who promoted this type of education?

The lack of students in short-cycle higher education in general, and in IUTs in particular, comes from its failure to attract students rather than from methods of selection for admission to the short-cycle stream; although figures concerning the rate of admission to the IUTs are not available, it is certainly lower than 60 per cent.[25] Even if only 40 per cent of all candidates for entry to the IUTs were actually admitted, there would be at most only one student in seven applying for admission to short-cycle education. Is this because it is a 'bad bargain'? Probably not. And yet there are few takers. What accounts for this?

The Pitfalls of Collective Choice

The significance of an answer to this question goes well beyond the particular problem of short-cycle higher education. It raises the entire problem of the logic of educational demand and of the relationship between this demand and the structure of society. It is tempting, in this respect, to try to prove that the former is no more than a derivative of the latter. After all, since the skills acquired at school generally tend to be put to use on the labour market, can one not conclude that in the final analysis academic achievement is determined by the labour market? And this gives rise to the teleological argument popular among sociologists, according to which the system of the division of labour necessarily determines – if this theory is correct – the structure of the school system, which in turn determines the educational achievement of individuals. In terms of aggregates, then, this would correspond to the 'needs' of the labour market or of the social structure.[26] The failure of the IUTs shows that the structure of educational demand may, on the contrary, tend to become incompatible with the 'requirements' of the social structure, even when governments make use of the means at their disposal in order to articulate the two. This is because the demand for education results from the aggregation of the independent individual decisions and is therefore by no means bound to be regulated, like a Leibnizian clock, to tick in time with the clock of the structure of society.

With the aid of the example of short-cycle higher education we can show that certain institutional combinations may, on the contrary, lead to a kind of structural maladjustment of the two clocks.[27] In order to clarify this we shall construct a simple model which simulates the situation prompting the authorities to encourage the development of short-cycle higher education in the first place, and which subsequently simulates the consequences of the creation of short-cycle streams.

The situation arising from the increase in the demand for higher education at the beginning of the 1960s in most European countries may briefly be summarised as follows: if we imagine a cohort of students entering university at that time, all the individuals in the cohort are naturally going to have to pay the costs arising from prolonged education lasting several years – four or five and sometimes more. Even if the costs of fees and supplies are low, their time at university will certainly entail a renunciation of earnings, as well as social and psychological costs – such as being placed in a socially marginal position – which are much harder to define precisely, but which are no less important. Naturally these costs are matched by anticipated or desired advantages which also include life-time earnings as well as social aspects, such as the complex set of social rewards which come not only in the form of income but also of prestige and power and to which sociologists normally refer as 'social status'.

Of course not all the students can hope for the same advantages. But one of the fundamental reasons which drove the authorities to develop short-cycle higher education was the fact that increased demand for university higher education was beginning to mean that a number of students were receiving remuneration and other rewards which were inferior to what they had desired and anticipated.

To simplify the argument let us imagine the cohort to consist of twenty students. Since our aim is to disclose the paradoxical results derived from the aggregation of the decisions of individuals, we have found it necessary to confine ourselves to small numbers; the size of the group dealt with does not affect the results of the model. Let us imagine, furthermore, that the cost of four years' education at university level, for example, is measurable in terms of a certain unit which, for the sake of convenience, we shall call a franc, and that these costs are identical for all.[28] Let us assume, finally, that the structure of the labour market is such that on the completion of their studies the twenty students will receive a benefit – the discounted value of the 'social status' minus cost – amounting to two francs for six of them, one franc for eight of them and no francs for six of them. These fictitious figures are significant only in terms of their interrelationships; their sole purpose is to stimulate the phenomenon of underemployment, which probably led governments to try to develop short-cycle higher education.

This model portrays a situation in which six out of the twenty students gain a return on their educational investment which no more than covers the value of that investment. The situation is naturally disadvantageous from the individual's viewpoint. But it is equally so for the society which pays the costs of the educational system.

This model does not contradict the proposition of the economic theory of human capital, according to which the average return on educational investment is positive.[29] On average the twenty students in our imaginary cohort will obtain a one-franc return on their investment. On average their remuneration will be greater than the remuneration of those who abandoned their studies on completion of their secondary education. Limiting ourselves to the economic remuneration, the model does not contradict empirical observations to the effect that life-time earnings rise, on average, in proportion to the level of educational attainment, and in particular are higher for those who pursue their education beyond the secondary level. But an average can signify a good many things, depending upon the variance associated with it.

Let us now suppose that the government, aware of the disadvantages in the situation briefly summarised in the model, seeks to remedy it by offering students a choice between long-cycle higher education, with its attendant risks, and short-cycle higher education. Short-cycle education has one obvious advantage from the student's viewpoint, namely that it reduces the individual costs of education: the loss of earnings occurs during a two-year period instead of four or five years. The student is able to 'settle down' earlier. (The short duration of studies, cited by more than four-fifths of the students in IUTs as justifying the choice of short-cycle education, is significant.[30]) Another advantage was that the authorities sought to introduce new teaching methods into the IUTs. The rates of success in the final examinations at the end of the IUT course are far higher than the rates of success between the first year and the *licence* in French universities, for example.[31]

Nonetheless governments have little control, other than very indirectly and partially, over the essential advantages which lie in higher social remuneration and social status. The only way in which government can intervene effectively is to ensure that the student in short-cycle higher education receives the kind of education which will make him attractive to prospective employers.

In France short-cycle higher education and IUTs in particular have been successful in this respect. If we confine our attention to the most easily identifiable and measurable criterion, namely money, then IUT students obtain incomes which on average are very close to those obtained by graduate teachers after much longer periods of study. Since graduates who go into teaching are by far and away the largest group of university graduates, this is a significant advantage.

According to our model, on average, short-cycle higher education leads to remuneration which is comparable with that obtained after the completion of long-cycle higher education. Our hypothesis was of an average return, after allowing for costs, of one franc for students in long-cycle education. We will now assume that, since it began, the short-cycle stream has also provided its students with an average return of one franc; after allowing for the cost of their education, the spread of the earnings of students in the short-cycle stream is considerably narrower than in the case of university graduates. To simulate this as simply as possible, we shall assume that all students completing the short-cycle course of study received a return of one franc after costs amounting to one franc and earnings amounting to two francs.

In our model which crudely simulates the structure of the choice placed before students by the establishment of short-cycle higher education, the twenty students making up our imaginary cohort now have the choice between short-cycle higher education, which guarantees them a return of one franc, and long-cycle higher education. If every student chose the latter, six would have a return of two francs, eight would have a return of one franc, and the six remaining students would have no return at all. If all twenty chose long-cycle higher education, then each could hope for an average return of one franc – the odds being six to twenty for two francs, eight to twenty for one franc, and six to twenty for obtaining no return at all. The short-cycle stream, on the other hand, guarantees a return of one franc. What may be expected to occur if all the students play the game skilfully? We shall further assume, for the sake of simplicity, that all twenty students are interchangeable and, in particular, that none of them thinks he or she is superior to the rest.

One possible answer to this question is that once the average returns to graduates of the two streams are the same, the shorter of the two courses will be sufficiently attractive to be chosen by a significant proportion of the twenty students. This is the solution which comes most intuitively to mind. This may also be the implicit diagnosis on which the government established short-cycle higher education. It may also account for the government's disappointment at the lack of popularity among students of this type of higher education. The intuitive solution is, however, mistaken: if all twenty students play the game skilfully, then none will gain by yielding to the attractions to the short-cycle stream, despite its apparent competitiveness.

Each student has the choice of two strategies: a short-cycle or a long-cycle stream. If he chooses the former, he can be sure of obtaining a return equivalent to one franc. If he chooses the latter, the remuneration he can expect will depend on the choices made by the others: if he alone chooses the long-cycle stream, then he can be sure of obtaining a return worth two francs, for lack of other competition. In this case return of his two francs is guaranteed and he has everything to gain by choosing the long-cycle stream. Hence the problem for each student is to calculate the return he can expect by permutating each of his two possible strategies so as to take into account all the various hypotheses regarding the behaviour of his fellow-students. For each student there are twenty possible hypotheses since the number of students, other than himself, in a position to choose the long-cycle stream is equal to any number between 0 and 19.

Because these students are assumed to be interchangeable, if any one of them supposes that a maximum of five students, apart from himself, will choose the long-cycle stream, he can then be sure to obtain a return of two francs. The problem becomes more complicated if one more student makes such a choice: in this case, our student has no more than six chances out of seven to obtain a return of two francs. Naturally the odds will be one to seven of obtaining an average return of one franc. In this case, then, his expectation of return will be $\{(6/7) \times 2\} + \{(1/7) \times 1\} = 1.86$ francs. By continuing to reason along the same lines, we can calculate the expectations of returns of our interchangeable student on the basis of various hypotheses concerning the behaviour of the other students[32] (table 4.10).

The result is clear: independently of the choice of the others, our student has an interest in choosing the long cycle rather than the

TABLE 4.10 *Pay-off Matrix for 20 Students for Short-Cycle and Long-Cycle Higher Education*

Student A's choice	Number of additional students choosing long cycle									
	0	1	2	3	4	5	6	7	8	9
Short cycle	1.00	1.00	1.00	1.00	1.00	1.00	1.00	1.00	1.00	1.00
Long cycle	2.00	2.00	2.00	2.00	2.00	2.00	1.86	1.75	1.67	1.60
	Number of additional students choosing long cycle									
	10	11	12	13	14	15	16	17	18	19
Short cycle	1.00	1.00	1.00	1.00	1.00	1.00	1.00	1.00	1.00	1.00
Long cycle	1.55	1.50	1.46	1.42	1.33	1.25	1.17	1.11	1.05	1.00

short cycle. In all cases but one, his expected return is greater if he chooses the short cycle. In one case – when the other nineteen students choose the long cycle – his expected return if he himself chooses the long cycle is equal to the benefit he would get if he were to choose the short cycle. As an experienced player, any student will consequently choose the long cycle. But as this student is not different from the other students, all students will choose the long cycle. Hence the 'solution' of the game will be that all students will choose the long cycle. Finally, in spite of their apparent 'competitiveness', the short-cycle institutions will not overcome the disadvantages which they were intended to eliminate: among the twenty students, only six derive a superior return from their choice, i.e., the students who receive a return of two francs. Eight students obtain a return identical to what they would have obtained by choosing short-cycle education. Six students receive no return, whereas if they had chosen the short-cycle stream they would have had a return of one franc.

This is clearly highly simplified as a model. For one thing it is not true that each student considers himself just as good as the others.[33] It is not true that all students are equally skilled players. But one can readily see that the disadvantages disclosed by the model would also emerge if the latter were made more elaborate in order to make it more realistic.

In other words, it is conceivable that the causes of the failure of short-cycle higher education are to be sought far more in the paradoxes arising from the aggregation of individual decisions than in cultural explanations such as the devaluation of technical training, etc. The structure represented by our model shows the outcome of a multiplicity of such individual decisions.

Can we really suppose however that a student is capable of calculating the mathematical probabilities of his returns depending upon this or that choice? It is true that real gamblers do not comply with the 'dominant strategy' in terms of the theory of games; were it otherwise, games of chance where a subscription is paid prior to redistributions – lotteries, *pari mutuel* betting systems, etc. – would never be half as successful as they are. We may nonetheless take it that the concept of a 'dominant strategy' is more or less perceived by the students.

Where prospects of remuneration are concerned, it is not unrealistic to think that students know what they are about. They know that some of them will enjoy high social status if they choose to pursue long-cycle higher education, even though some will not attain this level. They know that if they choose the short-cycle type of higher education, they can only hope to achieve rewards of a lower order.

As for the probability of obtaining these returns – the second factor in the calculation of the mathematical probability in question – this takes the subjective form of a sense of confidence in attaining this or that status. For some students this probability is experienced as a certainty.[34] For others it may belong to the realm of the possible, though in varying degrees.

Finally the notion of mathematical probability is itself implicit in reasoning which runs as follows: 'I have little hope of obtaining the *agrégation* – though one can never be sure; I have a reasonable chance of getting a *CAPES* and at worst I could always use my first degree to get an appointment as an assistant teacher.'[35] The sum of the products defining mathematical probability rests on envisaging a juxtaposition of more or less probable situations. But the act of 'summation' still remains to be done. Thus, for example, the judgement just referred to introduces a series of low probabilities of obtaining highly valued rewards. But at its conclusion it results in a better situation than one in which the only career envisaged is that of an assistant teacher. ('If I choose short-cycle higher education, I shall become a technician.') In other words it is reasonable to suppose that this kind of subjective assessment of the various possibilities takes into account the advantage – after making adjustments for the probability of obtaining them – of each possible outcome.[36]

The structure revealed by our model is different from the structure of the 'prisoner's dilemma'. Here some of the players at least win, whereas all the players in the prisoner's dilemma end by losing. It may well be that the difference makes the outcome of the present structure of educational choice even more gloomy than that of the prisoner's dilemma. At least in the case of the latter, the fact that everyone loses means that everyone can agree to the need to remedy the situation. For the same reasons everyone accepts traffic lights, even though we all dislike being delayed at a red light; we know that things would be worse for us without them. But here it would be much harder to obtain agreement to abolish the structure just described, since each person hopes to gain something from it. And this accounts for the caution with which Western European governments have gone about a policy of restriction of access to long-cycle higher education.[37]

While the collective pattern of decisions described here accounts for the failure of short-cycle education, the only way to avoid its undesirable consequences for the individual – and for society – is to lead individuals away from 'the state of nature'; that is, away from the disastrously competitive situation into which they have been plunged by freedom of access to long-cycle higher education. In contrast with this, in those countries – such as the United Kingdom, the United States and Yugoslavia – where short-time education has developed considerably, access to long-cycle education has traditionally been restricted. It should further be noted that it will also be more difficult to make the 'contract' here than it is to do so in the case of the prisoner's dilemma. It is after all harder to persuade individuals to agree to the suppression of a game in whieh there are both winners and losers – and in which consequently everyone has a chance of winning even if most of them lose – than it is for a game where everyone loses. This explains why there is strong opposition to the restriction of access to long-cycle higher education in those countries where this restriction is not traditionally accepted.[38]

Rousseau is one of the few authors to have identified this diabolical type of collective pattern of decision, in which the will of all is opposed, to the detriment of each and everyone, to the general will. It is quite probable that if called upon to vote on a proposal to abolish the game most future students and their families would reject the proposal, since no one would be prepared to hand over to an outside authority the task of deciding whether or not he might take part in a game in which he stood a chance of winning. As a result the individual and collective disadvantages to which the game gives rise would be preserved by the will of all.[39]

The model presented in the latter part of this article, together with its family of possible variants, suggests one possible interpretation of the inflation of educational demand which has characterised all industrial societies in the course of recent years. In addition it may serve as an analytical instrument for assessing the likely success of certain institutional changes. For example, without wishing to appear unduly gloomy, it is to be feared that the newly created French *maîtrise de sciences et techniques* will suffer a fate similar to that of the IUTs, and for similar reasons. This new degree was instituted in order to increase professional training in French universities. If the attempt fails, it will not necessarily be because of any 'culturally' deserved aversion for 'professional' studies on the part of students. Rather our diagnosis would be that such a degree in science and technology is likely to remain relatively unattractive so long as the 'high-road' to the doctorate, for example, remains open to all. In other words the attaching of 'branch circuits' on the long-cycle stream of traditional higher education does not look as though it is going to be very successful as long as the latter remains intact. The view that the failure of branch circuits of professional training can be interpreted more adequately in terms of the collective pattern of decisions engendered by existing combinations of institutional alternatives, rather than in terms of 'cultural' hypotheses, is supported by the fact that the 'professional' *Grandes Écoles* continue to attract large numbers of candidates. The failure of the IUTs cannot be accounted for by the fact that they are merely 'professional' colleges of lower level than, for example, the *École des Hautes Études Commerciales*; rather it is because they have to compete with the long-cycle streams of the university, to which access is open to all.

5 The Logic of Relative Frustration

This text, theoretical in nature, is intended as a contribution to a particular debate. This debate is concerned with the paradox in there being a relation between both inequality and satisfaction *and* material plenty and satisfaction. In fact classical sociology is full of paradoxical statements of this sort. For Tocqueville greater equality tends to produce envious comparisons: as they become more equal individuals find their inequality harder and harder to bear. C. Wright Mills has also taken up this theme. For Durkheim individual happiness does not increase in direct ratio to the quantity of available goods. The relation between happiness and goods has the form of a reversed U-shaped curve: on this side of and beyond a particular optimum satisfaction decreases. Again, for Tocqueville, dissatisfaction and frustration may grow when each person's opportunities begin to open out and improve. In *Marienthal*, Lazarsfeld observes the converse of Tocqueville's theorem: when an individual's future is blocked, recriminations against the social system may well be weak. Stouffer's works show that individuals may well grow more discontented with the social system to which they belong as it offers them what are, on average, better opportunities for success and promotion.

In short Tocqueville, Durkheim, Lazarsfeld, Stouffer and also Merton, Runciman and Hyman, authors who surely differ massively in their various methodological, theoretical and political orientations, agree to acknowledge the complex and (since there is no need to reject the word when it is given an exact meaning) *dialectical* character of the relation between material plenty and equality on the one hand, and between material plenty and individual satisfaction on the other.

By contrast there are many more recent authors who interpret this relation in a manner that would seem to have no other virtue apart from its simplicity: some clearly think that an intolerable and potentially explosive situation is created as soon as the poorest five per cent have a salary that is less than half the national average.

There are others who think that a reduction in inequalities is invariably, regardless of the context, positive.

The following text reaffirms its links with the sociological tradition. It argues that the paradoxical relationships that the classical works of sociology point to can be deduced from simple models inspired by game theory. The basic virtue of these models lies in their ability to show that (among other things) there is no simple way in which one can associate a particular degree of collective happiness, frustration or satisfaction with the various possible distributions of goods.

The simple models presented here bring out complex effects of composition (which may account for the paradoxical appeal of the propositions referred to above). They take up once more logical instruments analogous to those used in another chapter of this book, Chapter 4, 'Short-cycle higher education and perverse effects'.

> *Now let us consider the effect of this public prosperity on the private happiness of citizens. First of all, if these riches are distributed equally, it is certain that they will not long remain in this state of equality, or that, if they did, they would be as if non-existent for those who possessed them. For, in everything beyond immediate necessity the advantages of fortune only make themselves felt in terms of differences.*
> Jean-Jacques Rousseau, *Political Fragments*

The notions of relative deprivation and of reference group together make up a conceptual whole whose success is doubtless attributable to the way in which it allows one to account – with the help of commonsense propositions – for paradoxical observations. As Runciman notes, the two notions derive from a familiar truism, namely 'that peoples' attitudes, aspirations and grievances largely depend on the frame of reference within which they are conceived'.[1] Observation in fact shows that in most cases it is impossible to understand why an individual A will feel envious of B but not of C if one does not know 'the frame of reference' of A. How is one to explain why it is that A envies his right-hand neighbour's Peugeot if one does not know that A can hope to raise himself up to his right-hand neighbour's level but not to that of his left-hand neighbour? Suppose we use the excellent definition of relative deprivation proposed by Runciman: 'A strict definition is difficult. But we can roughly say that A is relatively deprived of when (i) he does not have x (ii) he sees some other person or persons, which may include himself at some previous or anticipated time, as having x (whether or not this will in fact be the case), (iii) he wants x and (iv) he sees it as feasible that he should have x. Possession of x may of course mean avoidance of or exemption from y.'

The difficulty with this definition, as Runciman acknowledges, is the notion of *feasibility*: people only desire what they can plausibly hope to obtain. But what rules determine the things that one can or cannot obtain? Does A's envy of B decrease in ratio to the feasibility of A obtaining the object x that B possesses? Suppose I take this argument a little further. By defining the notion of relative deprivation in terms of the concept of *feasibility* is one not setting up a kind of vicious circle? I understand that the Jaguar owner does not belong to A's reference group, a group that includes the Peugeot 504's owner. I also understand that A envies the second but not the first. But the first proposition sheds no light on the second: the notion of reference group is simply a rephrasing of the proposition that has it that A feels envious of the Peugeot 504 owner but not of the Jaguar owner.

I do not propose to analyse here the important literature to which the two notions of reference group and relative deprivation have given rise. I think however that it is fair to say that the following two propositions contain the most comprehensive summary of this literature:

1. The two notions make it possible to account for certain fundamental social phenomena. Take, for instance, Tocqueville's famous law. This law holds that the improvement of the condition of all may well increase rather than diminish the general sense of dicontent. When prosperity increases, Tocqueville writes, 'people seem, however, more uneasy and anxious in their minds; public discontent is aggravated; hate against all the old institutions increases [. . .] What is more, the parts of France which must be the principal focus for this revolution are the very ones in which progress is most apparent [. . .] it could fairly be said that the French have found their position increasingly unbearable as it became better.'[2]

One can clearly also postulate a link between the notions of reference group and relative deprivation and the law of Durkheim's that has it that the satisfaction that the individual experiences depends less on the plentiful supply of goods that are at the collectivity's disposal and more on the tendency the collectivity has to instil desires in the individual that are limited to what he can hope to obtain: 'Under this pressure, each, in his own sphere, becomes vaguely aware of the furthest point to which his ambitions may reach, and aspires to nothing beyond it if, at least, he is respectful of rules and has a docile attitude to collective authority, i.e., if he has a healthy moral constitution, he feels that it is not right to demand more. A goal and a limit are thus marked out for the passions. But this determination doubtless has nothing rigid or absolute about it. The economic ideal assigned to each category of citizens is itself understood to have certain limits, within which desires may freely move. But it is not without these limits. *It is this relative limitation, and the moderation that it entails, which makes men happy with their lot, while at the same time stimulating them, within reason, to improve it* (my italics, R.B.); and it is this average contentment that gives rise to that feeling of calm and active joy, that pleasure in being and living which, for societies as for individuals, is what characterises health.'[3]

Lastly I will call to mind the famous conclusion of *The American Soldier*, the book that marks the beginning of the literature on relative deprivation and on reference groups. Military policemen, who belong to a group in which promotion is rare, declare themselves satisfied with the system of promotion that governs their lives. Pilots, on the other hand, though belonging to a group in which promotion is frequent, declare themselves to be unsatisfied with the system of promotion.[4] Everything happens as if an objectively greater upwards mobility brought with it weaker overall satisfaction.

2. There is no doubt that the apparently paradoxical phenomena covered by Tocqueville's, Durkheim's or Stouffer's laws are fundamental ones. But that would clearly be the second conclusion that one would draw from an analysis of the literature, i.e., however useful the concepts of reference group and relative deprivation are, they only enable one to grasp very imperfectly the logic underlying these laws.

In the notes that follow I hope to show that the sociological notions of collective relative deprivation and reference group may be more clearly defined if one has recourse to simple models derived from game theory. These simple models suggest that the appearance of relative deprivation phenomena is, in some situations anyway, the 'natural' product of structures of interaction (of competition) within which individuals are located. In other words it would seem that some structures of competition incite a more or less significant proportion of individuals to participate in 'rivalries' from which some amongst them must necessarily emerge as losers. This proportion, and consequently, the general rate of deprivation, varies with the properties of these structures. I will devote the rest of this article to a presentation of these elementary structures of competition and to an analysis of certain of their logical properties. As the reader will observe, even extremely simple structures of competion give rise to relatively complex analyses. It is incidentally worth noting that the *counter-intuitive* character of the properties of these structures of competition may well explain their capacity to fascinate: the consequences that they entail correspond to data that are often observed but only with some difficulty explained.

On a theoretical plane the simple models developed below make it possible to specify the purchase that Tocqueville's, Durkheim's and Stouffer's 'laws' enjoy, to demonstrate that it is not a question of universally valid laws, as Durkheim thought, but of propositions which may be conditionally true. In other words it is not true that in general an increase in the opportunities or goods offered to individuals will in every case bring about the higher degree of dissatisfaction observed by Tocqueville. On the other hand it is true that the phenomenon can, in certain cases, occur. By 'certain cases' I mean as a function of modifications in the structures of competition that the increase in opportunities or goods offered to individuals by the 'social structure' has provoked.

We therefore arrive at a completely different interpretation of his law than Durkheim himself does. In *Suicide*, and perhaps even more clearly in *The Division of Labour*, Durkheim has recourse to propositions that are well established in the psycho-physiology of the period in order to explain that dissatisfaction may grow with the increasing number of goods on offer: 'Indeed, it is a truth generally recognised today that pleasure accompanies neither the very intense states of conscience nor those that are too weak. There is a pain when the functional activity is insufficient, but excessive activity produces the same effects [. . . .] This propostion is, besides, a corollary of Weber's and Fechner's law. It is not without reason that human experience sees the condition of happiness in the *golden mean*.'[5]

The reader will see below that this interpretation rests on hypotheses that are both needlessly ponderous and probably false.

As Runciman suggests, in the text quoted above, there is relative deprivation when there exists a good x that A possesses and that B does not have. The notion of relative deprivation does, in other words, imply the notion of competition for a good.

Imagine a simple competition model in which there is a group comprising N individuals. 'Society' proposes the following option to each of the N individuals: (1) They can either reap a profit $B (>C)$ for a stake C, with a probability that diminishes as the number of competitors rises; (2) or they can choose not to participate in the competition. This very general structure characterises a whole number of situations in which there is competition: should I 'invest' in order to try and be promoted to the rank of office head, given that the majority of my colleagues are doubtless driven by the same objective? I would like to make it clear that throughout the first part of this article I shall assume individuals are equal and regard each other as such. This hypothesis will be abandoned in the last part of the article.

It is worth introducing a methodological proviso at this point: I am aware that in many situations of competition individuals are not equal and do not consider themselves as such. It is clear enough that, through sociology, a statistical correlation between social origins and a whole range of other characteristics could be elicited. One is nevertheless entitled, from the methodological point of view, to neglect this fact during the first stages of the analysis. This strategy has the added advantage of highlighting in all its purity the *perverse* character of the effects of composition that structures of competition generate. In the last part of the analysis I will openly abandon the egalitarian hypothesis in order to postulate the existence of groups that tend to be endowed with different levels of resources. These groups can be called classes. One will not of course obtain identical perverse effects when one advances an esentially unrealistic hypothesis – that all are equal – as when one admits that classes do exist, but in either case one will still observe them. They tend, *ceteris paribus*, to be more marked when the egalitarian hypothesis is posited.

Quite apart from its methodological interest, recourse to the fiction of equality allows one to obtain a sociologically significant result, namely, that equality of opportunity does not necessarily lead to deprivation being minimalised. We thus come back to another of Tocqueville's classic themes, and one that C. Wright Mills later revives: that equal conditions tend to stir up rather than to curb envy. I will come back to these points later.

In order to fix these ideas in the reader's mind and in order to make the logic of interaction shown by the preceding model more concrete I propose to give its parameters an arithmetical value. Let N therefore equal 20: the set of individuals to whom the option is available comprises twenty individuals. Let us also imagine that stake and profit are quantifiable, which is clearly not always the case in social life, and that C, the stake, equals £1, while B, the profit, equals £5. Finally we will only allow $n = 5$ winners. Thus if fifteen out of twenty persons decide to put down a stake, only five of these fifteen will draw a profit of £5. The other ten will lose their stake. We will presume that the distribution between winners and losers is random and occurs through drawing of lots (it would naturally be possible to construct more complex examples but there is some interest in beginning with the analysis of the simplest cases.) What will happen? How many of the twenty potential players will in fact decide to re-enter the game? How many losers or frustrated people will the game create? In this example the answers to these questions are not difficult to provide. If we take just one of the twenty players and presume that he is perfectly well informed about the situation, he will make the following calculations:

1. If I suppose that I, Jones, am the only person playing, I know

that in staking £1 I am absolutely certain to get back £5. I will therefore make a bet;

2. This also applies if one, two, three or four colleagues play. In each case I am assured of a net profit of £4 (£5 profit less my stake of £1) since there are five winners;

3. If five of my colleagues play: there are six of us competing for the five winners' places. I have therefore five out of six chances of winning £4 (£5 profit less a stake of £1) and one chance of losing my stake, i.e., of obtaining a negative profit, or as one would be more likely to put it, a loss of £1. My 'expectations' of a profit therefore stand, in statistical terms, at $(5 \times 6)(4) + (1/6)(-1) = 3.2$. I clearly run the risk of losing my stake but I have a good chance of winning £4. It is likely that I will decide to make a bet;

4. If six of my colleagues play, my expectation of a profit will then be: $(5/7)(4) + (2/7)(-1) = 2.6$. I therefore make a bet;

5. If 7, 8, 9, 10....16, 17, 18 of my colleagues play, my expectations of a profit will diminish accordingly but will still be positive: the value of my possible profit, multiplied by the probability of obtaining it, exceeds the value of the possible loss incurred, multiplied by the possibility of suffering it. I have five out of nineteen chances of winning £4 and fourteen out of nineteen of losing £1. My expectation of profit is therefore $(5/19)(4) + (14/19)(-1) = 0.3$. Supposing I consider it quite reasonable to make a bet when my expectation of profit is positive: I will then bet on the assumption that the number of other gamblers is equal to eighteen. If everyone bets, my expectation of making a profit is still positive: $(5/20)(4) + (15/20)(-1) = 0.25$. I will therefore make a bet.[6]

We are therefore dealing with a structure of competition in which each person, regardless of the behaviour of others, reckons that it is in his interests to bet. As a result there will naturally be fifteen losers. The example simulates a situation of competition in which each of the group's members feels justified in entering the lists. Nothing forces potential players to rejoin the game, except the encouragement given by the fact that expectations of profit are positive irrespective of the number of players. The players therefore invest in the game not because of any constraint but because a good understanding of their individual interests inspires them to do so. Now the combined effect of these interests is to turn three-quarters of the group's members into losers. The structure generates a collective deprivation that can be measured in terms of the number of losers: in the above game, fifteen out of twenty individuals appear to be so deprived. Their contribution was the same as that of the five winners. It was no more unreasonable for them to bet than it was for those who came out of the game without losses. These individuals cannot help adopting the five winners as a reference group and therefore feeling *relatively deprived* in relation to them. In this case the structure helps to generate a level of dissatisfaction typical of the upper level. It perhaps helps to throw some light on Stouffer's observations: when promotions are relatively numerous it is in everyone's interest to bet on promotion. But all those not promoted (the majority in this case) are then deprived. Ease of promotion generates a considerable degree of overall frustration.

The previous game brings to mind the case of the aviators who figure in Stouffer's famous analysis. The game's structure offers individuals objective opportunities for profit – or, in another language, for promotion or increased mobility – that are by no means negligible. But it therefore encourages an excessive number of players and consequently a considerable collective deprivation.

Before proceeding any further I will introduce a new methodological proviso. In the previous model I used a fairly unpopular version of *homo sociologicus*. Sociologists tend to recoil from the idea of assimilating *homo sociologicus* to a calculating individual intent on pursuing his own interests. In fact the model does not at all imply such a narrow representation of the determinants of his behaviour. Although it would make my mode of exposition and argument far more ponderous, I could eliminate the apparently shocking nature of the hypotheses used. I could for instance suppose that individuals were moved not only by the idea of profit but by other motives (pleasure at playing, for example), or that some work out the lottery's value, in a more or less confused way, before deciding, whilst others decide to take part in the game because they believe their luck is in, or decide to abstain because they are plagued by ill-fortune (I will leave to one side the question raised by the unrealistic hypothesis of *equality* between individuals, which, once again, will be taken up again below.) I could put forward hypotheses as to the frequency with which individuals decide as a function of their own interests. It is not hard to see that, under a wide range of conditions (i.e., if one supposes that social agents do *on average* tend to follow their own interests rather than setting them to one side), my previous conclusions hold good, in the sense that a perverse effect will invariably appear. The brutal simplification implicit in positing a rational *homo sociologicus* does have the considerable methodological advantage of making the exposition and demonstration less ponderous. It would be purely and simply a misunderstanding to interpret this hypothesis as an ontological statement. It is also incidentally worth noting that if one postulates a minority of individuals who fail to recognise their own best interests and make their decision on the basis of irrational sentiments (ill luck, chance etc.), the collective level of deprivation will, paradoxically, be attenuated.

Suppose we now simulate the second case presented in Stouffer's classic analysis, that of the military police. Here promotion is, objectively speaking, rare. This feature can be represented by supposing that the number n of winners no longer equals 5, as before, but equals 2, for example.[7] Thus, the proportion of winners to group members is no more than two out of twenty. For the rest, I will keep the parameters of the previous example and consider military policeman Jones's line of reasoning:

1. If I, Jones, make a bet, and if at the most one of my colleagues also bets, I have a guaranteed win of £4.

2. If two colleagues bet, I have two in three chances of winning £4 and one chance in three of losing £1. My hope of winning is then: $(2/3)(4) + (1/3)(-1) = 2.3$.

3. If 3, 4, 5, 6, 7, 8, 9 colleagues bet, my chances of winning are progressively reduced and in the final case, become nil. In fact $(2/10)(4) + (8/10)(-1) = 0$.

4. If more than nine colleagues bet, my expectations of winning are negative and the 'hoped for' loss will rise in ratio to the number of people who bet. Then, for fifteen people betting altogether, Jones's expectation of winning is $(2/15)(4) + (13/15)(-1) = 0.33$. When there are twenty people altogether who bet, Jones's chance of winning amounts to: $(2/20)(4) + (18/20)(-1) = 0.50$.

What will Jones do? Imagine that he has no information about the possible behaviour of the others and that the same goes for them: each must then decide whether to participate or not in the game, given a totally solipsistic context.[8] In this case Jones and each of his colleagues reckon that, if there turned out to be 11, 12, 13. . . .20 people betting in all, this would result in an unfavourable situation in which expectations of profit would be negative (expectations of loss). Beyond solipsism a sort of solidarity must then be introduced: with no one having control over the behaviour of others, each will do everything in his power to ensure that the total number of people betting does not exceed ten.

It is worth giving this point some thought, for, in spite of the fact that the model's hypotheses tend to simplify things, the structure of interdependence that it generates is of extreme complexity. Let me repeat the proposition that I have just formulated: 'Each will do everything in his power to ensure that that the total number of people betting does not exceed ten'. In reality, although it is in everyone's interest to obtain this result, no one can assume responsibility for it, since it clearly depends on the collaboration of all. But a collaboration of this sort was ruled out by definition. Suppose we imagine that the lottery simulates a choice that the educational system offers a public of potential students: those who play clearly cannot, in such circumstances, confer amongst themselves. What should one do in such a contradictory situation? If Ego assumes that each will take his chance, it is in his interests to abstain. But everyone might reason like this. In reality Ego stands to gain most if, in the hope that the others will do likewise, he allows himself one chance in two of participating in the game.[9] If everybody acts thus, the number of participants will be of the order of a dozen. Interestingly enough the structure of interdependence commits the players to a form of tacit cooperation that I defined above in terms of the notion of quasi-solidarity. It is worth making at this point a methodological observation of the sort I had made above, although in a different context: the model attributes to policeman Jones the capacity to make subtle calculations. But it is important to recognise that the relevance of the hypothesis is purely *methodological*. In other words it is a caricature of the more realistic proposition that, in a situation in which upwards mobility is rare, the potential players will hesitate more before investing their energies in the search for a difficult promotion. In hesitating thus they will, without wishing to and perhaps without knowing it, be manifesting a behaviour of *quasi-solidarity*.

Let us now return to the model and suppose that each will allow his own bet to be decided by the toss of a coin. Let us suppose that Jones and the others employ this strategy. Each will then hope to gain: $(1/2)(0) + (1/2) [(2/10)(4) + (8/10)(-1)] = 0$.

This clearly is not a brilliant result but it is preferable to the one that Jones could hope to obtain by deciding, for instance, to allow himself more than a $1/2$ chance of participating in the game. The term in brackets does in this case become negative, since the coefficient of 4 would then be lower than $2/10$ and that of (-10) higher than $8/10$. Jones therefore imposes on himself, and consequently on the others, a negative expectation of profit.

One can in short admit that, in a situation of this sort, the behaviour of a rational player can broadly be described by supposing that he will allow a toss of the coin to decide his participation in the game. There will then be ten people betting (if we admit, for the sake of simplicity, that the twenty tosses of the coin will give heads ten times and tails ten times).[10] Once again a result like this is only a semblance of what one actually observes. But at the same time, it is not entirely unrealistic. One often enough finds that an individual who wants to obtain a good but perceives, more or less clearly, that the number of individuals who desire it make his chances of obtaining it purely 'random' uses a dice throw to decide whether or not to participate in the game.

Once this process of *self-selection* has occurred, we find that the situation for ten people betting is analogous to the first situation examined; out of the ten, eight will emerge losers and two as winners, since it was stated that only two individuals could win the £5 prize.

The game that corresponds to the second example – the one simulating the result given in *The American Soldier* for the military police – can in short be summed up as follows:

1. Ten potential players do not take part in the competition game. They win nothing, but lose nothing. Their non-participation in the game is the result of a considered and reasonable procedure. I have shown how this abstention can be interpreted as a result of the *quasi-solidarity* imposed by the structure of competition.

2. Two players bet and win.

3. Three players bet and lose.

What sort of consequences does this result lead to, with respect to frustration? The two winning players do of course have no reason to feel frustrated. As for the eight players who have made bets and lost, they will probably be tempted to compare their fate to that of the two winners, i.e., to consider them as their reference group: their *contribution* is equal to that of the winners, their *reward* less. This difference in treatment received will tend to be perceived as illegitimate, and frustration is in this case the most likely response to the situation. The case of the ten players who have abstained and have therefore won nothing has to be considered separately. The situation is different from that of the two other groups of players, for the zero value of their reward is the proper remuneration for the zero value of their contribution. From another angle their abstention has been described as the product of deliberation. But abstention only appeared to them to be a reasonable strategy because of the existence of the structure of interdependence. They can therefore consider themselves to be frustrated. Nevertheless frustration is very probably more likely here than when the players have lost their stake out of a feeling of resignation. I will define their reaction in terms of the notion of *resigned* frustration. One can conclude from this that the collective frustration engendered by the lottery is lower in this case than in the preceding model. More precisely, the number of individuals who are likely to feel frustrated and cheated at the outcome of the game, and who will therefore contest its legitimacy, will doubtless be lower in this case than in the preceding example.

This can therefore be summarised by saying that a frustration leading to *quarrels* will be least frequent in the latter case. It is worth noting, incidentally, that the model, in spite of the simplicity of the original psychological hypotheses, generates complex distinctions regarding the situations in which individuals find themselves at the start of the game, and therefore regarding the sentiments which ought to correspond to these situations. We have in short to deal with a situation that is objectively less favourable than the first one was for the potential players. In the first situation the number of potential winners was five, whereas in the second it is two. But, on the other hand, the first situation incites each player to participate in the game, while in the second it would be quite reasonable for each player to decide whether to participate in the game by tossing a coin. The first situation thus generates fifteen cases of frustration *leading to quarrels* in a group comprising twenty persons, while the second only produces eight cases of this type. In this latter case we therefore have a situation comparable to that of the military police analysed by Stouffer: there is less chance of promotion there than in the air force, but the general level of frustration produced by the system of promotion is much weaker. To be more exact frustration *leading to quarrels* is less likely to appear.

To conclude I will recall an important methodological observation: in the two cases analysed above, I presumed that individuals would evaluate in the same way a fixed profit and a lottery linked to expectations that are, mathematically, of equivalent value. In actual fact it tends to be the case that individuals only treat a lottery and a fixed profit identically when the expectations of profit linked to the lottery are higher than those in the case of the fixed profit.[11] In applying this principle to the results of the two examples above, I would conclude that my analysis gives a maximum estimate of the rates of frustration for both. But, whatever hypothesis one retains as to the value of the difference between the fixed profit and the expectation of profit, it is important to realise that the rate of frustration leading to quarrels is higher in the first case, although individuals' objective opportunities are greater.

It is of some interest to formalise the above argument. I will posit a group of N persons, who are then offered a possible win of B_1 for a stake $C_1(B_1 > C_1)$ or B_2 for a stake $C_2(B_2 > C_2)$, with $B_1 > B_2$, $C_1 > C_2$. If $B_2 = C_2 = 0$, one again finds the two situations cited in the previous section (either one tries to obtain B_1 with a stake C_1 or one does not participate in the game). Let n_1 and n_2 be the numbers of winners of lots B_1 and B_2 respectively (supposing $n_1 + n_2 = N$). It is worth noting, incidentally, that the fact of introducing positive values for B_2 and C_2 is of more interest at the level of sociological interpretation than at the formal level. In fact, in the case of B_2 and C_2 not being nil, the game amounts to proposing to the players an additional stake $C_1 - C_2$, with the clear option of abstaining, i.e., in this case obtaining nil (additional) profit as against nil (additional) stake.

When $x_1 (> n_1)$ players stake C_1, the expectation of profit $E_1(x_1)$ of a player also betting C_1 is:

$$E_1(x_1) = (B_1 - C_1)\frac{n_1}{x_1} + (B_2 - C_1)\frac{x_1 - n_1}{x_1}$$

$$= (B_1 - B_2)\frac{n_1}{x_1} + B_2 - C_1 \qquad [1]$$

The expectation of profit $E_2(x_1)$ of a player betting C_2 when $x_1 (> n_1)$ players stake C_1, is, however:

$$E_2(x_1) = B_2 - C_2 \qquad [2]$$

Thus when $x_1 (> n_1)$ players stake C_1, a player is advised to stake C_1 rather than C_2 if:

$$E_1(x_1) > E_2(x_2)$$

or

$$(B_1 - B_2)\frac{n_1}{x_1} + B_2 - C_1 > B_2 - C_2 \qquad [3]$$

More simply, it is advisable to stake C_1 if:

$$(B_1 - B_2)\frac{n_1}{x_1} \geq C_1 - C_2$$

or

$$\frac{B_1 - B_2}{C_1 - C_2} \geq \frac{x_1}{n_1} \qquad [4]$$

I will now apply this relation to the two examples given in the previous section. In the first example, $B_2 = C_2 = 0$. Potential players are in effect offered the possibility either of trying to win $B_1 = 5$ by betting $C_1 = 1$, or of not playing. Resolution [4] here becomes:

$$B_1/C_1 > x_1/n_1 \qquad [5]$$

In other words so long as the relation B_1/C_1 – which amounts to $5/1 = 5$ in the example given – is higher than x_1/n_1, it is reasonable for a player to stake C_1. Since x_1 cannot be higher than the total number of members of the group ($N = 20$ in the first example), and given that n_1 equals 5, x_1/n_1 cannot be higher than $20/5 = 4$. The example is therefore structured in such a way that inequality [5] is always satisfied for all possible values of x_1. It is therefore reasonable for each player to stake C_1.[12]

In the second example x_1/n_1 is higher than B_1/C_1, once x_1 is higher than 10, since $n_1 = 2$. The reader will recall that a player's expectation of profit does in fact become negative if the number of people betting exceeds ten.

This simple formalisation makes it easier for us to analyse the consequences of the system $\{B_1 - B_2; \ C_1 - C_2; \ n_1; \ N\}$. Suppose, for instance, we study the variations in the level of overall frustration, as defined by the proportion of individuals who find themselves in the tiresome position of acquiring at the high price C_1 the lot of least value, B_2.[13] If lot B_1 is considerably more attractive than lot B_2, or, to be more exact, if the difference between them is much greater than the difference in cost, to the effect that $(B_1 - B_2)/(C_1 - C_2) > N/n_1$, all potential players will stake C_1 and the rate of frustration will amount to $(N - n_1)/N$. If, on the other hand, $(B_1 - B_2)/(C_1 - C_2)$ amounts to $k/n_1 < N/n_1$, the number of individuals staking C_1 will be k and the rate of frustration will amount to $(k - n_1)/N$.

In order to study the relation between the structure of competition and the phenomenon of frustration, I have drawn up two tables. Table 5.1 gives the percentage $100x_1/N$ of players considered as a function of the relation between the additional advantage $B_1 - B_2$ and the cost of the additional stake $C_1 - C_2$ on the one hand, and the percentage of winners $100n_1/N$ on the other. Table 5.2 gives the proportion of frustrated members considered in relation to the different values holding between the stake $(B_1 - B_2)/(C_1 - C_2)$ and the percentage $100n_1/N$ of winners. The table brings out the complex manner in which the overall rate of frustration depends, on the one hand, on the individual being given back $(B_1 - B_2)/(C_1 - C_2)$ an increase in his investment, and on the frequency of high-level lots on the other. When $100n_1/N = 100$, the number of lots of high value is the same as that of the members of the group. Each person invests C_1 and receives a lot B_2. In this case none of the group's members is frustrated (last column in the table). When $(B_1 - B_2)/(C_1 - C_2) = 1$ (first line of the table) the number of investors will be exactly n_1: the first line of the table corresponds to a situation in which the number of individuals choosing the investment C_1 corresponds to the number of lots of value B_1. None of the group's members is frustrated, since the group is here divided into two categories: those who make a high investment C_1 and receive B_1 in return, and those who make a low investment C_2 and receive B_2 in return. One ends up here with a stratified system without relative frustration.

In every other case a proportion of the group's members appears to be frustrated. Thus when the rise in profit is twice as rapid as the rise in cost (second line of the table) and the number of lots of value

B_1 amounts to 30 per cent of the number of players N (fourth column of the table), for those making a bet to avoid an expectation of negative profit the percentage of betters $100x_1/N$ must be lower than $100\,(n_1/N)\,(B_1 - B_2)/(C_1 - C_2)$, that is, in this case, $100.0,\ 30.2 = 60$. Each individual will thus stake C_1, with a probability $6/10$, from which it follows that six out of ten individuals will stake (on average) C_1. As there are only three lots of value B_1 for ten individuals, three individuals out of ten will end up being frustrated.

The rest of table 5.2 may be reconstituted by applying [4] in an analogous way.

TABLE 5.1   *Percentage of Players as a Function of the Relation between the Stake and the Percentage of Winners*

expected gain $= B_1 - B_2$	Percentage of winners: $100\,\frac{n_1}{N}$										
$C_1 - C_2$	0	10	20	30	40	50	60	70	80	90	100
1	0	10	20	30	40	50	60	70	80	90	100
2	0	20	40	60	80	100	100	100	100	100	100
3	0	30	60	90	100	100	100	100	100	100	100
4	0	40	80	100	100	100	100	100	100	100	100
5	0	50	100	100	100	100	100	100	100	100	100
6	0	60	100	100	100	100	100	100	100	100	100
7	0	70	100	100	100	100	100	100	100	100	100
8	0	80	100	100	100	100	100	100	100	100	100
9	0	90	100	100	100	100	100	100	100	100	100
10	0	100	100	100	100	100	100	100	100	100	100

TABLE 5.2   *Percentage of Frustrated People as a Function of the Relation between the Stake and the Percentage of Winners*

expected gain $B = B_1 - B_2$ C C_1 C_2	Percentage of winners: $100\,\frac{n_1}{N}$										
	0	10	20	30	40	50	60	70	80	90	100
1	0	0	0	0	0	0	0	0	0	0	0
2	0	10	20	30	40	50	40	30	20	10	0
3	0	20	40	60	60	50	40	30	20	10	0
4	0	30	60	70	60	50	40	30	20	10	0
5	0	40	80	70	60	50	40	30	20	10	0
6	0	50	80	70	60	50	40	30	20	10	0
7	0	60	80	70	60	50	40	30	20	10	0
8	0	70	80	70	60	50	40	30	20	10	0
9	0	80	80	70	60	50	40	30	20	10	0
10	0	90	80	70	60	50	40	30	20	10	0

What general propositions can we deduce from these tables?

1. If we follow the lines in table 5.2 down the page we find situations in which the profits distributed to the group's members attain a greater and greater overall importance. The rate of frustration grows along with the hopes raised by investment, i.e., with the formal equivalent of those Durkheimian considerations as to the link between individual happiness and the limitation of desires: when n_1/N, for instance, amounts to 20 per cent, it is preferable, where the general rate of frustration is concerned, that the profits obtained by an additional investment should be weak rather than strong.

2. The highest levels of frustration occur in cases in which high-value lots are distributed among small minorities.

3. Moderate lots $(B_1 - B_2)/(C_1 - C_2)$ have the advantage of generating a moderate level of frustration, except when they are generously distributed.

4. Equivalent levels of frustration are obtained by distributing important lots parsimoniously or less important lots generously. Note, for instance, that when $100n_1/N = 30$ and $(B_1 - B_2)/(C_1 - C_2) = 3$, the overall rate of frustration is 60, and that the same rate is attained when the return on the additional investment amounts to 7 but the lots are parsimoniously distributed ($100n_1/N = 10$).

5. Generally speaking the curves corresponding to identical degrees of frustration have a complex trajectory. Comparison of tables 5.1 and 5.2 does nevertheless bring out the general shape of the phenomenon: in that part of the table representing the situation in which everyone bets ($x_1 = 10$) we find a linear progression of the overall rate of frustration, which is inversely related to the rate of winners. This 'plateau' is eroded at the point at which constraint is no longer operative (the 'slope's line of change' is the mode of distribution of each line in the table), and this *curve of maximum discontent* expresses a balance: expected gain $= k$/probability of winning.

The two preceding sections provide us with a general model through which we can formally define the different classes of situations of competition and study the proportion of individuals who, in each case, decide to enter the lists at such and such a level. Analysis confirms the basic intuition; namely that, in the vast majority of cases, the structures of competition determine the appearance of frustrated players, whose number, b, varies according to the characteristics of the structure. The preceding model is therefore a sort of theoretical machine that allows one to simulate, by simplifying them, the more complex structures of competition that one encounters in social life. The model's interest also lies in the fact that it provides a simple explanation for certain phenomena sometimes considered paradoxical in classical sociology. Thus by scanning, for example, lines 2, 3 or 4 of table 5.2 from left to right, one obtains a simple simulation of Stouffer's famous example: given the same relation of additional investment, overall frustration grows as the number of winners increases (up to a certain point, at any rate). It is therefore not at all suprising that satisfaction, with regard to promotion, is greater in a system in which it is in fact rare: in this case it is irrational to invest and consequently absurd to complain if one does not get any dividends. On the other hand in situations of competition in which it is rational to invest (frequent promotion, significant chances of mobility), the fact that for some dividends are nil is necessarily felt not merely to be frustrating but to be illegitimate: this resembles Homans' notion regarding the balance between contribution and reward.[14] But it so happens that situations of competition that culminate, at the individual level, in a balance between contribution and reward, are special ones (margins of table 5.2). In the majority of cases structures of competition determine whether participation in the competition is excessive or insufficient. These excesses are, moreover, a means normally used to select individuals with regard to the collective interest, it being left up to the collectivity to create the legitimacy of the selection thus effected.

It would now be of interest to ask what happens when individuals are no longer presumed equal or perceive themselves to be equal, as was the case in previous sections of this chapter, but have, for instance, different resources. To simplify, let us imagine that the competitive games in sections 1 and 2 are presented to two categories of potential players, whom I will call the rich and the poor. I am, in other words, using the very simplest hypothesis that one could advance with respect to the structure of a system of stratification: there exist two social classes. And, in order to avoid vicarious connotations, I use banal terms. One can then imagine that the difference in resources finds expression in the poor being more hesitant in taking risks. Thus it is not enough for them to know that applying a particular strategy gives a negative or positive expectation of profit. They also take into account the structure of the lottery that is offered to them. Thus one can imagine that the value of a lottery giving them an expectation of profit G is equal to G for rich and, for the poor, lower than G, in that the risk of losing is all the greater. Whatever definition one finally adopts here, there will still be less probability of the poor person making a high bet than of the rich person doing so.

Consider, for instance, the structure

$$n_1/N = 1/6, \ (B_1 - B_2)/(C_1 - C_2) = 4, \ N = 20$$

and imagine that there are six rich people and fourteen poor people. Suppose the rich person reckons one strategy as being at least of equal value to another if the expectation of profit associated with it is at least equal, and that a poor person adds to this condition a maximin-type condition: that the probability of losing should not be higher than r. To make this more concrete, imagine $r = 40$ per cent. That means that the poor person prefers the certainty of a nil profit to a lottery in which he would have fifty chances out of a hundred of winning £2 and fifty chances out of a hundred of losing £1. Even though the expectation of profit associated with the second strategy is positive, the poor person is presumed to prefer the first. Suppose we analyse this structure.

The strategy of 'investing' (betting C_1) gives, through [4], a positive expectation of profit if a maximum of 2/3 potential players take part in the game (bet C_1). The rich will therefore (if they are ignorant of the behaviour of the poor) bet C_1 with a probability of 2/3. Consider now the case of the poor. Given that $n_1 = 3$, the probability that a player will lose his bet exceeds $2/5 = 40$ per cent, once the number of people betting is higher than five. The result of these hypotheses is that the poor will bet C_1 with a probability of $5/20 = 1/4$.[15] Thus between three and four poor persons, on the one hand, and four rich persons, on the other hand, will bet C_1. Stratification therefore has the effect: (1) of attenuating the general rate of frustration; (2) of determining effects of self-reproduction of classes: the rich are the beneficiaries of the relatively more intense withdrawal of the poor.

One could introduce any number of further complications into the models outlined above. There is probably no point in doing more here than suggest those that are possible at the present stage in the argument.

1. Let us simply recall the family of variants that have just been outlined. It rests on the hypothesis of a preliminary *stratification* between potential players, this stratification having the effect of differentiating the players' attitudes with regard to risk.

2. One could also complicate things by making B_1 a function of n_1: by introducing, for example, the hypothesis that B_1 decreases with n_1. This sort of hypothesis is clearly useful for simulating those processes of competition for the acquisition of goods whose value, as is the case with prestige, sinks perceptibly with the rise of the number of people to whom they are distributed. This observation suggests that the logic of relative frustration may be thought to change with the nature of the goods considered (prestige, money. . . .)

3. In order to refresh the reader's memory, I will simply mention variants of a more mechanical nature, such as the one that consists of offering players the choice of three options: C_1, the necessary but not the sufficient condition for obtaining B_1; C_2, the necessary but not the

sufficient condition for obtaining B_2; C_3, the necessary but not the sufficient condition for obtaining B_3 (with $B_1 > B_2 > B_3$, $C_1 > C_2 > C_3$).

4. Instead of supposing that a stake, C_1, is the necessary (but not sufficient) condition for the acquisition of a lot of value B_1, one may suppose that the stake C_1 allows access to a lottery characterised by a particular distribution of lots, the stake C_2 allowing access to another sort of lottery.

5. It is worth noting, incidentally, that the model also provides the logical skeleton for a research project in experimental social psychology that would very probably lead to some very instructive results and would perhaps put one in a better position to understand phenomena like envy.

What I have tried to suggest is that simple competition models can readily provide an account of effects which have for a long time perplexed sociologists. They clearly show that the level of overall frustration does not necessarily decrease along with the diffusion of hopes of profit: an increase in opportunities for promotion for all may in fact lead to a still more rapid increase in the obstacles to promotion. The model's advantage lies in its clearly showing the sort of conditions under which this occurs, and its results make it possible to formulate more exactly the intuitive propositions advanced, in various forms, by Tocqueville, Durkheim and by those authors who used the notions of reference group and of relative deprivation, i.e., Hyman, Merton and Stouffer.

The model confirms Tocqueville's analysis of the effects of the differences between individuals being attenuated. Everything else being equal, when differences in individual resources are attenuated, one observes an increase in the number of cases of frustration of the sort that leads to quarrels. In other words the attenuation of distances between social 'strata' must, *ceteris paribus*, increase the level of frustration leading to quarrels. One should however insist on the limiting clause of *ceteris paribus*: if distances between individuals decrease, if, in other words, equality of opportunity increases, the general level of frustration tends – as an effect of this change – to grow; but this effect can be reinforced or, on the other hand, limited, as table 5.2 shows, when opportunities open to individuals grow as much as when they lessen. Consider, for example, line 8 of this table. There one sees that, when the number of winners goes from 10 per cent to 20 per cent, the rate of frustration shifts from 70 per cent to 80 per cent; but when the number of winners goes from 20 per cent to 30 per cent the rate of frustration falls from 80 per cent to 70 per cent. If one combines this result with the effect of a diminution or of an increase in the inequality of opportunities, it is clear that all possible configurations can in theory be observed. In other words an increase in the number of winners or, to shift from the language of games to that of sociology, an increase in social mobility may coincide with either an increase or a diminution in the overall frustration. It may also coincide with a constant level of overall frustration, in the hypothetical case of an increase in mobility and a simultaneous diminution in the inequality of opportunity having effects that would compensate for each other at the level of collective frustration.

One of the model's essential virtues therefore lies in the fact that it allows one to clarify the logical status of those results in classical sociology that I have cited throughout this article. It does, for instance, show that the proposition of Tocqueville's that has it that the attenuation in differences between individuals must increase frustration and envious comparison is, *ceteris paribus*, true. On the other hand the proposition linking increase in mobility to the level of frustration is only valid if one presents it as a possibility: it is *possible* (but not necessary) that the increase in mobility should provoke an increase in the overall level of frustration. The model thus has a double advantage. Firstly it completely eliminates the mystery contained in Tocqueville's paradox: it is sufficient to posit individuals preoccupied with the pursuit of their interests and to confront them with a lottery having a determined structure, in order to simulate Tocqueville's proposition. But from another angle the model shows that one can observe an inverse correlation between mobility and general level of frustration. That does not mean that one is faced with an independence between the two phenomena. They are, on the contrary, closely dependent on each other, but the direction of this dependence depends on the properties of the structure of interdependence linking the individuals.

The model does of course show, in the same way, that Durkheim's 'law' *may* in certain cases give the impression of being valid but in other cases may not be so. Applied to Stouffer's example, the analysis likewise shows that one could in other circumstances expect to find an inversion in the links observed. I mean that, as the model shows, one *may* encounter situations in which weaker promotion opportunities are associated with *greater* dissatisfaction, just as one *may* encounter the situation described in *The American Soldier*, in which a *lesser* dissatisfaction is associated with weaker promotion opportunities. This does not mean, let me stress once more, that opportunities for mobility and satisfaction are phenomena without any relation one to another, but that the structures of interdependence are different in the two cases.

These remarks have a corollary whose importance I would emphasise. It is in vain to wonder if, *in general*, an increase in mobility or in the accessibility of these *goods*, whatever the nature of these goods, or in the equality of opportunity, produces an increase in individual satisfaction. The question is not liable to a general answer. Not because individual satisfaction is a random phenomenon, and one that is independent of the individual's social position and of the opportunities that the collectivity offers him, but because the direction of the dependence in question rests on structures of interdependence.

The above notes are clearly just a sketch. But they do indicate a possible direction for research that could turn out to be important. They show that it is possible to construct a theory allowing one, for instance, to link the rate of overall satisfaction with the characteristics of situations of competition. They also show that it is possible, on the basis of the model that was fleetingly invoked in the final section, to analyse the problem of the reproduction of inequalities and handicaps by means of a 'light' model, i.e., one that does not imply the unwieldy and banal hypothesis which crops up so often in the work of certain sociologists, which has it that the persistence of inequalities is the effect of a dominant group oppressing a dominated one. Generally speaking it may be that the neo-individualist perspective[16] adopted here allows one to reiterate certain questions bearing on the study of social stratification. The models outlined above do clearly define the reference groups imposed on actors because of the conditions of interaction. They lead to definitions of the different types of frustration and envy and include, in filigree, a theory of *envy* in which this sentiment would not be the consequence of every single occurrence of inequality, as many sociologists implicitly admit, but a response to particular situations generated by definite structures of interdependence.

One could further complicate the preceding models by questioning the legitimacy of the structures of competition thus introduced: thus, if it is a question of choosing future doctors, a structure characterised by $(B_1 - B_2)/(C_1 - C_2) = 1$ is perhaps satisfying to the extent that it minimises the overall frustration. On the other hand it is definitely not the sort that will lead to the best and most motivated candidates being selected.

From another angle consideration of the theory – defended by authors like Jencks and Easterlin – that has it that industrial societies automatically generate phenomena of generalised envy and frustration suggests that, in terms of the perspective in use here, it is perhaps unnecessarily pessimistic.[17] As the present article indicates, it is not self-evident that every difference between two individuals generates envy and frustration. One must at least distinguish between that situation in which two individuals receive different rewards, each having made a similar contribution, and that situation in which each has made a different one. It is not certain that industrial societies, by improving the situation of all while at the same time maintaining and sometimes even aggravating relative differences, do for that reason generate frustration. Nor is it certain that, as Jencks would claim, overall frustration is narrowly tied to the distribution of goods being dispersed.

Finally the model developed above makes it reasonable to suggest that the real relation between the objective opportunities that society offers individuals and the level of collective satisfaction may be a negative one, as Durkheim and Tocqueville propose. The profound intuition of these two authors is quite opposed to the simplicity of the theory presented by Easton: 'We can expect that direct satisfaction of demand will at least generate specific support; and the longer such satisfactions are felt, the more likely it is that a higher level of political good will develop.'[18] In fact the preceding models show that one can only guarantee that a system will bring about a weak or a non-existent level of frustration if one advances the absurd hypothesis that it could eliminate every institution of competition. For the rest one must be prepared for the eventuality that, having succeeded in *increasing* and *levelling out* the opportunities of all, it will nevertheless see its audience decrease, because this improvement in the lot of all will have increased the general level of frustration, leading to quarrels.

6   Perverse Effects and Social Philosophy: Rawls's Theory of Justice

Those who reflect on the nature of industrial society constantly refer to what I shall here call programmed Utopias. The pessimist version has it that societies are vast organisations in which individual behaviours would inevitably be programmed. The optimistic version (see, for instance, the American sociologist Etzioni's book *The Active Society*) has it that industrial societies have to be corrected by improving their programming, i.e., by researching into better means of circulating information and by perfecting the retroactive mechanisms that link the different poles of a society (considered as an organisation) together.

Rawls's book, *A Theory of Justice*, is intellectually superior to most programmed Utopias. He has recourse to an impressive armoury of concepts. But he too tends to minimise the role played in social change by the perverse effects that social institutions and in particular individual freedoms invariably produce. We have known since Rousseau that there is always some cost involved in eliminating these perverse effects. Their social significance is in itself sufficient cause to doubt theories that argue for an implicit identity between societies and organisations. The distinction is actually a fundamental one. All the behaviours that take place inside an organisation are more or less ordered. They are the product of roles. In society, on the other hand, there are all sorts of behaviours (those that comprise the private sphere) that depend on individual free choice, and perverse effects are often the result, as several of the above texts suggest, of the accumulation of behaviours of this type.

Finally Rawls fails to realise that the distributive justice that he claims to define implies costs and that these costs may well be paid off in the all too familiar form of restriction of the individual's liberties.

This discussion of the Rawlsian theory of justice thus brings us to some of the fundamental questions that this book poses: the accumulation of micro-sociological actions will readily engender, at the macro-sociological level, effects that are in general too complex to be anticipated in all their detail and sufficiently ambivalent to leave a great deal of room for ideological and political conflicts. It is for this reason that the dialectic (in a restricted form) seems to me to be a better general paradigm for sociological analysis than cybernetics.

This text was originally published in *Revue Française de Science Politique* xxv, 2 (Apr. 1975) 193–221.

Difficult though it is to summarise in a few lines the 600 or so pages of *A Theory of Justice*, it is not impossible to do so provided one keeps to the essential. Rawls's theory of justice is in fact relatively simple in its main lines. It proceeds from a 'deductive' approach which derives directly from the contractualist philosophers: let us assume there to be men who are ignorant of the particular position which will be attributed to them in the society of which they are going to become members, not knowing even the generation to which they belong, possessing minimum knowledge of human nature and of societies, harbouring towards each other a basic feeling of neutrality which excludes envy, knowing that they appreciate 'primary goods' such as wealth, power and personal fulfilment, but knowing neither the exact list nor the relative utility of these goods. Let us then imagine that these men are presented with various conceptions of justice, that is to say principles which should govern their choices of social institutions. According to Rawls, the theory to which they would give pride of place over all other and in particular over all theories of the utilitarian or intuitionist type – I shall have occasion to bring out the exact significance of these terms subsequently – is that of *justice as fairness*: they would demand first of all that the basic liberties be equally distributed among all men (first principle); secondly that social and economic inequalities (1) be regulated in such a way as best to serve the interests of the most unfavoured individuals; (2) be attached to functions and positions to which all men have equal opportunity of access (second principle).

Without entering into Rawls's demonstration in detail, I shall briefly show how certain propositions are 'deduced' from postulates relating to the 'original position' (*i.e.*, 'the state of nature') as it is described by Rawls. Thus, once the contractants are assumed to be not envious, they have no reason to include equal conditions among their demands. More precisely, since they do not know what position they will occupy in society, they should prefer to an egalitarian system in which all men would have a certain quantity of 'primary goods' an inegalitarian system which would enable each person to be ensured of an at least equal quantity of primary goods.

Equal opportunity of access to positions is 'deduced' in a similar way: not knowing their aptitudes and talents, knowing merely that there exist natural inequalities between men, accepting moreover unequal conditions provided that these turn out to be to the benefit of the community and thereby to benefit each person, the contractants admit of the principle of competition for access to social positions. But they cannot admit that the outcome of the competition be predetermined by natural aptitudes for, in this case, they would have to envisage the possibility of their coming to occupy a low position in the event of their having small talent. If one assumes that the contractants subscribe, out of prudence, to this pessimistic hypothesis, it follows that *each person* should then consider favourable social positions to be reserved for *others*. In this case it would be impossible for them, since they are not altruistic, to admit the principle of unequal conditions. One therefore concludes that the acceptance of unequal conditions implies that equal opportunity be achieved, or in other words that such handicaps as are likely to affect the equality of the competition be neutralised. No limit to equal opportunity can therefore be deduced from the premises contained in the description of the original situation.

I fully appreciate that the summary which has just been set forth of certain essential points in Rawls's theory is a superficial one and does not do justice to its richness. It is however sufficient for an understanding of the following objections.

These objections, which lead me, as will be seen, to disagree radically with Rawls, are of two types. The first are of a logical nature. It does not seem to me that the laborious 'deduction' engaged in by the author of *A Theory of Justice* takes us a single step beyond the set of axioms which he lays down at the beginning. Rawls's 'original position' seems to me in this connexion less fruitful than the state of nature of the classical contractualists. The second series of objections come under sociology. Just as the Rousseauist myth of the 'savage' leads to a generative grammar of social justice, so Rawls's original situation and the theory to which it gives rise result in a theory of the legitimacy of institutions. But in this connexion Rawls must again bow down to both Hobbes and Rousseau. I do not think that the Rawlsian theory of justice enables us better to understand the feelings of legitimacy or illegitimacy evoked by the institutions of the societies with which he is first and foremost concerned, that is the liberal industrial societies.

Rawls's general approach is therefore identical to that of Rousseau: in both cases what is involved is deducing the terms of the contract from the characteristics of the state of nature. But, and this is even more important and all the more worthy of note in that Rousseau is mentioned only in passing in *A Theory of Justice*, Rawls's contractant resembles the 'savage' of the *Discourse on the Origins of Inequality* like a brother. Like him, he is good (neither envious nor malevolent), harbours towards his fellows a feeling of indifferent neutrality and has only a rudimentary knowledge of human nature and of societies. One even finds again in Rawls, transposed into modern language, the lexicographical order introduced by the *Discourse* between the instinct for self-preservation and the instinct for preservation of the species. This dual instinct corresponds textually to the feeling of 'limited altruism' (p. 146) which Rawls ascribes to his contractants, thus distinguishing them from the selfish *homo oeconomicus*.[1] The main point on which Rawls's contractant and Rousseau's 'savage' differ is the fact that the latter is assumed to belong to an affluent world whereas the former is faced with a society of 'moderate scarcity'. This notion of scarcity naturally goes hand in hand with the principle that the contractants, in this respect poles apart from Rousseau, prefer to possess a larger quantity rather than a smaller quantity of primary goods.

The axiomatic premise of the 'savage' was to turn out to be remarkably fruitful: it enabled Rousseau to sketch out the theory of what would today be called systems of collective action. Mention may be made here, to keep to only one example, of the hunting expedition in the second *Discourse*: two 'savages' meet up and decide to co-operate in a deer-hunting expedition; one of the accomplices, lying in wait for the deer, sees a hare go by and abandons his look-out post; result: on one side an empty-handed hunter and on the other meagre spoils.[2] The anecdote is an illustration of the celebrated 'prisoner's dilemma': each of the partners stands to gain by unilaterally betraying the other, but, by so doing, each obtains a lower retribution than the Pareto's optimum which cooperation would have ensured. It is clear from this that cooperation between individuals who are free to back down unilaterally from a contract may come to grief even when cooperation is to the advantage of each. This was a considerable discovery, since it demonstrates that it may be necessary to *compel* men to cooperate of whom it is assumed that they wish to act in accordance with their own interests and that they are aware of the advantage of cooperation. This theorem which is the very foundation of the *Social contract* has received a great deal of attention in the modern theory of collective action.[3]

I shall return to this point later. At this stage my intention is simply to show that the axiomatic premise of the 'savage' led Rousseau to discoveries whose originality is more clearly to be seen in comparing the Rousseauist contract with the Hobbesian contract: the latter aims at reducing the social costs of confrontation and rivalry; the former, at making cooperation possible in the both singular and fundamental illustrative case in which cooperation founders even when it is in each one's interest to cooperate and no one feels any hostility or even rivalry towards anyone else. The detailed discussion that Rousseau devotes in the *Discourse* to Hobbes' axiomatic structure clearly shows that the fundamental reproach which he addresses to the latter is in fact that he assumes the state of nature to be characterised essentially by the opposition of individual interests.[4]

Despite the kinship between Rawls's set of axioms and that of Rousseau, I do not think that the former is as fruitful as the latter or, at least, that Rawls has been able to draw such basic consequences from his axioms as Rousseau. In fact the theory of justice which is 'deduced' from this set of axioms does not really seem to me to result from it. I even suspect the principles of the theory of justice can be obtained only on the condition that the axiomatic premise of the original position be completed by the principles which are claimed to be deduced from it!

I shall limit myself in this connexion to showing that a key element in the Rawlsian theory of justice, the indifference principle, in no way results from the axiomatic premise of the original situation.[5] This principle corresponds to the first half of the second principle of justice according to which inequalities must be dealt with in such a way as to serve the interest of those who are most unfavoured. In order to distinguish this from other types of distributive principle, it is convenient to use Rawls's graphic presentation. Let us imagine then that we want to describe the way in which a primary good is distributed in a society. For this a system of rectangular coordinates can be used in relation to which the relative shares corresponding to individuals belonging to different classes are registered. In the simplest case two axes are used and the relative share falling to a representative of the worst-off class is shown on the x-axis and that of a representative of the best-off class on the y-axis. The fact that a 'representative' of each class is considered rather than the classes as a whole presents the advantage of eliminating the complication deriving from the differences in the numbers belonging to each class, which differences are not known by the contractant, placed as he is beneath the 'veil of ignorance' which is characteristic of the original position.

Thus, point A (figure 6.1) represents a distribution such that the representative of the worst-off class possesses a relative share of the primary good measured by the abscissa of A, whereas the representative of the best-off class has a relative share measured by the ordinate of A.

Let us now return to the line of reasoning by which Rawls claims to deduce the indifference principle from the premise of the original position. As the contractants are assumed to be not envious, the lesser or greater *equality* of the distribution does not make it possible to determine the relations of preference or indifference between

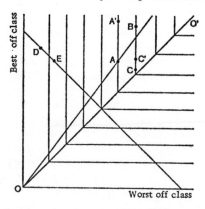

FIGURE 6.1   Distribution of a primary good between a representative of the best-off class and a representative of the worst-off class

hypothetical situations. Moreover it is assumed that the contractants are ignorant of the position which will be finally attributed to them in the society which they are joining. Lastly they know that this society is characterised by a situation of moderate scarcity and that they themselves wish to have at their disposal a greater rather than a lesser quantity of primary goods.[6]

As is easily imagined, the contractants in the original situation prefer *B* to *A* (figure 6.1). *B* corresponds to a more inegalitarian distribution than *A*. But, as they are not envious, they overlook this point and consider merely the fact that, regardless of their future position, whether they belong to the best-off class or to the worst-off class, their share will be better in *B*. If a society can attain states *A* and *B* they will therefore prefer *B* to *A*, even if distribution *B* is more inegalitarian. In the language of game theory, *B* is a *dominant* strategy: regardless of their future condition, their fate will be better if they choose distribution *B*. As the reader will have noted, I assumed in the graph of figure 6.1 that two distributions are egalitarian to the same degree when the relationship of the share which falls to the representative of the best-off class to that which falls to the representative of the worst-off class is the same. Thus, all the points on the straight line *OO'* are considered to represent identical degrees of inequality.

Let us now compare distributions *A* and *C*: if the contractant identifies himself with the best-off individual, he is bound to prefer *A* to *C*. If he identifies himself with the worst-off individual, he is bound on the contrary to prefer *C* to *A*. But being ignorant of his future position, he cannot identify himself with either one or the other. Being ignorant also of the proportions of the individuals belonging to the two classes, he is incapable of calculating and comparing the expectations corresponding to the two states and A and B. In this state of maximum uncertainty the only reasonable strategy, so Rawls argues, consists in the contractant minimising the risks which he runs, or in a word in choosing the situation which ensures him at all events of the greatest of minimums. From this point of view C is preferable to A, since the *maximum minimorum*, the maximin in short, corresponds to C. The contractant will consequently prefer C to A.

It is I think possible to be convinced by this argument although, as Barry rightly emphasises, games theoreticians are loath to admit that the maximin strategy is necessarily preferable to any other in the case of uncertainty as to the probabilities attached to the different possible rewards being maximum. But the contractant would undoubtedly take a considerable risk in using, for instance, the strategy sometimes recommended in situations in which a choice has to be made in conditions of uncertainty and which consists in assuming the probabilities of belonging to each of the classes to be equal. He would take an even greater risk in adopting the maximax strategy upheld by Barry.

Certainly it is possible to construct situations in which the maximax is patently a better strategy than the maximin in conditions of uncertainty. It is true that if I do not know what the weather is going to be like, I can reasonably go out without an umbrella and thus opt for the maximax (if it does not rain and if I am not encumbered with my umbrella, I shall be gratified) rather than the maximin (if it does not rain I shall be encumbered with my umbrella, but, if it does rain, I shall be protected). But the 'futile' character of the examples put forward by Barry clearly shows that the maximax strategy and, generally speaking, any strategy implying a degree of optimism greater than the maximin strategy cannot be upheld without difficulty in the case, which is that of Rawls, of the contractant gambling wiht his conditions of existence.

Let us consequently admit that from the axiomatic premise of the original situation it can indeed be deduced that the contractants are bound to prefer B to A and, *in terms of different considerations, C to A.* I have stressed part of the previous sentence because, whereas preference for B in relation to A is deduced directly from the premise, this does not hold good for preference for C in relation to A which entails the additional proposition according to which, in the absence of a dominant strategy, the maximin represents the optimum strategy in the case of a decision in conditions of maximum uncertainty.

But while it is possible to follow Rawls up to this point, it seems impossible to me to admit, as he does, on the basis of the axiomatic premise of the original situation, the indifference of the contractants when it comes to choosing between B and C. For, whatever the probabilities of belonging respectively to the most favoured class and to the most unfavoured class, a contractant who desires a greater quantity rather than a lesser quantity of primary goods is bound to prefer B to C. If he is destined to belong to the worst-off class he will have the same share in both cases. If he destined to join the best-off class, he is ensured of a greater share if distribution B is ensured by the society. According to the premise of the original situation, B and C cannot therefore belong to the same indifference curve; on the contrary, B must be preferred to C. One cannot see why, in other words, the contractant should adopt the maximin strategy to cate to his preferences when he has a dominant strategy at his disposal.

And yet this is the proposition on which the indifference principle is founded: the contractants prefer the distribution represented by point B or by point C to the distribution corresponding to point A; on the other hand they are indifferent when it comes to choosing between B and C since these two distributions do not stand out from the point of view of the fate reserved for the worst-off. This accounts for the appearance of the indifference curves in figure 6.1: so long as one is considering distributions in which the individual whose fate is shown on the y-axis is privileged in relation to the other, that is the distributions belonging to the space included between the y-axis and the straight line forming with it an angle of 45°, there is indifference on the part of the contractants between two points situated on a line parallel to the y-axis and preference for any point whose distance from the y-axis is greater than that of a given point. Naturally, when the individual whose share is shown on the x-axis is the worst-off (distributions belonging to the space included between the x-axis and the portion of the straight line at an angle of 45°), the indifference curves are parallel to the x-axis.

How can one get over this contradiction between the axiomatic premise and the indifference principle? Rawls's text contains in this respect a few suggestions which it is worth while examining. Thus it is stated that the contractants are assumed to be not envious when the inequalities do not exceed certain limits: 'He [the contractant] is not downcast by the knowledge or perception that others have a larger index of primary social goods. Or at least this is true as long as the differences between himself and others do not exceed certain limits and he does not believe that the existing inequalities are founded on injustice' (p. 143). Thus, beyond a certain degree of inequality, envy appears. It is therefore possible to imagine that indifference between B and C is due to the fact that B represents a degree of inequality situated beyond this threshold: the advantage that the contractant would obtain in choosing B, which in the most unfavourable case ensures him of the same quantity of primary goods as C, would according to this hypothesis be cancelled out by the envy which he would feel if he found himself placed in the unfavoured class. However apart from the fact that it is difficult to give a precise expression to this hypothesis of compensation, it is not compatible with the indifference principle. Indeed it implies that two distributions between which the contractant would be indifferent, appear on separate indifference curves. Thus it is possible to imagine that the rate of inequality to which distribution A' corresponds is such that A' and C are perceived as affording no difference between them. But again one comes up against a contradiction in that A' and C are situated on separate indifference curves. It is to be noted moreover that, according to the text referred to, envy appears only when inequality reaches a certain threshold. Consequently it is always possible to find two distinct points situated on the same indifference curve, both of them representing distributions situated this side of the threshold at which envy appears and such that one of these points must, according to the axiomatics of the original position, be preferred to the other. Let us assume for instance that C and C' have these properties. In this case C' must, according to the axioms, be preferred to C. And yet the indifference principle places the two points on the same indifference curve.

The text quoted above suggests yet another way of getting over the contradiction. According to the text, envy appears if inequality goes beyond a certain threshold of if, this being an alternative hypothesis, the contractant believes the inequalities to be founded on injustice. Is it not then possible to imagine that distributions B and C are considered as affording no difference because B is believed to be founded on injustice? If the hypothesis amounts to introducing a mechanism of compensation between the injustice of one distribution and the expectations with which it is associated, the previous diffculties crop up again. If it implies that the contractants first of all wonder whether two distributions are equally fair before determining their preference, then one of two things is possible: either B and C are believed to be equally fair and B is preferred to C, since it is associated with higher expectations, or B is believed to be unfair in relation to C and C preferred to B. Once again it seems impossible to deduce that the contractants will be indifferent when it comes to choosing between B and C.

In other words it is impossible, even taking into account the corrections which Rawls gives of the axiomatics of the original situation, to deduce from it that key element in the theory of justice which is constituted by the indifference principle. Even more curiously, one does not see how the indifference of the contractants when it comes to choosing between B and C is compatible with the notion according to which the inequalities should be adjusted in such a way as to serve the interests of the worst-off class. For, if a society can achieve either distribution *B* or distribution *C*, *B* and *C* giving to the representative of the unfavoured class the same share, the greater inequality of *B* is not justified. Once again it is not clear why *B* and *C* are considered to afford no difference in contradiction with the proposition according to which inequalities should be adjusted in such a way as to serve the worst-off.

To tell the truth, the only way to clear up these contradictions seems to me to assume that the contractant situated in the original position is identified with the representative of the worst-off class. Of course such an identification makes a good part of Rawls's book useless and reduces the 'deduction' of the indifference principle to a trivial repetition. But I confess that I see no other way of reconciling the axioms describing the original position with the indifference principle. I may add that one of the reasons put forward several times by Rawls for preferring the indifference principle to 'classical utilitarianism' (the theory according to which the general interest is satisified by the maximisation of the total quantity of goods) also seems to me to be in direct contradiction with his premise.

The utilitarian, he argues, prefers *B* to *C* (for instance, p. 188 *seq.*) because *B*, regardless of the distribution of individuals between the favoured class and the unfavoured class, corresponds to a greater total quantity of primary goods. But, he says, to assume the contractant to be sensitive to the total quantity of goods distributed amounts to either giving him the status of an outside observer and making him a judge where he is a plaintiff, or to considering him as altruistic, that is to say as sensitive both to the share which falls to others and to the share which falls to himself. Moreover the utilitarian perspective has the disadvantage of assuming the problem of the interpersonal comparison of utilities to be solved. The argument is valid if one considers two distributions such as *D* and *E* (figure 6.1) situated on a straight line such that the total of the goods which fall to the two classes is constant (I am disregarding here the hypothesis of convexity generally introduced by the utilitarians): the classical utilitarian's indifference as far as these two points is concerned does indeed imply that a contractant be either altruistic or taken for an outside observer. On the other hand the argument is specious when one compares distributions *B* and *C* in figure 6.1. In this case, the contractant characterised by an indifferent neutrality towards others, wishing to obtain a greater rather than a lesser quantity of primary goods, is bound to prefer *B* to *C*, even if the veil of ignorance prohibits him from knowing in advance what condition is held in store for him by the society.

In fact Rawls's axiomatic premise should have led him to a definition of the notion of rationality close to that which is to be found in certain games theorists:[7] it seems that, in the case of two distributions being such that one of them represents a dominant strategy, the contractants are bound, in view of the passions which are attributed to them by the description of the original position, to choose this distribution. As to the maximin strategy, it is possible to uphold this when two distributions are such that no dominant strategy exists. Instead, Rawls admits, in direct contradiction with his premise, that the contractants adopt the maximin even in the presence of a dominant strategy.

For reasons of space it is impossible for me to go any further in criticising the internal coherence of Rawls's theory. The foregoing objections seem to me to show sufficiently that his intention of creating a moral geometry is finally unsuccessful. One is therefore forced to admit that the second principle of justice stems from a theory of the 'intuitionist' type which is in contradiction with Rawls's actual intention. This lack of success however in no way detracts from the originality and the boldness of his undertaxis which at one and the same time explain and justify Rawls's perseverance in his undertaking and the interest to which it has given rise.

In the second part of this article I shall inquire into the other aspect of Rawls's objective: building a theory of the legitimacy of social institutions, that is to say an instrument making it possible to distinguish just and legitimate institutions from ill-formed or illegitimate institutions. As will be seen, the result once again does not seem to me to match up to the ambition.

In this second part I shall disregard Rawls's deductive intentions and shall consider the theory of justice as an intuitionist theory. As will be remembered, this theory includes two principles of justice of which the second is itself divided into two sub-principles. Let me remind the reader of them:

1st principle: the basic liberties must be equally distributed among all men.

2nd principle: (1) social and economic equalities must be regulated in such a way as best to serve the interests of the most unfavoured individuals; (2) they must be attached to functions and positions to which all men have equal opportunity of access.

These two principles form the core of the Rawlsian theory of justice. It should be added that, according to Rawls, they are ordered: the first has priority over the second and the second part of the second priority over the first part. In other words the basic liberties cannot be distributed in an inegalitarian manner even on the assumption that this would have the consequence of improving the fate of the most unfavoured ones. It will be noted incidentally that, according to Rawls, a certain inequality of liberties can however be admitted in certain historic conditions if this inequality allows a society to emerge from a state of collective poverty. He refers in this connexion to phases of development largely outgrown by the industrial societies.

Likewise any deviation from the principle of equal opportunity is illegitimate even if it helps to improve the fate of those who are most unfavoured. The ordering of the principles amounts in other words to excluding from the primary goods whose distribution obeys the indifference principle, on the one hand the basic liberties and on the other opportunities: it is not possible for the contractants to accept to trade equal liberties and equal opportunity for a greater quantity of primary goods, for instance wealth or power.

The reasons for this ordering were briefly set forth above with regard at least to the two parts of the second principle of justice. It was seen that the contractants can only accept unequal *conditions* under the twofold proviso that they turn out to benefit those who are most unfavoured and that equal opportunity in competing for employment be ensured. But the latter condition dominates the first one: the contractants indeed base themselves on the pessimistic eventuality that their talents, of which they are ignorant, are modest; in this eventuality the favourable conditions which may be offered by a society are assumed by everyone to be attributed to the others; not being altruistic, they cannot accept unequal conditions at this price. Equal opportunity conceived as a corrective to the initial handicaps is therefore a necessary condition for their acceptance of unequal conditions. As is seen, the demonstration is achieved by a new application of the maximin principle.

The logical anteriority of the first principle of justice (equal distribution of liberties) in relation to the second is deduced in a similar manner: the contractants cannot accept to trade an unequal distribution of liberties for an equal distribution of opportunities or an improvement of the share of the worst-off member. It will be noted in this connexion however that the Rawlsian theory, as a result of its formalism, leads to no particular conclusion concerning the content of the liberties: it concludes merely that they must be equally distributed.

Several passages in Rawls's text indicate that, according to him, the basic institutions of liberal industrial societies and particularly of American society obey these principles of justice and that consequently they should be recognised by the contractants as being legitimate.[8] In a word Rawls conceives liberal industrial societies as societies whose institutions tend asymptotically to guarantee for everyone equal basic liberties and opportunities and to preserve only the inequalities necessary to improve the lot of the worse off members.[9]

One cannot avoid emphasising at this point that Rawls's deduction results in a theory of inequalities close to that developed by many functionalist sociologists and of which Davis and Moore have given a particularly explicit formulation.[10] For these authors the inequalities of wealth, of prestige and of power are necessary to the operating of any society characterised by the division of labour: from the time that a society comprises a system of social positions differentiated according to the level of competence, the size of the educational investment or the extent of 'experience', remunerations must be proportional to investments if individuals are to be incited to invest. Any system based on the division of labour therefore implies a system of stratification and inequalities. But since the division of labour helps to increase social output, the inequalities turn out to be to everyone's advantage. Naturally, so that the process of selection governed by the inequality of the remunerations attached to the different social positions may operate in optimum manner, there must be as close to perfect equal opportunity as possible.

A basic difficulty in Rawls's theory of justice, as well as in the functionalist theory of inequalities of Davis and Moore, resides in the illegitimate application to global societies of a pattern which at a pinch is only applicable to entities of lesser complexity, such as organisations. To confine ourselves to the second principle of justice, it is possible without too much difficulty to imagine an organisation which obeys operating laws such that (1) equal opportunity be ensured for the members of the organisation in competing for the best-paid jobs; (2) inequalities in remuneration be regulated in such a way as to ensure optimum social output and thus turn out to be to the advantage of everyone. Class-social analyses were made of this model by Max Weber. But the question is whether it can be applied to societies without any major change. In my opinion the reply is no. In this case the inequalities which appear at the global level cannot, even as an approximation, be deduced from a model of the functionalist type.

Without expanding on this point here, I will say merely that the basis for the gap between the organisational level and the level which, with Parsons, we may describe as the 'societal' level lies particularly in the fact that the societal level includes many classes of behaviour which (1) may be adopted without consulting or being approved by someone else; (2) have marginal external effects close to zero; (3) may, when they are *aggregated*, have considerable external effects. It is exceptional for the three properties to be present simultaneously at the organisational level. It would not be difficult to show that not only Rawls but also many sociologists are not fully aware of this fundamental distinction and are thus led to consider societies as complex organisations. Consequently they readily attribute the responsibility for the undesirable phenomena which are observed in societies to institutions and/or to particular groups, and fail to see that many of the phenomena which appear at the societal level derive neither from the ultimate aims of institutions nor from the wishes of particular groups. We shall examine in what follows several examples of situations characterised by notable effects of aggregation.

Let us consider the example of the relation between social and economic inequalities on the one hand and unequal educational opportunity on the other. It has the advantage of showing that at the level of global societies, *institutions* may be incapable, even when they set themselves that goal, of simultaneously meeting the two-fold Rawlsian requirement of equal opportunity and the 'optimization' of ineqalities. Thus legitimate basic institutions, in Rawls's sense, may coincide with social mechanisms whose results are illegitimate.

Everyone knows today that school education is far from being equally accessible to all. Some theories attribute this state of things to the fact that the school, on account of its very function, transmits and places a value on a culture which is the property of the upper classes. Thus, as the children of the upper classes are better prepared by the family context to meet the requirements of the educational system, they consequently have a greater chance of attaining a high educational level. If this theory were sufficient, Rawls's principle of justice would be satisfied by measures aimed at compensating, particularly during the first years of school education, for the cultural inequality produced by the family background.

In reality it is not difficult to show that this theory explains the lack of equal educational opportunity only to a small extent. This inequality seems essentially to stem from the fact that, as I have endeavoured to show elsewhere, according to the social class to which an adolescent belongs, the continuation of school attendance beyond each point at which alternatives are offered in the course represents variable socio-economic costs and benefits.[11] Thus the usefulness of continued school attendance increases in terms of the social class of origin: the higher the latter is, the greater is the usefulness of continued school attendance. Certainly measures have been taken in most of the industrial societies to reduce the number and the inflexibility of the points at which the educational system branches up. The extension of compulsory education to the first years of the secondary course tends, for instance, to reduce the number of these points and thus to promote equal opportunity. However, except in a utopian system in which all the children would follow a common course for a number of years which would be the same for everyone, a certain number of points at which alternatives are offered must be maintained, this being simply a result of the existence of a system based on the division of labour. Consequently the inegalitarian effects deriving from the link between the social class and the usefulness of continued school attendance are multiplied by the number of times that there exist points at which alternatives are offered. This exponential effect explains why it is that, even in a country such as the United States in which a wide range of institutional reforms aimed at reducing unequal educational opportunity has been applied over the last decade, this inequality remains sufficiently marked for an adolescent originating from the upper level of society to have ten times a greater chance of obtaining a college degree than an adolescent of modest social origin.

If this analysis is correct, it sets an insurmountable difficulty in the way of the Rawlsian theory of justice. If indeed it is true that the costs and benefits of continued school attendance vary in terms of the social position occupied by families and that institutional reforms of the educational system cannot in themselves, except in the hypothesis of a Utopian educational system, neutralise this effect of the stratification system, it follows that any stratification system inevitably gives rise to a considerable degree of educational inequality. Thus one comes up against a contradiction as far as Rawlsian theory is concerned, according to which the inequalities attached to jobs and functions can be justified only if equal opportunity of access to these jobs and functions is achieved. How can these principles be reconciled with the fact that, concretely, socio-economic inequalities or, to speak in the language of the sociologists, the stratification system is the ultimate cause of unequal educational opportunity and, as a result, inevitably gives rise to unequal opportunity of access to employment? In reality it is difficult in this connexion to imagine a social system conforming to the two parts of the second principle of justice, if at least one does not want to violate the first principle, for instance by taking authoritarian measures to limit access to education to the upper classes.

In reality Rawls's theory is based on a reductive representation of societies: it admits that feelings of justice or injustice produced by a social system apply to the explicit aims of institutions rather than to the complex social effects to which they give rise. Moreover it cannot be otherwise once the hypothetical contractants are assumed to have only a limited notion of the complexity of social mechanisms. The hypothesis aims at making the contractants free from the prejudices which they would have if they belonged to an actual society. But is it not absurd to derive the feelings of injustice experienced by the members of real societies from the feelings of injustice attributed to contractants devoid of any precise view with regard to societies? To this question I would be tempted to answer positively and, since Rawls dwells at length on the fact that his approach derives from Kant, I will add that Hegel, in particular the Hegel of the *Grundlinien der Rechtsphilosophie*, seems to me to be a better starting point for a theory of social justice.

More precisely the functionalist model implicitly used by Rawls leads him to be not fully aware of the often 'contradictory' character, in the sense of Hegelian and post-Hegelian dialectics, of 'basic institutions' or, as he says again, of the 'basic structure' of societies: as we have just seen, nothing can be done for instance to prevent inequalities from simultaneously having the dual effect of increasing the social production of certain primary goods and of giving rise to a not negligible inequality of opportunity.

A general question which is implicitly raised by Rawls's theory of justice is therefore whether industrial societies may be considered as systems whose basic structure leads to consequences compatible with the principles of justice. In the following remarks I shall attempt to show that it is possible to go on adding to the examples which reveal the 'contradictory' character of certain 'basic institutions'. What I mean by this is that on the one hand their consequences obey the criterion of indifference and the criteria implicitly used by Rawls and, on the other, they run counter to them.

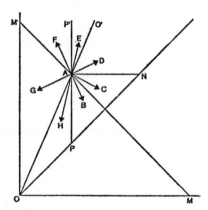

FIGURE 6.2   Possible combinations between four distributive criteria

In order to make the discussion clearer, let us take up again Rawls's schematisation and represent the distribution of a primary good by a system of two rectangular coordinates (figure 6.2). Let us imagine that a particular distribution *A* be given. The area *O'AN* contains vectors simultaneously obeying Rawls's criterion of indifference, Pareto's criterion (no one obtains a situation more unfavourable than that which he had at the starting point), the equality principle (the inequality of the distribution decreases) and the utilitarian criterion (the total quantity of goods increases). In the area *P'AO'* the criterion of equality is not met but the other three are. In the area *P'AM'* only the utilitarian criterion is met. In the area *M'AO* none of the four criteria is met. In *OAP* only the criterion of equality is met. In *PAM* the criterion of equality and Rawls's criterion of indifference are met. In *MAN*, apart from these two criteria, the utilitarian criterion is conformed to.

As has been seen Rawls's theory *officially* includes only the criterion of indifference, but the axiomatics lead to the others being taken into account: the utilitarian criterion comes into play, since everyone is assumed to desire a greater rather than a lesser quantity of primary goods; the criterion of equality also comes into play, since envy appears beyond a certain threshold of inequality and since inequalities must be justified. Lastly a just society is one in which the advantages of those who are the most favoured cannot be reduced without prejudicing those who are the least favoured. Its over-time change therefore obeys Pareto's criterion.

Over and above the inconsistencies of the theory, several passages clearly confirm that, according to Rawls, a society which obeys the principles of justice must undergo an evolution which simultaneously conforms to the four criteria. This proposition emerges with perfect clarity on p. 104 of *A Theory of Justice:* '[. . .] it seems that the consistent realisation of the two principles tends to raise the [contribution] curve closer to the ideal of a perfect harmony of interests.' Here is what this means: the 'contribution curve' represents the possible distributions in a given society, at a given moment, of a primary good. It has the form shown in figure 6.3. According to the criterion of indifference, a just society will choose distribution *M*, which maximises the relative share of the worse-off. In contrast a 'classical utilitarian' would choose distribution *N*, which maximises the total quantity of the good. But the important proposition is, if the principles of justice are consistently realised, the contribution curves will shift towards the line of equality (towards 'the ideal of a perfect harmony of interests'): the distribution will therefore shift in time from *M* to *M'*, with the effect that the four criteria previously singled out (equality, indifference principle, Pareto's criterion and the utilitarian criterion) will be met. Thus, although the principles of justice do not explicitly contain more than one of these distributive criteria, their realisation is supposed to lead to an evolution of the distribution of primary goods conforming with the three others.

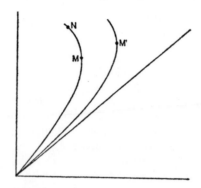

FIGURE 6.3 'Contribution curves' describing the possible distribution of a primary good between a representative of the best-off class and a representative of the worst-off class

What I should now like to suggest with the help of a few concisely developed examples is that the 'basic structure' of industrial societies in no way guarantees a Rawlsian evolution of the distribution of goods. One can indeed easily identify sub-systems of collective action simultaneously producing vectors belonging to different areas on the space covered by figure 6.2 and, as a result, being unequally acceptable from a Rawlsian point of view.

Let us first of all consider the problem of income distribution. It may be said that during the last few decades it has evolved in Rawlsian fashion in most of the industrial societies: the situation of the worst-off members has improved more or less steadily. But it is difficult to admit that economic inequalities result, as Rawls would have it, from a functional necessity. Certainly the comparatively high incomes of garbage collectors in the USA can be accounted for by the need to incite a sufficient number of persons to carry out a task which would otherwise not be much in demand. But it is impossible to account for *all* the differences in incomes in this manner. It is well known that mechanisms foreign to Rawls's functional analysis explain to a large extent the intensity of economic inequalities as well as their stability over the last few decades in most industrial societies.

One of these mechanisms is the difficulty of increasing beyond a certain threshold direct taxes, the effects of which may in theory be more easily egalitarian, at the expense of indirect taxes. As Olson has shown, this 'difficulty' results from the very logic of collective action:[12] let us assume that N persons desire a *collective* good, that is to say a good which will benefit everyone once it has been produced; let us imagine that its total cost is equal to C, that its total value V is equal to twice its cost and that V/N is the value of the good for any individual in the community. Let us admit furthermore that everyone can, without risking any penalty, withdraw unilaterally from the operation. In this case it is easy to show that in general conditions the structure of collective action is that of the prisoner's dilemma: although each person has an interest in obtaining the collective good, no one has any advantage in paying the price for it. The good will therefore not be produced.[13] Let us in fact consider any individual (i); the first line of the matrix below corresponds to the remuneration which he receives in paying his share, the second to the remuneration which he receives in not paying (it is assumed that $N = 10$, $C = 10$, $V = 20$). Naturally these two types of remuneration depend on the number of payers. The columns show the individual's profit in terms of the number of payers other than himself. Consulting this matrix, it is immediately seen that strategy $\bar{P}$ (not paying) is dominant:

	No. of payers other than i									
i's strategies	9	8	7	6	5	4	3	2	1	0
P (paying)	1.00	0.89	0.75	0.57	0.33	0.00	-0.50	-1.33	-3.00	-8.00
$\bar{P}$ (not paying)	2.00	2.00	2.00	2.00	2.00	2.00	2.00	2.00	2.00	0.00

However the others behave, each person therefore has an advantage in not paying, although everyone has an interest in acquiring the collective good. The only solution to the dilemma consists, as has been known since Rousseau, in *compelling* the individuals to follow their own interests.

This basic structure explains, according to Olson, the necessarily coercive character of direct taxation as well as the feeling of it being an intolerable imposition beyond a certain threshold. In contrast indirect taxation is perceived as being indistinctly incorporated into the price to be paid for the acquisition of an individual good even if, like direct taxation, it contributes to the production of collective goods. The structure of the prisoner's dilemma does not therefore appear in the case of indirect taxation. Hence its generally more 'painless' character.

The relative importance of indirect taxation to a large extent explains, as is shown for instance by Nicholson in regard to England, the limited character of the transfers achieved by the tax system, the stability of the transfers in time and the relative importance of inequalities in income.[14] It is clear that this explanation is totally foreign to Rawls's functional analysis. From it is directly deduced that a society does not necessarily evolve from the point of view of the distribution of economic goods according to the canons of the Rawlsian theory of justice: let us refer to figure 6.2 and assume there is an open choice between path *AE* and *AD*. Once the two paths are possible, Rawlsian theory considers *AD* to be legitimate and *AE* to be illegitimate. And yet, assuming that solution *AD* is obtained by a policy consisting in the relative increase of direct taxation, it may give rise to, or threaten to give rise to, sufficient protest for the political authority legitimately to consider it as being contrary to the general interest: the conclusions of the theory of justice would then be in contradiction with the general-interest principle on which however it claims to be founded. Alternatively path *AD* could be taken at the cost of reinforcing the hold of the political authority over those whom it represents. But this 'solution' once again contradicts the Rawlsian theory of justice, according to which the second principle cannot be realised at the expense of the first.

It is interesting to note that Rawls (p. 278) upholds in this connexion the principle of a proportional tax on consumption, which he prefers to a graduated income tax. The reason for this is that, if inequalities in income are assumed to be justified, their adjustment cannot be justified. Taxation then loses its redistributive function and retains only its function of financing *collective* goods. Rawls undoubtedly recognises that, while his preference for consumer tax is deduced from the principles of justice, the imperfections of real societies may justify recourse to other forms of taxation. But he does not see that, once a proportion at least of the inequalities are due to non-functional causes, it is impossible to determine whether and to what extent they are legitimate.

This example shows in summary form that Rawlsian theory, by its lexicographic ordering of the principles of justice, is not fully aware of the 'dialectical' character of the values introduced into these principles. From another angle it shows that, without any doubt in the societies with which we are familiar, inequalities, at least a proportion of them, exist for reasons other than those postulated by the indifference principle. Consequently it is absurd to found the legitimacy of inequalities on their contribution to the lot of the most unfavoured member.

I shall now consider an example in which it is seen that the distribution of a good evolves in a satisfactory manner from the point of view of the Rawlsian theory of justice but that it gives rise to a progressively more inegalitarian distribution of another good: the first of these goods is education. Statistics reveal to us that in all the industrial societies the average level of instruction has steadily risen over the last two decades. From another angle the distribution of this good has become more egalitarian. However it is easy to show that the development of education has probably given rise to a consequence which works in the opposite direction: the average educational level of individuals in professions associated with a high social status has indeed risen more quickly than that of individuals in professions of middling status, which in its turn has risen more quickly than the average educational level of individuals occupying the lowest positions.[15] If one admits the hypothesis that income depends not only on occupational status but also, and independently, on the level of instruction, it follows that the development of education as such may have contributed to increase economic inequalities.[16]

Let us now return to the diagram in figure 6.2 and consider in isolation from the universe to which they belong the two goods or variables which we have just been considering. The foregoing analysis indicates that a society which chooses a particular 'path' in respect of the evolution of the distribution of a good (education) at the same time affects in advance the path which will be taken by the distribution of another good (income): in the hypotheses considered a more egalitarian progression of education is associated, all other things being equal, with a more inegalitarian progression of income. It is clear that the Rawlsian theory of justice does not make it possible to deal easily with this type of system in which trends of the Rawlsian type characterising the distribution of certain goods are accompanied by a mounting inequality in the distribution of other goods. Using the diagram in figure 6.2, Rawls's hypothesis is that the distribution of primary goods in a society obeying the principles of justice follows paths such as *AB*, *AC* or *AD* characterised both by an improvement in the condition of the most unfavoured member and by an increase in equality. It has just been seen however that this condition can be achieved for one of the goods and, for this very reason, not be achieved for others: the over-time change of the distribution of education according to one of the three paths *AB*, *AC* or *AD* is associated with an evolution of the distribution of income according to path *AE*. At the same time the foregoing analysis makes it possible to isolate another non-functional cause of income inequality.

The case of education is such as may afford many other examples which contradict Rawls's optimistic evolutionism. I have shown elsewhere that the fast growth of the demand for education in industrial societies during the last two decades has had complex effects, some of which have once again the structure of the prisoner's dilemma: the 'basic institutions' of the industrial societies have had the effect that from one period to the next, during the last two decades, the growth of the demand for education has been faster in the lower classes than in the middle classes and faster in the middle classes than in the upper classes[17] giving rise to a slow but indisputable increase in equality of educational opportunity. However the equalisation of educational opportunity has not itself been accompanied by an equalisation of social opportunity or, if the term is preferred, by an increase in social mobility, that is to say by a reduction of the social heritage. This phenomenon, which characterises all the industrial societies, is to be explained by the fact that the growth in the demand for education has caused a particularly rapid devaluation of average educational levels: thus, in the period 1950–70, adolescents of upper social origin in a large proportion, and in a proportion which increases in time, attain a higher level of instruction; but a not inconsiderable proportion of them continue to attain merely average levels of instruction, the social expectations attached to which decrease in time. It results from this that their social expectations appear on an average to be scarcely affected during the period. The same conclusion applies to the other classes: thus adolescents of lower social origin derive practically no benefit in terms of social expectations from the relatively fast rise in time of the average level of instruction for this category, for at the same time as they have more and more frequently gained access to higher levels of instruction, these have turned out to be associated with diminishing social expectations.

Possibly the general growth of the demand for education is to an extent responsible for economic growth and consequently for the general rise in the standard of living. But the logic of the aggregation of individual actions results in the fact that, when each individual demands more education than a similar individual would have demanded in the previous period, the social expectations of each remain stable. Each must therefore have a higher educational level from one period to another so as to preserve the same chances of not falling to a lower position or of rising to a higher one.

The system which has just been described can be summed up with the help of the diagram in figure 6.4: equal educational opportunity has evolved in the direction AB: the representatives of each social class have had access to a growing quantity of education in the course of time and inequality between the classes has decreased from this point of view, as is marked by the fact that vector AB is situated below OO'. The inequality of social opportunity, that is to say the intensity of the social heritage, has for its part remained stable. This phenomenon is shown graphically by the loop AA. If one admits of the existence of a causal relationship between the development of education and economic growth, the first variable has had the effect of raising everyone's standard of living: this consequence may be symbolised by vector AD. However a previous analysis showed us that it was possible for the growth of the demand for education also to give rise to inegalitarian effects from the point of view of the distribution of income. It is therefore possible that in this respect AC more faithfully represents the evolution of the system than AD. AE

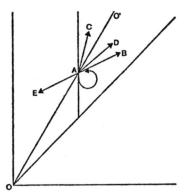

FIGURE 6.4 Vectors associated with a particular sub-system of collective action (see text)

finally represents the prisoner's dilemma effect which results from the system: on account of the logic of the aggregation of individual actions, the individuals of *each* class have had to pay a mounting cost in time, in terms of the period of school attendance, so as to preserve the same social expectations.

It would not be difficult to imagine other examples of sub-systems leading or capable of leading in the same way to 'contradictory' evolutions, that is to say to effects of which some are acceptable and others inacceptable from the point of view of Rawlsian criteria, these effects being *indissociable* from each other. In conclusion I shall consider an idealised sub-system which is particularly interesting inasmuch as, in contrast with the previous sub-system, it produces exclusively unfavourable effects.

Let us imagine a simplified economic system constituted by a duopoly. One of the firms, *A*, takes the initiative to spend money on advertising. If the advertising is assumed to be effective, the advertising investment of firm *A* will attract a part of the clientele of firm *B*. The latter will then endeavour to get its customers back by in its turn committing an appropriate amount of expenditure to advertising. If it is not possible for the market to be extended, or merely to a small extent, the main effect of advertising will be to increase production costs. If the duopolists cover the increase in production costs by a rise in prices, the net effect of the expenditure on advertising will be to impoverish the consumer and to institute a sort of indirect tax for the purpose of financing advertising agencies.

Naturally this model is not meant to be interpreted as a faithful reflection of reality: the market of a product is not necessarily inextensible; in certain cases advertising serves to provide information, it may help to enlighten the consumer and provide an impetus towards innovation. The sole point that I wish to demonstrate by way of this crude model is that the entrepreneur's freedom, that is to say the faculty accorded to him of taking unilateral measures may lead, when at the same time anyone else has exactly the same freedom, to consequences which are unsatisfactory on two counts from the Rawlsian point of view: if the previous model is assumed to be extended to cover the whole of an economic system, it gives rise to a levy on the consumer's purchasing power which is not only unjustified but which also has distinctly inegalitarian effects. In the language of the diagram in figure 6.2, the model simulates a system following the course of path AG.[18] The difficulty which this case sets in the way of Rawls's theory of justice resides in the fact that the 'basic institution' of the freedom of the entrepreneur also gives rise to sub-systems whose chief effects are acceptable or desirable according to the Rawlsian criteria of justice. In this case, as in the previous ones, a Rawlsian judge who had to rule on the affair would have to conclude that there were no grounds for proceeding: the theory of justice does not allow for 'basic institutions' being able to give rise to 'contradictory' effects.

I shall limit my examples here. They seem to me to show that it is difficult to consider Rawls's theory as a generative grammar making it possible to distinguish legitimate institutions from ill-formed institutions. Undoubtedly the liberal industrial societies conform to the Rawlsian model in the case of basic liberties and particular primary goods. The standard of living of the most unfavoured individuals has gone up over the last few decades; basic political liberties tend to be, as is demanded by the first principle of justice, equally distributed. But it is impossible to agree with the Rawlsian interpretation of the inequalities to be observed in these societies: indeed, inequalities are not exclusively explicable – far from it – in terms of their contribution to the smooth running of the social system and thereby to the fate of the most unfavoured members. Their persistence is to be explained to an extent which is certainly not inconsiderable by the difficulty of transferring the financing of the production of collective goods from a system of indirect taxation to one of direct taxation in a system in which the power of coercion of the political authority is assumed to be limited. It has also been seen that the *freedom* afforded to all, at a formal level, to 'choose' their educational level may be considered to be one of the factors which has contributed to the persistence of inequalities. The Rawlsian ordering of the principles of justice and of the values which they include has the basic defect of not taking proper stock of the interdependence between the pair coercion/freedom and the pair equality/inequality, despite the fact tht this was noted by the pioneers of political theory, Hobbes, Rousseau and others.

Generally speaking Rawls misjudges the complexity of sub-systems of collective action which together constitute that which is called a society. Not without a certain naïvety, he admits that the distribution of primary goods in a society whose basic institutions are in conformity with the principles of justice must undergo an evolution which satisfies not only the indifference principle but also Pareto's criterion, the egalitarian criterion and the utilitarian criterion. The educational crisis which is affecting the industrial societies is not however unrelated to the fact that the development of the educational system has helped to increase the social marginality of *all* young people. Unless the feeling of having one's place in the society to which one belongs cannot be considered as a 'primary good' we have here the example of a good whose distribution has evolved unfavourably (vector *AG* in figure 6.2). During the same period, the development of education has undoubtedly contributed to the improvement of the lot of the most unfavoured individuals (vector *AD* in figure 6.2). But, if one considers the history of industrial societies over the last two decades, the two vectors appear to be indissolubly linked. In the language of figure 6.2, the 'basic institutions' of the industrial societies relating to the educational system have therefore given rise to a system of radiating vectors of which only some cross the Rawlsian indifference curves in the prescribed direction. The same is true of another basic institution, the market. The last example shows that it can produce effects obeying neither Pareto's criterion nor even Rawls's indifference criterion. But it also, in other respects, gives rise to desirable consequences in Rawls's sense and possibly in Pareto's. Naturally it is possible – and desirable – to seek to change institutions in such a way that the non-Rawlsian consequences of a system be neutralised. But this change generally gives rise to consequences with regard to the conduct of the other 'vectors' representing the distribution of primary goods and bearing at the same time on the application of the *values* included in the first principle of justice (liberties) and in the second part of the second principle (equal opportunity).

I should like to avoid creating the impression that I am setting Rawls on trial. He does not explicitly write that his theory of justice may be considered as a theory of the legitimacy of the institutions of industrial societies. But it appears obvious to me that this aim underlies the undertaking. If it is not explicitly formulated, it is perhaps because the lack of success is obvious: not only does Rawls's theory not help to explain the crisis of legitimacy which, in various forms, has stricken the industrial societies since the beginning of the sixties, but it also claims implicitly to convince us of the illegitimacy of that crisis. It thus constitutes the optimistic counterpart of the pessimistic theories according to which the 'basic structure' of the industrial societies necessarily leads to a growing deterioration either of the relative situation of the worst-off individuals or of the situation of everyone. For Rawls, the basic institutions of the industrial societies produce vectors of the type AB, AC and AD (cf. figure 6.2). For the pessimists, the vectors are of type AF or of type AG. The first variant, more traditional and more frequently represented in Europe, is illustrated by theories according to which the 'basic structure' of the industrial societies necessarily gives rise to an increasingly inegalitarian distribution of certain primary goods (for instance, power), the sum total of which is assumed to be constant: consequently, the condition of the most unfavoured individual can only deteriorate. The second variant, which is more specifically American, corresponds to theories according to which the 'basic structure' of the industrial societies gives rise to a deterioration in the condition of everyone (cf. Herbert Marcuse, Paul Goodman).

The truth of the matter is that the basic institutions of the industrial societies produce sub-systems of collective action characterised by a radiating structure of vectors which represent their effects. It seems to me to be a major task of political sociology, and one which hitherto has been fairly neglected, to analyse these sub-systems of collective action.

Unless Rawls is claiming to teach us not what industrial societies are but what they should be. In this case, the present article would show that the Rawlsian model is fundamentally Utopian.

All in all I do not think that a deductive theory of justice is possible. Moreover it has been observed that Rawls's theory is deductive only in appearance. In the course of the 'deduction', the basic axioms are gradually corrected, shades of meaning are introduced and they are rounded out by propositions which are on occasion incompatible with the axiomatic premise of the original position. To use the language of Rawls, only a theory of the *intuitionist* type seems to me to be possible. I mean by this that a society may ideally be considered as being characterised at a given stage by a set of configurations of vectors such as those in figure 6.2, each configuration corresponding to a sub-system of collective action. These configurations may give rise to positive feelings on the part of social groups, but also negative feelings not only of injustice but also of absurdity, alienation or constraint, which feelings are clearly not reducible to each other although Rawls seems unaware of the fact. Thus the appearance of a 'prisoner's-dilemma' effect may give rise to a feeling of absurdity rather than injustice. These feelings and their various expressions by way of political institutions, but also social conflicts and ideologies, seem to me to provide the only yardstick for measuring the legitimacy or illegitimacy of institutions.

7 Social Determinisms and Individual Freedom

Contemporary sociology may often take the form of a sociology without a subject. *Homo sociologicus* is either described as if he were programmed by 'social structures' or as if he were determined by his social origins and his social position.

In the following text I have tried to show that this determinist paradigm is both useless and costly. By denying the social agent the faculty of choice, of decision-making, of creation and innovation, the sociologist succumbs to the temptation that is endemic to sociology, namely, sociologism. He is then afflicted with a kind of blindness. Once determinism is everywhere, what difference is there between the bout of fever that confines me to my bed, the penal sanction that dissuades me from fulfilling certain of my desires, and the limited nature of my resources which forces me to leave certain consumer goods well alone?

The determinist paradigm, or more properly, determinist paradigms, take their toll of the sociologist. They make it impossible for him to conceive of and *a fortiori* to explain phenomena as significant as social conflicts and social change.

The history of sociology shows that if the temptation of sociologism seems like a chronic illness ravaging it, the best sociologists have always known how to keep clear. Notions of choice, of decision-making, of anticipation and of freedom play an essential role in the work of Rousseau, Tocqueville, Marx and Merton.

Without these notions it is impossible to account for the advent of Merton's unintended consequences, Marx's contradictions, Sartre's counter-finality and in general the emergence of what I here call perverse effects.

I want however to make it clear that I am not advocating a return to the definitive criticisms that Durkheim made of Spencer's contractualism. In general sociology has had good reasons to mark out the limits of utilitarianism. A rational *homo sociologicus* cannot serve as a general paradigm for sociology. But there are tendencies in sociology that would seem to favour the concept of the individual who is always 'acted upon', and this concept is of even less use. Between the rational *homo oeconomicus* and the manipulated man of modernist sociology, the paradigm of *intentional* man would seem to be at present the most effective one. It is, in any case, the one used by sociologists whose work has best withstood the wear and tear of time.

It goes without saying that one's lack of knowledge about the social agent's past sometimes makes his present *intentions* quite opaque. It is clear that such intentions are in general incomprehensible if one does not take into account the structural constraints inherent in his social position. But it does not in any sense follow from this that the social agent's behaviour is determined. *Intelligible*, yes. *Determined*, no. This distinction is a fundamental one and entails serious consequences for both one's resources and one's method.

I do not claim to give a definitive answer to any of the complex questions raised here. Some of the points made (such as the account given of the success of *sociologism*) are hardly more than rough sketches. I fully intend to take up these points again in future publications. But I thought that it would serve some useful purpose if I were to close this book with an attempt to grapple with the fundamental questions implicitly raised in the preceding texts.

> *The important thing was to realise a division into three categories inserting between natural phenomena, i.e., those that are independent of human action, and artificial and conventional phenomena, i.e., those produced by human design, a distinct and intermediate category comprising those non-intentional patterns and regularities that one encounters in human society and that it is social theory's task to explain.*
>
> Friedrich von Hayek, *Studies in Philosophy, Politics and Economics*

The most effective way to grasp the epistemological status of a discipline is probably to identify the main paradigms in use there. An implicit definition of this kind has the advantage over an *explicit* one, in that it maps the contours of the discipline more effectively. It also enables one to assess the degree of logical integration of the products of that discipline and eventually allows one to elicit what I would call isomorphisms between disciplines, by which I mean the shared use in several disciplines of identical paradigms. An analysis of this sort also allows one to discern epistemological similarities between disciplines whose contours are often the result of more or less complex processes of institutionalisation.

The notion of paradigm may itself be defined in several different ways. Merton, for example, gives an implicit definition when he talks of the paradigm of functional analysis.[1] This term's popularity would seem to derive originally from the Kuhnian theory of scientific revolutions.[2] Kuhn uses this term in a very general and complex sense. For him a paradigm is a set of propositions that forms the basis of agreement from which a tradition of scientific research develops: 'By choosing it (the term "paradigm") I mean to suggest that some accepted examples of actual scientific practice – examples which include law, theory, application, and instrumentation together – provide models from which spring particular coherent traditions of scientific research.'[3] I will myself use the term in a more specific sense. I will use it to designate the language *in which the theories or, eventually, important sub-sets of theories generated in the framework of a discipline are formulated.*[4] Ideally one would take a rough sample of theories and one would identify the different paradigms by identifying the language or languages in which these theories are at root construed. This is of course to set out the project in an *ideal* form. Although the classification that I present below rests implicitly on a large number of sociological theories, it has no pretensions to being the product of a systematic 'sampling'.

Two Paradigm Families

If one casts a rapid glance over sociological analyses and theories there is a first and basic distinction that catches the eye and is enough in itself, I believe, to define two paradigm families. The main sub-families that make up these families will emerge at a later point in the argument. There will also be an opportunity to analyse the relations between the two families. For the time being this basic distinction will suffice.

Forget sociology for the moment and consider two different newspaper accounts of traffic accidents:

1. 'Mr X, an important industrialist who, according to eye-witnesses, seemed quite tipsy when he left the restaurant at the end of a business lunch, crashed his vehicle into a tree.'

2. 'The two drivers, who were heading straight for each other in the central lane of a three-lane carriageway, were said by eye-witnesses to have flashed their lights repeatedly. Head-on collision was inevitable.'

In the first example, the journalist uses a causal kind of model to explain why the driver's behaviour was bound to end in an accident. His behaviour was due to his drunkenness, he must have lost control of his reflexes. There is nothing especially surprising about his drunkenness either, for are not business lunches known for the richness of their fare? The accident is thus explained by referring it to the states that preceded it: the driver was an important industrialist; that explains his participation in a business lunch; this made excessive consumption of alcoholic drinks likely; and that deadened his reflexes and therefore made an accident more likely.

In the second example the analysis implicit in the journalist's account is completely different. The two drivers must have jobs of some sort but no reference is made to them. They must have come from somewhere, but their immediate past is not mentioned. The journalist's analysis definitely suggests that the accident was due to both drivers' efforts to emerge as 'winner' in a foolish game in which each by flashing their lights indicated that they would not give way or let the other overtake.

The two explanatory schema are totally different. In the first a causal schema accounts for the driver's behaviour, but in the second the actors' intentions and the way in which they represent the things they have to do to fulfil these intentions play a crucial part. The journalist moreover thinks it worth while to specify the kind of road (three-lane) involved. This is vital, for the motorists could not have played what game theory calls *the chicken game* on a two-lane road or a dual carriageway. In other words it is the road's structure that is thought to make the two drivers' behaviour possible. Nothing of course compels them to fall into the absurd trap of the chicken game. But once the accident has been noted, to understand it one only has to argue that it was the road's structure that made the game possible, and that it was the drivers' intentions in the moments just preceding the accident that made it inevitable.

These simple examples would seem to illustrate quite well the basic distinction advanced here: some sociological theories use a language that suggests that the social phenomenon to be explained is produced by juxtaposition or by the composition of a set of actions. In what follows I will take *action* to mean a behaviour that is goal-oriented. Sociology will therefore be said to belong to the family of *interactionist* paradigms.

Other theories use a language that suggests that the social phenomenon explained is produced by behaviours that are not, in any definite sense, actions. In this case the particular behaviours are not described as being oriented towards goals that subjects strive, more or less consciously, to reach. They are, on the contrary, described as being solely the result of elements *prior* to the behaviours.

Existing semantic associations persuade us that actions, as I understand the concept, are a sub-set of *behaviours*. However, for brevity's sake, and excepting those contexts that are totally unambiguous, I have decided to use the term *behaviours* to mean only those behaviours which are not actions.[5] I will call the set of behaviours and actions *acts*.

When *behaviours* (in the sense defined) are taken to be the sole determinants of a social phenomenon I will call the paradigm then used a *determinist* paradigm.

The reader will observe that these definitions correspond to the two simple examples I used as my point of departure. In the first example the social phenomenon to be explained (the accident) may be convincingly analysed as being the result of what I call a behaviour. In fact this behaviour is *explained* by elements and events *prior* to it (the man *was* a businessman, he *did* indulge himself etc.) In the second example however the accident is explained in terms of actions, i.e., acts that are goal-oriented, *intentional* acts.

Two examples borrowed from the social sciences provide an additional illustration of the distinction between the two families made here.

Henry and Short, in a study of suicide and murder,[6] argue that these two variants of aggression (aggression against oneself, aggression against the other) should properly be considered as *responses* or *reactions* to unbearable situations. There is no point in presenting here these authors' arguments as to the probability of each of these two variants occurring. It is enough to note that the arguments advanced lead them to conclude that there is some sort of correlation between a set of variables to do with social and economic status and the probability of an aggressive behaviour appearing. A statistical verification of the existence of these correlations then follows. One is dealing here with an analysis belonging to the family of *determinist* paradigms. The statistical relations the analysis is designed to explain are interpreted as being the result of acts described as behaviours. Thus one of Henry and Short's hypotheses is that the black American woman, given that she has a higher familial status than the black man, will (all else being equal) far less often behave in a blatantly aggressive way.

All Henry and Short's arguments are of this sort. If one group is less aggressive than another, elements *prior* to the appearance of the aggressive behaviours are held to explain this fact (relative status within the family, social and economic status etc.)

I want now to define one of my terms more precisely: in speaking of a *determinist* paradigm I mean to refer to those paradigms in which acts are always explained in terms of elements *prior* to these acts. Let B be one of these acts and A a prior element used to explain B.

Analysis sometimes makes it possible to conclude: 'if A (prior to B) then B'.[7] In both cases I will talk of determinist paradigms. A model will be taken to determinist if and only if it explains an act exclusively in terms of elements prior to this act. The distinction that bears on the strict or probabilistic character of the links between elements, which would be crucial in other contexts, will therefore be disregarded here.

My two examples illustrate the basic opposition, and whilst my chosen vocabulary has mnemonic advantages, its use may well spread confusion. I will quickly explain what I mean. In the first place one should strictly talk of 'actionist' rather than 'interactionist' paradigms. Action is always in one way or another interaction, but this feature does not concern the opposition considered here: it is simply that I have refrained from coining a neologism that would perhaps prove unnecessary. Secondly the reader must have noted the unusual sense that the word 'determinist' is given here: take the case of the actor placed in a situation in which he is forced to choose. His behaviour may be predicted and one can therefore talk of *determinism* in the usual sense. But since this behaviour is described in terms of action, I will say that the description belongs to the interactionist paradigm.

Here, borrowed from economics, is a classic example of a theory belonging to the family of interactionist paradigms, the famous spider's-web model.[8] The model is meant to explain a very widely observable phenomenon, that of the emergence of economic cycles. The model posits two actors or, in fact, two classes of actors: the producers and the consumers (of a given product). Secondly their acts (producing and consuming) are interpreted as actions (acts meant to bring about particular ends). The producer wonders what quantities to produce in the coming year, his plan being to maximise his profit. But this depends on the current market price, a factor presumably quite outside the control of any one producer. The following refreshingly simple argument is then advanced: each producer will *anticipate* a price close to the one at which the product settled the previous year. A classic proposition from supply and demand theory is also introduced: all else being equal, a producer will tend to manufacture a particular product in quantities that increase in direct ratio to the anticipated price. The consumer will meanwhile consume more and more as the product's price falls. In short, classic supply and demand curves appear, curves that intersect at an equilibrium point. The rest of the analysis is straightforward: if the anticipated price is lower than the equilibrium price, the producers produce less than the consumers would be willing to consume at the price; the eventual price will therefore tend to be higher than the anticipated one (and higher than the equilibrium price). In the next financial year production will be higher than equilibrium production. The price will therefore fall below the equilibrium price. It is easy then to see that if this line of argument is pursued further, the model causes cyclic phenomena (*vis-à-vis* prices and quantities produced) to emerge.

This analysis is typical of interactionist paradigms: the ends that the actors have in mind are held to account for their actions (the consumer wants to get maximum satisfaction from his purchases, the producer wants to maximise his profit); it is then demonstrated that the composition of these actions engenders cyclical phenomena analogous to those empirically observed.

My second example was taken from the field of economics because analyses of the *interactionist* type are common there. One could even argue that economic theory as a whole uses paradigms of an interactionist kind. Things are different in sociology: interactionist and determinist paradigms appear together, with a frequency that varies with the period of sociological theory considered and the kinds of problem tackled by the sociologist.

Interactionist Paradigms: Four Major Types

Before tackling these questions I must consider the actual forms that the two main paradigm types in sociological theory assume. I will begin with interactionist paradigms. I would hold that it is worth distinguishing between four major types of interactionist paradigm in sociology. I will therefore try to give a brief description of each type before stopping to consider them in greater detail. Whilst I trust that the classifications presented in this text are of some use, I do not of course claim that they are the only ones possible.

SUB-TYPE a: INTERACTIONIST PARADIGMS OF THE MARXIAN TYPE

The reason for the above appellation will become apparent later. In these paradigms subjects' actions are described as if they depended on their free will alone. More specifically it is presumed that each subject's freedom of action is in no way limited by commitments, tacit or explicit, entered into with respect to others. The spider's-web model illustrates this quite well: The actors' behaviours are described as if they were determined by individual preferences, to the exclusion of all agreement, contract or mutual commitment. Compare this with the very different example that Parsons gives of the doctor asking a sick person to undress, an action structured in terms of the doctor's tacit commitment to the sick person.[9] Marxian-type paradigms are in short characterised by what is taken to be a lack of mutual commitment between the actors. Secondly individuals' preferences are considered *self-evident*. They are, in other words, taken to be independent variables; they play a vital role in the explanatory schema but do not themselves require analysis. The spider's-web model illustrates this second feature too: it presupposes that the producers want to extract the highest possible profits from their production and that the consumers tend to curb their consumption of a product if, all else being equal, its price goes up. These propositions need no explaining and can be read as primary propositions.

The situation of interdependence analysed in the spider's-web theorem obviously presupposes the existence of a social and institutional context, that of the market. This observation would hold good for all the examples analysed below and for any others too. A structure of interdependence, if defined in a socio-institutional vacuum, would be indeterminate, unanalysable and therefore of no interest. So I will not bother to repeat below the fact that the structure of interdependence or of interaction (the two words are synonyms here) invariably presupposes the socio-institutional context that defines it.

SUB-TYPE b: INTERACTIONIST PARADIGMS OF THE TOCQUEVILLEAN TYPE

This appellation too will be justified later. In this sub-type the actors' actions are also assumed to derive exclusively from their free judgement, and nothing resembling a commitment, an agreement or a contract binds them together. In eighteenth-century terms this type of relational context would be described as a *state of nature*: the actors in the spider's-web theorem, the motorists who all arrive at the Place de la Concorde at the same time, these situations may each for their own particular reasons be interpreted as states of nature. The motorists are not all in the same place because they decided by by mutual agreement to meet up there. The producers and consumers did not decide by mutual agreement to provoke fluctuations in prices and in production. The traffic congestion in the Place de la Concorde and the economic fluctuations cited here are *emergent* social phenomena that derive from the composite or aggregate effect of quite separate actions.[10] Depending on the language one wants to use one could also talk of effects of interaction. But interaction necessarily entails a state of nature: the actors can choose to ignore or to recognise the fact that their behaviour has an effect on others. Here then is the feature that allows one to distinguish Tocquevillean (*b*) from Marxian (*a*) paradigms: in sub-type *b* the actors' preferences, namely the ends that they have in mind, are not accorded the status of independent variables. In other words they are treated not as self-evident but as requiring explanation. Consider the question of choice of jobs. This sort of action differs from these considered in the spider's-web model because a different order of things has to be explained. There is no point in carrying out detailed research in order to argue that Mrs Jones changes the contents of her shopping-basket in a way that corresponds exactly with the relative variations in price of the products that she usually buys. On the other hand the fact that there are some jobs that women tend to choose less than men do indicates a difference in *preferences* that needs to be explained. To sum up: sub-type *b* can be differentiated from sub-type *a* on the grounds that preferences do not there have the status of independent variables and that consequently propositions describing actors' *preferences* do not have the status of primary propositions.

SUB-TYPE C: INTERACTIONIST PARADIGMS OF THE MERTONIAN TYPE

Here the state-of-nature hypothesis is jettisoned. In other words the main feature of the categories of action considered consists in the fact that the agents carrying them out have no alternative but to take account of their effects on others. The actions that a teacher performs when teaching are of this kind. To explain why Mr Jones discourses on the chemical composition of water in front of a group of children who listen to him more or less attentively, I will use a totally different paradigm from the one that helped me to understand why Mrs Jones changed the contents of her shopping-basket. Mr Jones plays a *role*, as sociological theory generally puts it. In discoursing on the chemical composition of water, he fulfils a *contract*. It is not a question of course of a contract in the legal sense. Mr Jones's hours of work are legally fixed. But the contract also includes some unformalised aspects: Mr Jones knows, for example, that he will elicit signs of approval or disapproval from his pupils in using humorous asides well or badly.

Sub-type *c* is therefore to be distinguished from the two preceding sub-types on the grounds that interaction between individuals does not occur in a *state of nature* but under conditions that the notion of *contract* (if one were still to use eighteenth-century language) describes well: here individuals cannot make up their minds without taking into consideration, among other things, the effects of their actions on others. As this definition makes clear, I do not in any way attribute a voluntaristic and judicial kind of meaning to the notion of *contract*. In fact it corresponds very closely to what Rousseau would have called a restriction on 'natural liberty' or a restriction of the individual's *autonomy*.

To sum up: in theories belonging to sub-type *c*, interaction will tend to occur in a *contractual* context. Depending on circumstances, these theories will either treat the actors' preferences as immediately intelligible facts or as phenomena requiring explanation. But since this distinction scarcely applies to the present paradigm, I will disregard it here.

It is incidentally worth noting that the two terms of the dichotomy 'contract/state of nature' do between them subsume situations that it would, in another context, be important to differentiate. There are, for instance, situations that are 'states of nature' in which I can make up my mind without taking others into account; there are others in which I can make up my mind without taking the *interest* of others into account but not without taking the *existence* of others into account (situations of interdependence that are, with respect to others, of a strategic nature only). If every 'contract' situation is one in which I have to take account of others' *interests*, my sense of *obligation* may thus assume many different forms.

Please note that the opposition between 'contract' and 'state of nature' denotes limit cases. Thus the legal liberalisation of abortion does not *ipso facto* cause the linked moral constraints on the family unit to disappear. Legal liberalisation is therefore not enough in itself to bring about a context in which a 'state of nature' obtains and in which a family unit, regardless of the outside world, would be able to decide quite freely for itself. Legal liberalisation does nevertheless produce a qualitatively significant increase in autonomy. Similar observations would also apply to Rousseau's interpretation of the notions of contract and 'state of nature': even after society has been constituted the 'state of nature' persists. A society's members are still free, within certain limits, to get rich at the expense of others.

SUB-TYPE d: INTERACTIONIST PARADIGMS OF THE WEBERIAN TYPE

This final example is still within the family of interactionist paradigms: actors' behaviours are seen as being imbued with intentionality and therefore as being *actions*. But here aspects of these actions (the structuring of the system of preferences, choice of means necessary for the attainment of the desired ends, skill in engineering this etc.) are thought to be determined by elements that are *prior* to the actions. This is always more or less true, of course: every action implies the mastery of certain techniques (communicatory or physical) or of certain forms of knowledge whose acquisition is necessarily prior to action. But these elements may play a completely secondary role and may in many cases be disregarded. Thus, in analysing the form of interaction that takes place between Mr Jones, the chemistry teacher and his class, it is hardly worth noting that the teacher must have learnt chemistry before teaching it. But there are situations to be analysed in which any account of the differences between categories of actor depends on making some reference to elements *prior* to the actions analysed. But it is extremely important to note that this does not rule out the treatment of individuals' behaviours as goal-oriented. In other words the determinant quality of elements prior to the action does not deprive this latter of its status as *action*. To take a simple example: in assembling the contents of her shopping-basket Mrs Jones seeks to maximise her satisfaction, but the fact that her basket may well be different from Mrs Bright's is attributable to a difference in the socialisation process that the two persons have undergone. Mrs Jones's liking for and Mrs Bright's dislike of sea food may well date back to their childhood.

Sub-type *d* is interesting because it introduces elements of a *determinist* type (in the sense in which I have defined this term) into explanatory schemas belonging to the family of *interactionist* paradigms.

I admit that these distinctions (between the four sub-types of interactionist paradigm) are fairly abstract. Their significance and, I believe, their epistemological importance will become clearer in what follows. The four sub-types will then be illustrated by means of concrete examples drawn from sociological analysis.

To round off this discussion of interactionist paradigms I would like to make two fairly general observations. The first concerns the deliberately unsystematic nature of the classification presented here. By combining the criteria set out here (presence/absence of determinist elements, preferences given/preferences to be explained, state of nature/contract) one would arrive at a systematic classification. But it is not worth specifying all of the eight types that these three criteria in combination produce. On the other hand if one considers the kind of work currently being produced in sociology, the four types presented here correspond to recognised and significant research traditions.

I want, secondly, to point out (and I will expand on this later) that the preceding classification seems to me to be, from a history-of-sociology perspective, a fundamental one. It would therefore be interesting to survey the attempts that various sociologists have made to reduce sociology to one of the preceding paradigms. In positing the notion of role as the logical atom of sociological theory, Parsons's 'general theory', for example, excludes paradigms *a* and *b*. Yet the history of sociology clearly shows that these paradigms have been widely used by classical authors like Marx and Tocqueville. Parsons defines sociology in a way that practically rules out the analysis of systems of interaction not ordered by contractual constraints, and this perhaps explains why his general theory has not been more widely acclaimed. From another perspective it may perhaps be possible to show that some analyses are problematic because they are situated within a faulty paradigm. Thus the works of Gordon Tullock that analyse criminality exclusively in terms of a Marxian type paradigm (sub-type *a*) are open to serious objections.[11] It is almost certain that this paradigm cannot be systematically used in the analysis of this class of phenomena. Conversely the fact that type *a* and *b* paradigms sometimes seem to sociologists to lie outside their discipline, despite the use classical sociologists have made of them, has clearly been detrimental to the progress of sociology itself. The preceding classification is, in the end, of interest because it causes the isomorphisms I spoke of earlier to appear: paradigms of the *a, b, c, d* sub-types rephrase distinctions that are of greater significance, epistemologically, than the distinctions between the disciplines where they are used.

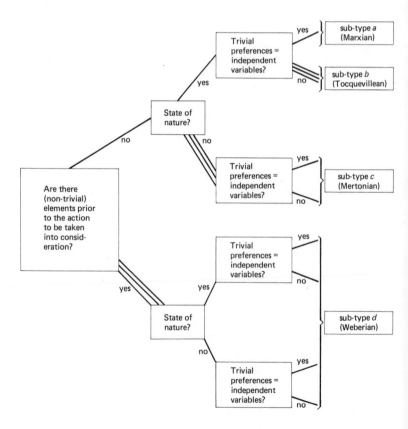

FIGURE 7.1   Types of action paradigms

I will return to this set of observations in the last part of the article. First of all, though, I will examine the four sub-types of paradigm in detail. I will thus, through the use of concrete examples, be able to give a more exact account of their significance.

To make things easier for the reader I have summarised my definitions of the four sub-paradigms by means of the tree diagram in Figure 7.1 (the triple branches represent the distinctive features corresponding to the comparisons sub-type b/a, sub-type c/b, sub-type d/c).

Paradigms of the Marxian Type

The reader will recall that Marxian-type paradigms are those in which individual actions are assumed to be *unrelated*, in the sense that the social agent performs them without having to take account of their effect on others, and in the sense that preferences are obvious enough to enjoy the status of independent variables. I qualify this paradigm with the adjective '*Marxian*', because there is no doubt that Marx is the classical sociologist who uses it most often[12] (I choose the term 'Marxian' rather than 'Marxist' simply because it is the *form* and not the *content* of Marx's theories that concerns me here). Consider a classic example, that of the falling rate of profit, as set out in the third book of *Capital*. This law is so well known that it seems fair enough to summarise it in a couple of lines: there are in society two categories of actor, the two classes (capitalist and proletarian). All else being equal, the profits that the capitalists appropriate rise with rises in overall production and with falls in the ratio between fixed capital to wage labour or variable capital. But there is a 'contradiction' between the two variables determining the overall profit. It is in fact in the capitalist's interest to increase his productivity, that is, to reinvest a part of his profit in order to acquire faster and more effective machines, thus making it possible to manufacture a product in shorter labour time. But in doing this he helps to lower the rate of profit and pledges the capitalist system to a process that culminates, at the limit, in the suppression of profit. It matters little if the law of the falling rate of profit is true or false. What is of interest here is the reappearance of features of the type a paradigm. The economic structure of capitalism tempts the capitalist to raise his productivity levels, and the capitalist who does not comply with the others in adopting this strategy is bound to be quickly eliminated. He is in effect compelled to offer his product at a loss or at a price higher than the market price. The capitalists therefore choose the strategy of a rise in productivity levels. But in doing this they help to erode the very basis upon which profit is founded. It seems legitimate to analyse the actors' behaviours as unrelated actions. Preferences are however too obvious to need explanation: the capitalist prefers a higher to a lower overall profit.

It is incidentally worth noting that the example of the law of the falling rate of profit illustrates very clearly one of the basic meanings of the obscure notion of 'dialectic': the capitalists do capitalism, and, consequently themselves, a bad turn.[13] The dialectical contradiction here assumes the form of a paradox of *composition*: the individual profits that the actors derive from their action are necessarily accompanied by an undesired collective cost.

The case of Marx is particularly relevant to my perspective here. Parsons has shown that the Marxian axiomatic is very dependent on the utilitarian position.[14] It is in fact hard to contest this, for Marx does consistently explain the behaviour of social agents, in terms of the pursuit of individual interest. Parsons's assertion is not as surprising as it first appears. One only has to reflect on Marx's familiarity with political economy and political philosophy at the end of the eighteenth and during the first half of the nineteenth century, and on the way in which these disciplines were rooted in the utilitarian philosophical tradition (consider, for example, Marx's admiration for Mandeville.)[15] His analyses are of course different from those of the classical economists but Marxian man is a close cousin to the *homo oeconomicus* who derives from the philosophical tradition of the eighteenth century. The paradigm used in the law of the falling rate of profit, throughout *Capital* and in many other of Marx's works, also occurs in most eighteenth-century political and sociological theory, particularly in the *Social Contract* and in the *Discourse on the Origins of Inequality* of Jean-Jacques Rousseau.[16] I try below to give a brief answer to the following basic question: why should a paradigm that played a crucial part in both eighteenth-century political and sociological theory, and in Marx's work, be held in such scorn by sociologists? It comes to dominate economics in the same epoch, and most noticeably from the moment at which that discipline becomes separate from the other social sciences and enjoys a more and more unchallenged institutional autonomy.

Marx therefore seems to me to be the sociologist who most consistently interpreted social change as the result of effects of composition. He posits social agents exclusively preoccupied with the pursuit of immediately decipherable interests in which they are free to disregard the effect of their action on others. He writes in *The Holy Family* that 'History is nothing if it is not the activity of men in pursuit of their objectives.' Not only the law of the falling rate of profit, not only Marx's economics as a whole, but also his entire analysis of social change and of historical development is characterised by the concept of a 'state of nature', by preferences conceived as trivial and by the blatant effect of the relations of production on preferences (given my perspective here, historical monographs such as *The 18th Brumaire* should be put to one side.) I cannot develop this argument much further but it seems clear to me that Marx's dialectic is fundamentally derived from the same principles as inform Adam Smith's 'invisible hand' or Hegel's 'cunning of reason'. These dialectical effects can however only arise within an axiomatic in which the social actor is described as obeying a particular logic, one summed up by the Hayekian notion of *limited rationality*. A dialectical structure, like the prisoner's dilemma (a structure that characterises not only the law of the falling rate of profit but also, in a general way, the Marxian theory of social change), can only arise if one assumes both actors with preferences, intentions and a limited knowledge of the means available to them, and structural constraints that limit their possibilities of action. It is for this reason that I would hold that von Mises goes astray when in *Human Action* he accuses Marx of *polylogism*. It is not true that in Marx's analysis of social change differences in class position are conceived as producing differences in the logic of the actors' behaviour. Proletarians and capitalists are *equally* utilitarian and in the sway of the limited-rationality principle. Differences in class position are expressed in structural constraints on action but not in the logic of action.

Having in this way tried to justify the tag of 'Marxian' attributed to the first sub-type of interactionist paradigms, it is worth giving some examples of its use in recent sociological and political theory.

1. Social stratification theory often has recourse to it. One theory has been the object of a particularly large number of commentaries and discussions and, for all its flaws, is worth citing here. I refer to Davis and Moore's theory,[17] a theory whose real significance would seem to lie in its attempted identification of some of the basic causes of social stratification. Let me however stress that below I interpret their arguments slightly differently, giving them a more analytic form. The models underlying their theory may be illustrated by the following line of reasoning: imagine a social system with a division of labour. Let there then be two sorts of sets of professional tasks T_1 and T_2 such that, if a person has undergone an apprenticeship qualifying him to perform tasks T_2 he is equally well equipped to carry out tasks T_1, the opposite not being true. In that case an apprenticeship geared to the set of tasks T_2 is longer and therefore more costly than one geared to the set T_1. Next imagine a central authority that fixes the rate at which the two sorts of task and the corresponding jobs are, in economic and social terms, rewarded.[18] Suppose moreover that individuals are free to choose their careers (T_1 or T_2) and that the central authority opts for equal pay. It is not hard to work out that in this case young people, once they are of an age to

choose one or the other of the two possible forms of training, will all opt for the apprenticeship that leads to a mastery of the tasks T_1 but not the tasks T_2. The system therefore leads to a drying-up in recruitment for careers of the T_2 type. This consequence is presumed to be collectively undesirable, and the government may avoid it by having recourse, if it has to, to the various forms of *constraint* at its disposal, in order to steer individuals towards one or the other of the two sorts of training. Or it may resort to what is perhaps the simpler strategy of setting up a system of *wage differentials* for people working in *métiers* of the T_1 or T_2 type.

But suppose that there is no government or, less drastically, that there is one but that it no longer has any control over choice of jobs or wage levels. Let T_1 and T_2 also correspond to services rendered to shareholders. Under these conditions it is clear that those individuals with a higher level of competence would be able, whatever happened, to force the shareholders to supply them (in return for services that they alone were able to render them) with higher wages than less qualified individuals would be able to demand.

Through the composite effect of individual actions the system therefore generates a macro-social phenomenon, namely the emergence of wage differentials and, more generally, of *stratification* phenomena.

I would argue that this simple model represents the most fruitful possible interpretation of Davis and Moore's theory. Its most significant intuition is contained in the following proposition: stratification phenomena must be interpreted as effects of composition.

In short the development of theories of social stratification since the Second World War clearly shows that theories belonging to the Marxian paradigm type have very real possibilities.

It is therefore worth pausing to consider an empirical result that by itself suggests the importance of this class of paradigm for the analysis of stratification phenomena. Table 7.1 shows that there is absolutely no parallelism at all between changed attitudes to segregated housing in the United States and the growth of segregation itself. While acceptance of the principle of integration makes considerable progress, actual segregation stays constant.

This contradiction is interpreted in the following way: the existence of segregated housing does not represent what people in general feel, i.e., some fervent wish for life in a neighbourhood composed of people belonging to the same racial group. It represents, rather, an effect of composition. In choosing a home individuals consider first of all their means and their preferences as to kinds of housing. But suppose we push the argument further and posit that they attach *no* significance whatsoever to the ethnic

TABLE 7.1   *Index of Residential Segregation in Terms of Race: 109 towns in 1940, 1950, 1960, and the Percentage of Whites approving of Residential Segregation in 1942, 1956, June and December 1963, 1965 and 1968*

	South		North	
	Residential segregation	% of Whites approving residential integration	Residential segregation	% of Whites approving residential integration
1940	84.9		85.5	
1942		12		42
1950	88.5		86.3	
1956		38		58
1960	90.7		82.8	
1963 (June)		44		68
1963 (December)		51		70
1965		58		81
1968		57		83

Source: James Coleman, *Resources for Social Change*, (New York: Wiley, 1971) p. 31.

composition of their environment. It is still a simple matter to show that effects of segregation may appear. These would be the *undesired* result of the composition of choices made in a context in which availability of resources and ethnic affiliation are statistically linked.[19] This interpretation of the contradiction in table 7.1 reveals a structure comparable to that of the spider's-web theorem or to that of the law of the falling rate of profit. It effectively accounts for the persistence of segregated housing by invoking the play of effects of composition that the actors did not intend.

2. In the last few decades paradigms of the Marxian type have been extensively used in the field of political theory.

I will therefore sketch very rapidly the theory of Olson's that treats of participation in voluntary associations such as political parties, unions or professional associations.[20] Olson takes the following social phenomenon as his point of departure: it is clear that, empirically, voluntary associations very often attract a small number of participants in spite of the obvious appeal of the services offered and the fact that they are well placed to render these services to their potential public. Thus, globally, unionisation rates in most societies in Europe and North America seem to be relatively weak. They also seem to remain constant over time, in spite of industry's general tendency to assume an ever more concentrated form.[21] How is this global phenomenon to be explained? The unions are clearly in a position to provide very real services, starting with wage rises. Wage earners are unlikely to be unappreciative of this kind of service. Political parties are likewise in a position to be of use to individuals: their programmes invariably contain 'promises' appealing to significantly large numbers of individuals. Now it is obvious to everyone that these promises would be more likely to be kept if the party that formulated them was to accede to power. Why is it then that the number of party militants in all the Western European democracies and in North America tends to be, when contrasted with the number of persons who declare their interest in the parties' programmes by voting for them at elections, extremely small? One theory has it that such a lack of political participation would be due to a disaffection stemming from the quasi-identity of the parties' programmes. If this theory has a virtue, it lies in the fact that it explains, or at least goes some way towards explaining, why rates of abstention at elections are lower in France than in the United States. It clearly doesn't explain why, beyond the differences in party structure in each particular country, the proportion of militants is *in every case* very low.

To account for these phenomena Olson resorts to a very simple theory. The services rendered by organisations like parties and unions may be characterised as essentially *collective* services. Economists say that such organisations provide collective *benefits*, that is, benefits that are necessarily advantageous to all the members of a group.[22] Thus when a union wins a wage rise for a particular professional category, this rise applies to all the individuals within that category. The wage rise does of course represent an increase in each person's pay packet. But to the extent that this service is necessarily rendered to a whole *set* of individuals, it does in itself represent a collective service.

There are, according to Olson, serious consequences arising from the essentially collective nature of the goods and services provided by organisations like parties or unions. Here, in a simplified form, is his analysis: imagine that the potential public, or to use Dahrendorf's term,[23] the 'latent group', to which a union offers its collective services is pretty large. Each member of this latent group is bound to consider that their subscription to and, more generally, their participation in the voluntary association will at best make it slightly more probable that the association will provide a particular *collective* service. Because of the individual benefits that they have been promised, everyone naturally wishes and hopes that the particular collective service will indeed be offered. But since each individual correctly sees that nothing he does can have much real effect on the eventual provision of the service, and since the cost of participating is, *for him*, quite high, he is not likely to decide of his own accord to participate in the association. Because of individual preference, self-sacrifice, ideological interest or altruism, or for other reasons, there will certainly be some who will opt for participation. But the existence of these sorts of motive will be counter-balanced by the existence of diametrically opposed ones. One cannot therefore, all in all, expect to see high participation rates. Whilst each person may individually favour the service being provided, it is no one's real interest to participate in the providing of it. This conclusion may be stated in another form, if, for instance, you imagine an individual who could make the eventual provision of a collective good more likely but could not therefore feel more hopeful about gaining enough from his action to compensate him for the cost of his participation.

Olson's theory does more than just explain the low participation rate so often observed in voluntary associations. It also accounts for certain apparently paradoxical phenomena: the fact, for example, that some voluntary associations try to win from the public authority the right to *force* the members of their potential public to participate. Olson's theory also makes it easy to interpret something like the *closed shop*, which would otherwise make little sense. How does one explain why an association has to force individuals to join when it provides essentially welcome services?

This theory also makes it clear that voluntary associations have another strategy apart from *coercion* for boosting their numbers. This entails the provision of *individual goods* in parallel to the *collective goods* usually provided by voluntary associations. This corollary explains, or may in some cases explain, the different levels of participation in different associations. Thus an association for professional scientists does normally, as a matter of course, provide collective goods and services. But if, alongside these collective benefits it were to provide some individual benefits, it would stand every chance of boosting its membership. Some medical associations do, for instance, offer legal aid in case of professional misconduct. Similarly if a union is so placed institutionally that it can both win wage rises (collective benefits) and further its members' careers in some way (individual benefits), it is sure to have a far greater number of people participating than if other institutions limit its function to the provision of collective goods and services. Take the French educational system: the successful unionisation that has occurred there only makes sense if one considers the provision of individual benefits that the teachers' unions are able, thanks to the other institutions, to guarantee (alongside the provision of collective goods and services that is their *raison d'être*).

3. The sociology of education is an area of sociology that has, in the last decade, proved very popular. I want finally, therefore, to

mention the renewed importance that paradigms of a Marxian type have enjoyed in this area.

Consider, for instance, a macro-social phenomenon such as the increasing 'demand for education' that we have known since the Second World War. How does one explain this phenomenon? There is one fundamental fact that immediately springs to mind: if one consults any industrial society's statistical records there is invariably some correlation (more or less strict according to circumstances, and in fact often quite loose) between social rewards and educational level attained. In other words individuals *on average* enjoy economic and social rewards that correspond to their educational level. This is an empirically established fact. But it is important to stress the proviso just italicised: *on average*. I mean here to emphasise the fact that, if one takes two particular individuals, an inversion may be noticeable between rewards and educational level attained. In other words although individuals from the higher educational level *on average* enjoy higher rewards, it often happens that with two individuals selected at random the link between the two variables is inverted. To produce a positive correlation between rewards and educational level, such cases just have to be less frequent than the opposite kind. In other words, in spite of the positive correlation between reward and educational level, there is a very high chance that an individual will attain a lower level of remuneration than his neighbour even if he has attained a higher educational level.

To make these notions more concrete, imagine a social system in which there were only two educational levels. Suppose moreover that the statistical structure of rewards empirically associated with each level can be represented by figure 7.2.

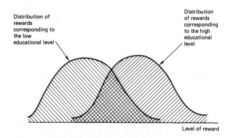

FIGURE 7.2   Distributions illustrating the meaning of the correlation between educational level and rewards

The cross-hatched area in the diagram represents the relative importance of the inversions mentioned above. The diagram shows that individuals with high educational qualifications tend to be better rewarded. However the cross-hatched zone contains two sub-populations (corresponding to the superimposition of the two distributions) of individuals that are rewarded in exactly the same fashion. Yet one of the two sub-populations is of a lower educational level and the other of a higher level.

Now imagine a whole series of family units or individuals who, for the sake of simplicity, will be taken to have exactly the same cultural, economic and other resources, and who are called upon to *choose* between the two levels. This simplification may well be unrealistic but its elimination would not effect the conclusions in any way. Imagine moreover that when the family units or individuals are faced with this decision, they perceive more or less clearly that the rewards that go with the two educational levels have a structure like that of figure 7.2. Although I have no way of proving this, there are some surveys that suggest that this is a realistic hypothesis. I want finally to propose an inertia hypothesis like that advanced in the spider's-web theorem: the individuals will presumably take it for granted that figure 7.2's structure holds good for the future.

How will individuals behave in these circumstances? Without going into details, it is quite clear[24] that, in the most general conditions, there may well be a much higher proportion choosing to invest in education in order to reach the highest levels than in the situation represented in figure 7.2 (in this figure, the spread of the two distributions indicates that the two educational levels are pretty equally shared out among the whole population). For this conclusion to be valid, the difference between the economic, social and psychological costs that go with the two kinds of academic career would need to be much the same as the difference between the rewards anticipated. As a last resort one could easily create a situation of rampant educational inflation in which it would be to no one's advantage to choose the first type of educational level.[25]

I cannot dwell any longer on this new example of an interactionist paradigm of the Marxian type. The relations between the actors are actually of the 'state-of-nature' sort. The educational level chosen by each does have an effect on the rewards that each of the others may expect from their educational level. Even though particular decisions have this sort of interdependence it is still a question of a relational context in which each *can freely* decide, and without having to consider the effects of his decision on the others. From another angle 'preferences' do not demand a special form of explanation. It is simply argued that each person tries to take a decision that will be likely to secure him the best social rewards. It is in fact pointless to restrict the argument to economic rewards alone, and it can easily be generalised by defining status as a flow of rewards that the subject enjoys his whole life, rewards that are bestowed in several different forms (prestige, income, power).

A more complicated version of this model could be presented. It would enable one to study the effects of the existence of *social classes*, i.e., of sub-groups whose distribution of resources varies. This factor is bound to produce differing perceptions as to the risks that different elements in a set of options imply. An individual who expects figure 7.2's structure to be reproduced will perhaps consider the risk taken in trying to get to the high educational level as roughly equivalent to the cross-hatched surface. But one also has to argue that one's capacity to take risks depends on one's financial resources: someone with £1000 to his name will be far more likely to risk £1 than someone with £2 in all the world. With this in mind one can proceed to study the effects of this basic aspect of social structure (social classes) on decisions regarding education and one can highlight the complex effects of interdependence that ensue. When the demand for education becomes dramatically inflated, stratification will lessen the intensity of this inflation. The lower classes will however suffer because of this.

I have dwelt at some length on this example because I wanted to point to the potential importance of Marxian-type paradigms in a domain where they are not customarily applied.

A quick glance at any compilation of texts will in fact show that work in the sociology of education has developed quite separately not merely from the kind of paradigm discussed in this section but even from the family of *interactionist* paradigms.[26] Sociologists of education will tend to analyse educational behaviours not as *actions* but as *behaviours* (in the sense in which I defined these concepts at the beginning of this article). Educational 'choices' are, in other words, interpreted as deriving more or less mechanically from a process of conditioning in which social origin plays a major part. I will come back to this point when I reach the chapter on determinist paradigms.

The renewed application of Marxian-type paradigms in sociological domains has therefore met with considerable resistance, for it disrupts some well-entrenched traditions and interests. Those who object to the use of this type of paradigm usually argue that the advances made by *Tiefenpsychologie* render any model of *homo sociologicus*, recalling as it does the high period of rationalist psychology, quite redundant. But many classical sociologists have nevertheless used this model and it does provide a satisfactory explanation for many different behaviours. It does not explain every behaviour, admittedly, and only a lunatic would claim to account for a neurotic's behaviour in terms of this model. But it would be equally unreasonable to want to provide a systematic account of any and every behaviour in terms of a complex psychological model. When a passer-by crossing the street looks to right and to left his actions can be explained without having recourse to the unconscious, to alienation, to false consciousness. Sociologists working in areas like education would seem to have paid dearly for intending so obstinately to use a complex psychology anywhere and everywhere. A complex *homo sociologicus* can all too easily generate a simple, even a simplistic, sociology. The preceding examples do, I believe, indicate that Marxian-type models, *in spite of* and to some degree *thanks to* the simplicity of the *homo sociologicus* concept employed, often bring to light effects of interaction of a great structural complexity.

I will return to this point later, for it would seem to me to be of great epistemological significance. First though I will continue with the discussion of the other paradigm types.

Paradigms of the Tocquevillean Type

The second sub-type of interactionist paradigm features an *individualist* interpretation of actions (individuals make their choices within a state of nature) and a *social* interpretation of systems of preferences. The reader will recall that it is this second characteristic that typefies what I have called paradigms of the Tocquevillean type, a type of paradigm that may be distinguished from the preceding one by the fact that systems of preference (and especially the *valorisation* of alternative actions) are analysed in terms of data characteristic not of individuals but of the social system to which they belong.

I will, to start with, try to justify the terms I have used to designate this kind of paradigm. It would be of interest on some other occasion to show quite systematically that this paradigm characterises Tocqueville's work. Here I want only to cite an example taken from *The Ancien Régime and the Revolution* to justify my assertion that it does indeed belong to the class of paradigms just defined.

First of all consider the way in which Tocqueville explains why, at the end of the eighteenth century, capitalist agriculture and commerce did not grow at the same pace in France and in England. Administrative centralisation in Ancien Régime France had, he argues, proceeded so far that the state enjoyed more prestige than in England, and the state's offices, its 'places', were more sought after and more numerous. Consequently when a landowner was faced with the choice of staying on his estates and encouraging production there, or of obtaining royal office in some town or other, he would tend to choose the second:

The posts available under the Ancien Régime were not the same in all cases as they are today, but they were, I think, even more numerous: indeed, the number of minor civil servants was legion.

Within no more than sixteen years, from 1693 to 1709, it would seem that some forty thousand new official posts, for the most part open to members of the lower middle class, were created.... There can be few, if any, parallels for this intense desire of the middle-class Frenchman to cut an official figure; no sooner did he find himself in possession of a small capital sum than he expended it on buying an official post instead of investing it in a business. This deplorable propensity had a worse effect than the guilds or even the *taille* on the progress of trade and agriculture in France.[27]

But the final sentence reminds us that we should not forget the obvious attraction of the tax exemptions offered to those who set themselves up in town:

[. . .] The urban middle class, acting as a group, had many means of reducing the impact of the *taille* and sometimes of escaping it altogether; whereas an isolated member of that class, living in the country on his own land, had no such means of escape [. . . .] This, by the way, is one of the reasons why there are so many more towns, small towns especially, in France than in most other European countries.[28]

There then you have some of the basic reasons offered by Tocqueville for the limited growth of French capitalist agriculture in contrast to that of the English.

Tocqueville tends to argue like this: the behaviour of individuals is not ordered by transcendent norms. It is not the product of social structures. It is not a result of the influence of the environment. In any given social context social actors are described as doing nothing more than seek to further their own interests. These individual *choices* do then, in combination, produce macro-sociological effects (the underdevelopment of commerce and agriculture), which are explicable in terms of the structures of interaction created by the social context. There are, to be more specific, four fundamental aspects to this analysis. Tocqueville first defines quite precisely the *macro-social* phenomena that he seeks to explain, for instance the different town sizes occurring in France and England or the different levels of agricultural growth in the two countries. Secondly he regards these macro-social phenomena as having the status of effects of composition *vis-à-vis* elementary actions. Thirdly these actions are taken to obey the logic of individual interest. Fourthly the *values* ascribed by the individuals to the alternatives offered them depend on the particular features of the social system into which they are inserted.

The model of *homo sociologicus* that serves as backdrop for

Tocqueville's analysis is definitely more complex than the one encountered in the examples presented in the preceding section. In contrast to traditional eighteenth-century political philosophy, Tocqueville does not consider it useless or uninteresting to try and explain the hierarchical order in which an individual places his different objectives. This order does not obey the principle that Parsons dubbed the *randomness of ends*.[29] In fact quite the opposite: it is the social structure that helps to determine this hierarchy. It is therefore the historical effects of administrative centralisation and of various fiscal institutions that encourage the French landowner to neglect his estates. But a proprietor's decision to leave his estates is far from being the result of external constraints (possibly interiorised), nor is it the manifestation of some aetherial sort of determinism. It is the result of a free choice whose logic is, *roughly speaking*, based on utilitarian calculation. One can in short say that for Tocqueville the hierarchy of values attributed to possible objectives is not, as it is in the classical tradition, an *independent* variable, i.e., one that can be disregarded: if administrative centralisation had not occurred there would not have been so many state posts. Nor would they have had the same prestige and consequently the same *value* in Ancien Régime France. In the astute analyses of social stratification developed in *Democracy in America* the same sort of pattern occurs: the slight rewards that status brings would not have the same value and would not be so sought after if advancing industrialisation had not furthered the mechanisms of competition.

There are two things to be clarified here. These first two paradigm types differ, for in the first case, but not in the second, preferences *have to be explained*. This distinction is not identical to the usual one made between *endogenous* and *exogenous* variables. Its purpose is rather to stress that in some but not in all actions *any* observer whatsoever is thought to be able to understand the actor's system of preferences. Any observers will thus understand why (*wozu*) a passer-by looks to right and to left before crossing the street. In other situations, where the action is of a different kind, one will presumably be dealing with an action obeying a system of preferences that are *opaque* to all observers (why does Tocqueville's merchant want a royal post so desperately?). Two types of possible relation between *observer* and *actor*'s preferences therefore serve to distinguish the two paradigm types (immediate understanding or opacity). The distinction between these two types of relation has nothing to do with the distinction (to me a confused one and anyway of little use here) between the different ways in which individual preferences may be determined (for instance determination by social structures and determination by human nature).

In contemporary sociology and in the history of sociology it is not difficult to find numerous examples that call to mind interactionist paradigms of the Tocquevillean kind. I will briefly consider three of these:

1. The first is taken from the work of the American sociologist Robert Merton. In an article first published in 1936 and reprinted in more or less its original form in his famous theoretical work *Social Theory and Social Structure*, Merton argues that one of the most fundamental tasks of sociological analysis is to uncover the unforeseen consequences of human actions,[30] i.e., to decipher what I call here *the effects of composition of individual actions*. I would also draw the reader's attention to the fact that in the first lines of his text Merton cites both Mandeville and Marx.[31] This citation seems to me highly significant.

Merton does however use a more general paradigm than that most frequently used by Mandeville and Marx. In his text he argues quite explicitly for the abstraction – in analyses that deal with phenomena like financial panics – of the effects of social structure from the system of interaction. If it is rumoured that a bank is insolvent, its clients will hurry to withdraw their investments. The prophecy contained in the rumour is thus realised, not because it is inherently true but because it sets off a whole chain of actions that culminate in an effect of composition that the prediction sums up quite effectively. This analysis of *creative*[32] or *self-fulfilling prophecy* obeys a logical schema with a structure analogous to that of the preceding examples. There are other analyses however, like those that deal with the logic of racial prejudice, that fall within the Tocquevillean paradigm:

> As a result of their failure to comprehend the operation of the self-fulfilling prophecy, many Americans of good will (sometimes reluctantly) retain enduring ethnic and racial prejudices. They experience these beliefs, not as prejudices, not as prejudgements, but as irrestible products of their own observation. 'The facts of the case' permit them no other conclusion.
>
> Thus our fair-minded white citizen strongly supports a policy of excluding Negroes from his labour union. His views are, of course, based not upon prejudice, but upon cold hard facts. And the facts seem clear enough. Negroes, 'lately from the nonindustrial South, are undisciplined in traditions of trade unionism and the art of collective bargaining'. The Negro is a strikebreaker. The Negro, with his 'low standard of living', rushes in to take jobs at less than prevailing wages. The Negro is, in short, 'a traitor to the working class', and should manifestly be excluded from union organisations. So run the facts of the case as seen by our tolerant but hard-headed union member, innocent of any understanding of the self-fulfilling prophecy as a basic process of society.

Our unionist fails to see, of course, that he and his kind have produced the very 'facts' which he observes. For by defining the situation as one in which Negroes are held to be incorrigibly at odds with principles of unionism and by excluding Negroes from unions, he invited a series of consequences which indeed made it difficult if not impossible for many Negroes to avoid the role of scab. Out of work after World War I, and kept out of unions, thousands of Negroes could not resist strikebound employers who held a door invitingly open upon a world of jobs from which they were otherwise excluded. History creates its own test of the theory of self-fulfilling prophecies. That Negroes were strikebreakers because they were excluded from unions (and from a wide range of jobs) rather than excluded because they were strikebreakers can be seen from the virtual disappearance of Negroes as scabs in industries where they have gained admission to unions in the last decades. The application of the Thomas theorem also suggests how the tragic, often vicious circle of self-fulfilling prophecies can be broken. The initial definition of the situation which has set the circle in motion must be abandoned. Only when the original assumption is questioned and a new definition of the situation introduced, does the consequent flow of events give the lie to the assumption. Only then does the belief no longer gather the reality.[33]

For a further clue, return to our instance of widespread hostility toward the Negro strikebreakers brought into industry by employers after the close of the very first World War. Once the initial definition of Negroes as not deserving of union membership had largely broken down, the Negro, with a wider range of work opportunities, no longer found it necessary to enter industry through the doors held open by strike-bound employers. Again, appropriate institutional change broke through the tragic circle of the self-fulfilling prophecy. Deliberate social change gave the lie to the firm conviction that 'it just ain't in the nature of the nigra' to join cooperatively with his white fellows in trade unions.[34]

This analysis in short reveals two *structures of interaction* corresponding to the two periods that Merton refers to (the years after the First World War, the years following the *New Deal*). In the former period one can identify the following pattern· Whites 'note' that blacks are strikebreakers and they therefore tend in all good faith to bar them from the unions. This occurs because various aspects of American social structure (the blacks' economic circumstances, underemployment etc.) put the blacks in a position from which many of them can only find work by strikebreaking. On the one hand employers are often quite happy to appeal to strikebreakers. On the other hand the unions, by barring blacks, lessen their chances of finding jobs other than those that the 'strikers' create. Thus the logic of their situation leads the blacks to act like strikebreakers, just as the French merchants described by Tocqueville are driven by the logic of their situation to behave differently than their British counterparts. After the New Deal, conditions altered: whites no longer excluded blacks from the unions and the blacks thus found their situation radically changed. They warranted the whites' trust just as they had warranted their mistrust in the preceding period.

In this analysis the macro-social phenomenon that Merton seeks to explain (the non-admission of blacks to the unions) is conceived as an effect of composition. The actors confronting each other (blacks, white unionists) pursue their respective interests such as they conceive them to be. The black job-seeker's interest is in finding work. The white unionist's interest is in not admitting strikebreakers. When with the New Deal the structure of interaction alters, the blacks can find a job without acting like strikebreakers. The change in the structure of interaction accounts for the change observed at the level of individual behaviours.

2. I take my second example of a Tocquevillean paradigm from a recent study in the sociology of education, done by an economist, Louis Lévy-Garboua.[35] The following macro-social phenomenon had to be explained: since university degrees have in both the *middle* and *short* term fallen perceptibly in social value (measured here in terms of the socio-economic level of jobs that the students on average obtain) why are there not fewer people seeking university places?

Lévy-Garboua tries to answer this question by positing an effect of composition of individual actions obeying the logic of interest: those who have passed through the secondary system keep on enrolling in the university because it is to their advantage to do so. In spite of the social devaluation of university degrees, the level of social rewards still tends to depend on educational qualifications: there is a statistical correlation between the two variables. Someone with his *baccalauréat* therefore benefits from enrolling in the university. But between 1960 and 1975, say, the logic of the student's situation has changed: the differential advantage that he can hope to reap after his period at university has declined in importance. Lévy-Garboua therefore argues that the student copes with this new situation by exploiting the leeway that the institutions allow him to modify the various *costs* of obtaining a university degree. The student adjusts by reallocating his available time, spending less of it studying and preparing for university exams and correspondingly more of it doing paid work. These immediate financial rewards (and perhaps also the feeling of being slightly less marginal in a social sense) compensate for the losses that he would otherwise have suffered because of the devaluation of the differential advantage that a university degree brings. Each student will naturally tend to modify his own behaviour to fit that of his elders, and students will therefore tend to be more and more part-time, and this process represents an additional effect of composition. This effect will also have considerable influence on the university system as a whole.

3. My third example is effectively an extension of the second one. It comes from a study in progress on French intellectuals. One of the macro-social phenomena encountered in this study concerned the difference between France and the United States in the frequency of what one could call the 'McLuhan effect'.[36] Some explanation is called for here. There is an article by Lewis Coser[37] that analyses some cases of resounding intellectual success in the United States (McLuhan, Reich, Segal), and in it he argues that American intellectuals may seek to reap a social reward for their productions on a double market. The first sub-market is attached to and may even depend on a specific institution, the university system. This system shares out the various kinds of gratification that it has at its disposal (honours, 'recognition' etc.) after a slow and complex assessment of the worth of what an intellectual produces. If one extended Coser's hypotheses one could feasibly argue that the very nature of this evaluative process implies that the knowledge produced obey a *scientistic* ethic. The criteria applied when awarding the different sorts of gratification are therefore themselves *scientistic*: texts must be written in a language that the sub-group of university members competent in that field of research can understand and they must be only minimally original, in the scientistic sense of the term etc.

But there is a second system offering gratification in various forms and it is this that intellectuals like McLuhan and Reich have exploited. Here the intellectual 'grabs' not the university milieu but the milieu that one could call intellectual. His product will therefore be phrased in such a way that it is picked up very quickly by the intellectual press. It is up to the intellectual to produce something that the press will deem 'interesting' or worthy of being presented to the readers. Recourse to this system of gratification presupposes that the product deals with a theme of pressing general interest, that the analyses presented are both free of cumbersome technical detail and yet at the same time arouse (if possible) profound feelings, and that the conclusions can be summed up in a few simple propositions without reducing the 'depth' of the argument. Recourse to this system does naturally offer certain advantages. It frees the producer from the constraints of the scientistic ethic. It can provide quicker and more tangible rewards. It allows one to reach several different markets at once. It also has its disadvantages: it is able to confer a certain notoriety but this is often short-lived. One could even argue that it has a built-in tendency to be so, for large-circulation periodicals necessarily have a quick turn-over in stars. Professional reviews, however, are not in any position to consecrate someone as a scientific authority, such a thing only occurring after a long process of evaluation. From another angle scientism presupposes continuity, accumulation of knowledge and relative originality, whilst aestheticism is founded on rupture, absolute beginning and radical originality.

There is not, of course, a totally free choice between the two reward networks. A sociologist or an economist has more latitude than a physicist does, and personal idiosyncrasies will also determine the likelihood of a person being rewarded by one network rather than another. But the important thing to note here is that the *difference* in accessibility of the two sorts of choice depends on the kind of social system to which the actors belong. If you compare France with the United States, for instance, you will find that the McLuhan effect has assumed a far greater significance in the former country, although in the last decade both have been more and more affected by it. If one considers the leading figures in some of the social sciences, it is clear that in France they are to a very great extent and in the United States to a very limited extent the product of the McLuhan effect. In other words gratification is more rarely ensured by the intellectual network in the United States than it is in France.

How does one account for this macro-social difference? One could more or less ascribe it to the very limited number of symbolic rewards that the institutional structures of the French university system make available. Potential producers are therefore encouraged to address the 'intellectual' network instead. A particular feature of the social system to which the actors belong (in this case the structure of the university system) would thus seem to affect the way in which intellectual producers are encouraged to behave. Differences between the French and American university structures do therefore help to explain why the McLuhan effect should be much more prevalent in the latter. Other macro-social phenomena may also be explained in this way and may therefore be legitimately described as effects of composition. The above analysis therefore shows that, when the 'intellectual' network of rewards becomes more compelling for producers, their work (in the areas where this is possible) is bound to become less marked by a scientistic ethic. Originality in the literary sense then replaces scientific innovation, and the ideal of an impersonal and universalist writing is abandoned in favour of forms of research concerned with stylistic questions; a more or less ineffable *intuition* replaces *analysis* and Hegel's absolute knowledge replaces the bounded scientific kind.

This example is useful because it shows that the Tocquevillean paradigm can be applied in several extremely diverse areas, including the so-called sociology of knowledge. The fact that institutional structures may, in Shils's[38] phrase terms, favour a *romantic* or a *scientistic* ethic, the frequency of the 'McLuhan effect' and other macro-social phenomena characteristic of intellectual life may, as I have tried to show, be interpreted as effects of composition. Actors pursue their individual interests. Both the general structure of systems of preference and the fact of choosing one option rather than another depend on particular features of the social system in which the actors are placed. This is clearly therefore a situation in which a paradigm of the Tocquevillean type applies.

Paradigms of the Mertonian Type

It is worth remembering that the paradigms considered in the two preceding sections have a feature in common: the macro-social phenomena treated there are assumed to be the result of the composition of choices and, more generally, of individual actions occurring in the kind of context described above as a 'state of nature'. The blacks in Merton's analysis, the students in Lévy-Garboua's work, the intellectuals in my own analysis may and do act without considering the effect of their actions on others. In the years after the First World War the blacks did not serve their employers' interests because they had reached an agreement with them, and it was not after debating the matter that certain French intellectuals came to subscribe to a professional ethic of a romantic kind. The students did not reach an agreement with anyone before altering their timetables and substituting various paid activities for scholarly ones.

These examples make it clear that the state-of-nature context is of real use, and not merely in economics but in sociology as well. James Buchanan defines economics as the science of markets[39] or, in other words, the science of structures of interdependence in which typically each individual freely pursues his own interest. This definition seems to me an ideal one and I doubt very much if it accords with actual economic theory, but I will leave that to the better judgement of the economists. I am, however, certain that in sociology there are innumerable situations in which the macro-social phenomena studied there derive from the composition of actions appearing in a 'state of nature', i.e., an institutional context that leaves the individual free to make up his own mind without reaching an agreement with others, without winning the approval of others and above all without risking the moral and legal sanctions that might (because of the effect of his actions on the well-being of others) ensue.

In order to cover the whole gamut of sociological paradigms it would therefore seem to me to be vital to distinguish between those actions occurring in a state of nature and actions occurring in a contractual context. Traffic jams or ideological congestions constitute systems of interaction. There is congestion because n individuals turn up at the same place. But it is the convergence and juxtaposition of n decisions, each taken separately and without a thought for their effect on others, that results in the n persons finding themselves all in the same place. On the other hand the meeting of an administrative body represents a system of interaction in which n persons have agreed beforehand as to the time, place and object of the meeting. To dispense with a notion like that of role (of little use in the first example) would be to deprive oneself of any really effective means of analysing the pattern of interaction in the second example.[40]

Secondly I would argue that both kinds of context concern the sociologist. It does not therefore seem to me to be feasible to define sociological theory in terms of concepts such as role that imply situating oneself theoretically in the second kind of context. However important role theory is, it seems to me out of the question to regard it as the basis of a general sociological theory.

I have decided to call paradigms Mertonian (they could as easily be called Parsonian) when they display the following features: (1) the individual actions studied are thought to arise in a contractual context; (2) as in the preceding example, these actions are fundamentally self-seeking; (3) the manner in which preferences are structured may be considered either as given or as to be explained.

Merton may well be the sociologist who has used this paradigm most and formulated it most clearly, but it is essential to note that on many occasions he has had to resort, as the examples in the previous section show, to other paradigm types.

Since everyone acknowledges that this paradigm belongs traditionally within the sociological domain, I will be briefer here.

The concept of role is, as I have shown, central to this type of paradigm. This suggests that some structures of interaction only make sense if you refer to the actors' more or less explicit mutual commitments. Thus the fact that Mr Jones is at present engaged in offering his thoughts on the composition of water to a group of adolescents only makes sense if one knows that Mr Jones is a teacher, that his role consists of the dispensing of forms of knowledge belonging to a particular domain (chemistry), to a particular audience (his pupils), according to patterns that are partly compulsory (the curriculum, for instance), which he may have discussed with the relevant parties, or which he may have adopted because they seemed to suit him (the question, for instance, of a more or less authoritarian style).

Role theorists insist (and Merton has formulated this point in a particularly striking way) that unexpected effects of composition may occur in any structure of interaction whatsoever, whether it is in a 'contract' or a 'state-of-nature' context. As Merton has stressed, these effects of composition tend to be the result of three basic characteristics. First of all, social roles are rarely so strictly defined that they leave the actor no leeway to interpret. This leeway may in some cases be broad enough to affect the structure of interaction as a whole. From another angle an individual x is generally implicated in not just one role but in a set of roles. Thus x may be a family man, a boss at the office, a believer, a unionist and a member of a sports club. The effect of these different elements, often incompatible one with another or contradictory, is to allow x to define his set of roles more or less strictly. He may, for instance, have to favour a liberal style of interpersonal relationships in one role and an authoritarian style in another. Finally the one institutional structure will probably force the individual to assume not just one role but a whole series. Thus an employee will deal with both subordinates and superiors, and he may have relations with the clientele of the business employing him or with those working for firms associated with his. There are different roles linked to each of these types of relation. The social position of an individual x should, in Mertonian terms, be described in terms of both the multiple roles that he assumes (*status-set*) and in terms of the series of elements (*role-set*) for which these roles allow. The concept of *role-set* refers to the different types of relation and to the diversity of roles that characterise the individuals' position in each institution.[41]

The variability, multiplicity and individual complexity of roles are the three crucial ingredients that give rise to unexpected effects of composition within structures of interaction characterised by a contractual context. These effects are rightly considered by Merton to be in many cases the root cause of social conflicts and, more generally, of social change. Their analysis is therefore one of sociology's fundamental tasks.

In order to flesh out this brief account I will quickly run through some examples illustrative of this paradigm.

1. My first example depends on an analytic schema derived from Peter Blau's work.[42] His presentation is purely didactic in intention but, freshly interpreted, it does I believe throw some new light on the causes of the American university crisis of the 1960s.

Consider the *role-set* linked to the status of university professor in the United States. The role-set comprises many different elements. The professor is a 'teacher' and also a 'researcher'. These two roles imply a host of different relations: with students, with the administration, with the scientific community and the different institutions through which it expresses itself (scientific reviews, regional, national and international professional associations), with the backers of research funds, with journalists and with many other persons and institutions.

One of the students' central demands during the university crisis of the sixties concerned the return of the teaching body from research to teaching. The students bitterly reproached their teachers for only showing a limited degree of interest in teaching as such and for devoting most of their time and energy to research.

As Blau's remarks suggest, Mertonian notions illuminate this macro-social phenomenon. Sociological enquiries in fact show that those students engaged in confrontations in the 1960s were considered to be some of the very best.[43] Moreover the universities involved were those with the largest number of scientific stars. The students were probably right to complain that their teachers were neglecting their teaching responsibilities. But, from another angle, the teachers' interpretation of their role was not totally unfounded either: research work, when it produces noteworthy results, may well achieve recognition with national or international scientific authorities. For a teacher, on the other hand, and even one who is exceptionally well qualified from a pedagogic point of view, it is extremely difficult to win any recognition for his abilities outside of his own narrow circle or at best outside the institution to which he belongs. This is partly because an objective *assessment* is easier in the first case and partly because it is only research work that can give a teacher some visibility outside the institution to which he belongs. The best universities therefore tend to attract the best teachers. But because of the way roles are structured the social definition of *quality* may be reduced quite simply to the quality of research work. The best universities are therefore those in which the teachers, being brilliant researchers, tend to attach minimum importance to their responsibilities as teachers and identify only slightly with the university to which they belong. The logic of the role structure in the big universities then produces in the teachers who are least well known for their work, a strong feeling of identification: they belong to a prestigious institution but themselves enjoy little visibility and therefore tend to emphasise those aspects of their role that are directly linked to the institution. But the striking thing is that the institution owes its prestige to those who have every reason, given the opposite interpretation they could well give of their role, to feel very little allegiance towards it. This theory suggests that in the less prestigious universities one would expect to find less variation in the range of allegiances owed to the institution, and in the last analysis there might well be fewer tensions within the teaching body, between the teaching body and the administration, and also between the teaching body and the students. This is one of the reasons why the most criticised universities and those most hit by political confrontations in the 1960s were in general the best.

2. My second example is also taken from the sociology of education. It reiterates, in an altered form, an analysis that I gave of the reasons for the malfunctioning of the French university after 1968. I will restrict myself to a quick summary of this.[44]

Various studies together show that, in spite of the efforts made to put indirect controls on the demand for higher education, it has continued up until very recently to grow. One result of the lowering of social expectations tied to the university degree has been that students, as we have seen, spend less time preparing for their degrees. 'Teachers' are therefore also led to interpret their role differently. The Germano-American model of the research seminar becomes inappropriate to many disciplines, and teacher-pupil relations that favour a very small investment of time (outside of meeting up with teachers) come to seem more appropriate. This explains why students have again, once the passions of 1968 were quieted, demanded courses of the authoritarian sort so attacked in 1968, because they do at least allow the minimal amount of time to be consecrated to study. The other possible solution is the discussion meeting inherited from 1968. These meetings may still be called research seminars but the teacher simply plays the part of 'cultural animator'. The two parts of this demand may seem mutually contradictory but this is only on the surface: seminars that allow each person the maximum spontaneity and authoritarian courses in the classical tradition are both possible solutions to the same problem, that of altering the teacher-pupil interaction to fit the new structural constraints that weigh on the pupil.

I could provide endless examples of this sort. The sociology of organisations does of course use Mertonian paradigms a great deal, and the works of authors like Blau or Crozier automatically spring to mind here. Suleiman's work on top-level French bureaucracy[45] is a recent example of this genre and includes almost exemplary illustrations of the contradictions to which complexity of *role-sets* can lead. I do not want to do more here than mention Suleiman's analysis of the complexity of roles that the juxtaposition of ministerial cabinets with the administrative directions of the ministers produced.

Paradigms of the Weberian Type

This kind of paradigm has a basic feature: it is held that some aspects of actions (the structuring of systems of preference, the choice of the appropriate means etc.) must be analysed in terms of certain other aspects that preceded the actions. To account for Mrs Jones's shopping habits it may well be necessary to know that she has already had occasion to buy a particular object and knows how to use it. For cognitive reasons (she knows and remembers the object) or for affective ones (it brings back pleasant memories), she may well prefer it to a product sold at much the same price that could be put to much the same uses. *In the real world* there is not a single action that goes unaffected by this sort of element, if only because every action presupposes the operation of cognitive elements that in their turn imply an apprenticeship pre-existing the action. But, as the above examples show, there are numerous circumstances in which it is pointless to take these elements into account, either because they are essentially trivial, as the cognitive aspects of every human action are, or because they do not affect the explanatory schema. It has to be recognised however that these distinctions are difficult to maintain. Consider, for instance, Merton's analysis of the vicious circle in which unemployed blacks were caught just after the First World War: the analysis does not work if the whites' belief in the blacks' incapacity to demonstrate their loyalty to the principles of union membership is disregarded (i.e., a cognitive element). But in this case the *belief* only persists because it is reinforced by the effects that it gives rise to. It is explained by the system of interaction but at the same time constitutes an essential element in the explanation of that system. It is for this reason that I thought it more appropriate to classify this type of example in the preceding family.

There are other circumstances however in which elements occur that are indisputably both *prior* to the action, *not trivial*, and *indispensable to the analysis*. When all these conditions pertain, one is dealing with what I would call, because of its frequent occurrence in Weber's work, a Weberian paradigm.

Bernstein's studies on the relation between educational success and social origins represent a modern example of the use of this type of paradigm. In his opening hypothesis he asserts that family relations will tend to have different effects at very different levels and that this difference depends on the class to which the family belongs. Thus, when a mother wants to make a child change its mind, she will more willingly use *order* in the lower class and *persuasion* in the upper class. But order and persuasion are manners of relating that involve linguistic and, more generally, communicational techniques of varying degrees of complexity. Indeed in the second example (that of the upper class) they are bound to be more complex. The mother who wants to avoid having recourse to order has to present a more or less elliptical picture of the consequences that will ensue if the child chooses O_1 or O_2. She has therefore to make her own neutrality with regard to the different options seem credible, or, if she wants to make it clear that one of the options would be unpleasing to her, she has to indicate that that this *externality* belongs to a more general set.[46]

Bernstein's main hypothesis is therefore that these different modes of relating to a child produce differences that were not actually intended. By using a strategy of *persuasion*, the upper-class mother at the same time introduces the child to skills that the educational system will itself teach him, and he will therefore serve his apprenticeship to that system with far greater ease. By depicting the consequences that would ensue from both O_1 and O_2 she introduces him to the classificatory skills involved in grammatical analysis. By suggesting that the set of consequences associated with O_1 proves, after analysis, to be more favourable, she solves a kind of equation in which the unknown factor posited at the beginning (O_1 or O_2?) is given a value. It may be that in this way she introduces the child indirectly to the *circuitous ways* of algebra.[47]

Bernstein's analysis fits well with the type of analysis I defined above: because class differences produce different sorts of familial relationships, middle-class children when they arrive at school have already served a kind of educational apprenticeship and one that working-class children are far less likely to enjoy.

I will take the liberty of briefly referring here to a second example from the sociology of education, namely, the theory of educational *choices* that I have myself used. This theory is in fact situated within the framework of a Weberian-type paradigm.[48]

Alain Girard's writings,[49] which closely parallel numerous other studies done in various different national and institutional contexts, point to the existence of very regular statistical correspondences between three types of variables: social origin, prior educational success (an independent variable) and selection (a dependent variable). Thus prior educational success is statistically linked to questions of social origin, and the higher the person's social origin the better chance he has of educational success. Theories like Bernstein's may account for this link. From another angle, for the same level of success a link between educational aspiration and social origins is observed. Given the same level of success it is upper-class pupils who will tend to aim for the highest careers. But an interaction phenomenon (in the statistical sense of the term)[50] arises: the differences between classes as regards aspiration lessen as prior success increases; the link between success and aspiration is correspondingly stronger the lower the class of origin. This effect of interaction may typically be represented by the information whose structure is given in table 7.2.

TABLE 7.2   *The Typical Structure of Statistical Relations Between Social Origin, Educational Success and Vocation*

	percentage of pupils with a higher vocation when prior educational success is	
Social origins	High	Low
High	80	75
Low	70	40

It is clear that the 'effect' of social origin on aspirations is weak if prior success is high (80%–70%) and strong if it is low (75%–40%). Conversely the effect of success is weak in the upper class (80%–75%) and strong in the lower class (70%–40%).

I have used a simple enough theory to account for this structure. It consists of the juxtaposition of a number of empirical facts. Firstly I note that the cognitive effects that account for the link between social origin and success cannot satisfactorily explain the class differences evident in table 7.2. Class difference is still apparent when equally successful groups are compared. It is no easier to argue that the access to educational information enjoyed by different classes or the high value attributed to education as a means to success in themselves explain the table's complex statistical structure. This theory might hold if there was an evident success-selection link that was constant in relation to social origin, but in fact it varies. If there was an evident success-selection link that held constant in relation to social origin instead of *varying*, this theory could be defended. The postulated effect of sub-cultures within classes does not account very convincingly for this variation, and a second sort of evidence has therefore to be introduced: when a family clearly wants to point its child towards, say, long-cycle rather than short-cycle secondary education it will tend to have an implicit understanding of the *risks* it is taking. If previous performance at school does not bode too well for the future, a child's family may well decide that there is too much of a *risk* involved. Let me formulate this more precisely: faced with a decision about schooling a family will have at least some notion as to how *useful* or valuable the different options are, it will consider the risks involved in choosing one or other of the paths, and will also appreciate the risks involved in basing such a decision, more or less decisively, on the prior performance of the child at school.

One therefore arrives at the logically interesting proposition that adherence to this explanatory schema makes it difficult to account for the structure observed. On the other hand if another sort of evidence (and one that leads us directly to a Weberian type paradigm) is superimposed on this schema, it is easily explained: namely that the subject's class of origin (or the class to which a family now belongs) will crucially affect his choice of one or the other option. If their current success is mediocre, the family unit will consider itself 'satisfied' if the child has reached an academic level enabling him to aspire to a social status equal or higher than his own, even if this status is not especially high. A well-placed family unit will on the other hand strive (I ought to add: more often than not) to 'push' the child so that he doesn't fail (even if he doesn't enjoy a great success). My argument therefore is that the social level to which options O_1 and O_2 provide access is valorised by family units, not in any absolute sense but by virtue of their own social level. I am therefore led to advance, as quite central to the explanation, the notion that the social situation of the family affects the structure of the system of preferences. We are indeed within the framework of a Weberian paradigm since, if propositions pertaining to a determinist syntax are introduced, they nonetheless apply to a model that interprets the behaviour of family units as intentional, in other words as *actions*. In contrast many a contemporary analysis of the relation between social origins and aspirations has recourse to determinist models which consider family behaviour patterns as false choices imposed by social structures, which are described as being lived as authentic choices by introducing the more or less complex hypotheses of alienation or false consciousness. The proliferation of determinist models for the analysis of educational inequality is due to a misapprehension. Lower-class families would seem to be less ambitious in educational terms. In this they are perhaps acting against their *interest*, but not necessarily against their *preferences*.[51] If they were acting against their preferences their behaviour would indeed be irrational. The misapprehension derives from the sociologist arriving at a diagnosis of *irrationality* through comparing his own system of preferences with that of the individuals he observes. Such a comparison is clearly unwarranted: the notion of a subject's *objective interests* is one of a normative kind and therefore one that can only hold in the context of a normative sociology.

Determinist Paradigms: From Sociology to Sociologism

I will now tackle the problem of determinist paradigms. The reader will recall that two main paradigm families were, at the beginning of this article, counterposed: *interactionist* paradigms, analysed at length in the preceding sections, and *determinist* paradigms. I would remind the reader that by determinist paradigms I mean those paradigms in which a social subject's behaviour is interpreted *solely* in terms of elements prior to it. All *acts* in determinist paradigms are, in other words, treated as *behaviours*: the finality that informs the subject's actions is either considered secondary and with no real explanatory power or false (in the sense in which one speaks of *false* consciousness). Remember too that by determinism I do not mean strict determinism. In other words propositions phrased in the language of *determinist* paradigms take the form '*A* (prior to *B*) explains B'. In the case of strict determinism, these propositions assume specific forms: '*A* (prior to *B*) is the necessary condition for *B*', '*A* (prior to *B*) is the sufficient condition for *B*', and '*A* (prior to *B*) is the necessary and sufficient condition for *B*'. But here I only want to consider the general case. In the general case the word 'explained' in the proposition '*A* (prior to *B*) explains *B*' can assume any one of the three meanings that it has in a strictly determinist situation or when it has a strictly statistical meaning. The proposition is then equivalent to '*A*'s variance (prior to *B*) helps to *explain B*'s variance'. If *A* and *B* happen to be dichotomous attributes, the proposition may also be translated: 'If attribute *a* is observed then attribute *b* is (more often) observed'.[52] My perspective does not require that these different possible significations be distinguished.

But I must insist on the distinction between determinist and interactionist paradigms, in that the former treat the acts of social agents as being *wholly* explicable in terms of elements prior to these acts (structural constraints, socialisation processes etc.).

I devote just one section to determinist paradigms. I will justify this unequal treatment of the different paradigms – it favours interactionist paradigms over the others – in terms of the thesis defended here. I maintain that, however much they are used in sociology, it is essentially the *descriptive* qualities of determinist paradigms (I will explain what I mean by 'descriptive' below) that make them interesting and that, apart from that, they are nothing more than *reduced* versions of certain types of interactionist paradigms and are therefore of limited scientific interest.

I will now try and give a brief account of the three types of reductionist and determinist paradigm that figure regularly in the sociological literature and therefore seem worth distinguishing. I will then say something about the only form of determinist paradigm that seems to me a legitimate one. I have dubbed these three types *hyperfunctionalism*, *hyperculturalism* and *totalitarian realism*. I will consider each briefly in turn.

A. HYPERFUNCTIONALIST PARADIGMS

These paradigms represent a reduction of paradigms of the Mertonian type. The reader will recall that they belong to the clas of interactionist paradigms, a class with structures of interaction featuring a 'contractual' context. The concept of *role*, and its corollaries, the concepts *norm* and *value*, are indispensable here, for without them it would be impossible to describe individual acts and systems of reciprocal expectation that preside over systems of interaction. If I refer once more to the example of Mr Jones explaining the composition of water to a group of adolescents, it is only in order to point out that his behaviour is only comprehensible in terms of his being a chemistry teacher. As we have seen, in paradigms of this Mertonian type *roles* are thought of as guides to action. But these guides always offer a margin of indeterminacy. Individuals are free to interpret things in different ways, *status-sets* and *role-sets* are complex, and these three aspects of the situation are in themselves enough to explain why the contractual relations implicit in roles simply do not *determine* individuals' behaviours. There is another vital point that I would want to add to this one. The functionalists (if it is acceptable to designate by this term those who favour Mertonian-type paradigms) are well aware that some but not all of the observed actions of an individual are amenable to analysis in terms of roles. Thus Mr X *hic et nunc* treats of chemistry in front of a group of adolescents *because* he is a chemistry teacher. But role-theory cannot tell us why it is that a moment later the same Mr X, after hesitating between reading and taking a walk, chooses to take a walk. For actions arising in a 'state-of-nature' context role-theory is useless.

Hyperfunctionalist paradigms draw their inspiration from interactionist paradigms of the Mertonian type and quite simply erase the four basic distinctions cited above. Hyperfuntionalism may also be described in terms of the following axioms:

1. Every action arises in a 'contractual' context (in other words, no action arises in a 'state-of-nature' context).

2. *Role-sets* and *status-sets* are composed of complementary and non-contradictory elements.

3. The leeway for interpretation of the elements in the *role-sets* and *status-sets* is either non-existent or of no real interest.

The first axiom rules out some very basic distinctions, Consider, for example, a teacher who decided to divide his time equally between teaching and research. Role-theory can account for this choice. Or take the dentist who refuses to answer when a patient asks him what the best toothpaste is. Role-theory explains this behaviour too. But it would be absurd to use role-theory to explain why a young man decided to try and be a dentist or a teacher, or why Mr X decided to go this evening to see such and such a film. Hyperfunctionalist theories make out that choice of subject to study or job-choice are both consequences of the global role that his social origins imposed on the subject, and they thus eliminate this basic distinction entirely. There clearly are more or less strong statistical correlations between social origins and type of studies followed or type of job chosen, but that does not therefore prove that social origins can be thought of as a sort of super-role steering the subject's each and every behaviour. The second and third axioms successfully complete the first: the super-roles to which the subjects bow down are taken to be non-contradictory. The hyperfunctionalist will therefore try to show that there are convergent norms and values in various areas of behaviour that correspond to each particular type of social origin.

Apart from their tautological character, my main objection to this type of theory is as follows: they erase some clearly well-founded distinctions and introduce in their place arbitrary assimilations that do not offer any tangible advance in our knowledge and understanding of the phenomena studied. I do not see what is to be gained by considering actions as different as choice of studies and demonstrations of allegiance to medical deontology as being of the same nature.

B. HYPERCULTURALIST PARADIGMS

Hyperculturalist paradigms are a reductionist version of Weberian-type paradigms. As we have seen, the explanation of an action always implies propositions of a *determinist* type. To account for the composition of Mrs Jones's shopping basket one has to observe her tastes, her habits and many other elements that are *prior* to the particular action. Every action may well, *in the real world*, depend on elements of this type, but for the purposes of analysis they may be treated as *pertinent* or *non-pertinent*. This of course depends on the problem to be solved. If the frequency of accidents on three-lane highways or the behaviour of French landowners at the end of the *Ancien Régime* are the things to be explained, there is no point in having recourse to elements prior to the action (excepting trivial actions, of course: the drivers involved in accidents were driving in cars, the proprietors *were* landowners before buying a royal post). There are other cases in which the explanatory schema necessarily includes a consideration of elements prior to the action. But, as I have stressed, these elements may easily be incorporated into an interactionist syntax.

Hyperculturalist paradigms thus represent the sort of reduction in which action is the exclusive result of elements prior to the action.

The analytic schema is therefore as follows: Mr X's present action derives from his earlier interiorisation of such and such norms and values.[53] Schemas of this sort are often used to explain why individuals behave in a way that seems to work against their own interests. Sociologists use them generously to account for the statistical weight of an individual's social origins on his future.

Actually such schemas rarely have much credibility. Classes do assuredly have different value systems and socialisation can indeed cause behaviours ill-adapted to the interests of the acting subject to appear, but an explanatory schema that reduces an action to the effects of socialisation should always be treated very warily: the most *ritual* of acts are often incomprehensible if it is not realised that it is the presence and persistence of favourable institutions and structures of interaction that makes their ritual character possible. I may well have been raised to carry out a particular act, but if I find myself in an environment where it is difficult or harmful for me to carry it out, it is virtually certain that I will give it up and that I will adapt my behaviour to the new environment (except in the special case where costs of adaptation exceed those of non-adaptation). However well I have 'interiorised' the precepts of ecology, I shan't walk the streets of Paris indefinitely with a pile of papers I would like to get rid of, if a wastepaper bin takes a long time appearing on the horizon. In the domain of political sociology Suleiman has shown how easily a person can change role by changing function.[54] I don't see any special reason to suppose that patterns installed during the socialisation process are so systematically inflexible in relation to the changes in situation and social position that individuals may from time to time undergo. By introducing reinforcement (or non-reinforcement) effects one could probably try and maintain the stimulus-response schema that is the final result of the more or less complex detours of hyperculturalist-type paradigms. But it is hard to see what advantage this model enjoys over interactionist paradigms.[55]

C. TOTALITARIAN REALISM

I have borrowed the term 'totalitarian realism' from Piaget:

> Among the different forms of sociological explanation, there is . . . totalitarian realism: the whole is a 'being' that imposes its constraints, modifies individuals (imposes its logic on them etc.) and therefore remains heterogeneous to individual conscious-nesses such as they would be if considered separately from their socialisation.[56]

The 'totalitarian realism' paradigm may be treated as a reduction of interactionist paradigms of the Tocquevillean type. The reader will recall that in this type the structure of individual preferences depends on the particular features that, sociologically, characterise the system in which the individual is. These features partly determine the framework of individual action, at least to the extent that they determine the structure of the options available to individuals and the relative value of the different options. The case of the French merchant during the *Ancien Régime* is relevant here. Because of differences in institutional structures, this merchant and his English competitor were faced with a quite different set of choices. Circumstances do of course arise in which the options are so markedly different in value that no one will hesitate over the option to choose: the capitalist will be eliminated sooner or later by his competitors if he does not increase his enterprise's productivity.[57]

This is a limit case (in which choice is always a forced choice imposed on the individual by the 'social structure') but totalitarian realism treats it as a general paradigm. An *action*, a choice taken or a decision made are each treated here as if they were the apparent product of freely chosen ends and as the *real* product of the determining effect that social structures have on individual conduct. At worst this position culminates in that old story in which the individual is made out to be nothing more than the support of social structures, and in which the freedom of choice that the 'naïve' observer ascribes to actors is totally illusory.

Social life is clearly full of situations in which options that are in theory open are in fact limited by the cost that 'social structures' ascribe to them. Even if I were to be seized with a violent desire to assault the police officer who had just fined me, the fulfilment of this desire would have such serious consequences that I would very probably restrain myself. Social *institutions* could not exist without *limited*, and in the last analysis, *forced* choices: they all, from the simplest (doors or red lights) to the most complex (moral institutions), restrict the number of actually available choices. There are also systems of interaction that produce patterns in which the freedom enjoyed by individuals reduces people's options in general to the level of forced choices: whatever his actual wishes are, the capitalist has to increase his production the minute the others do.

But it would make little sense to eliminate the acting subject from sociology and to propose instead that every choice is really a forced one. There are clearly patterns that recur in social life but this does not imply that individual behaviours may be deduced in a more or less simple way from social structures, nor that they should be seen as the direct product of these same structures. Totalitarian realism is certainly a very attractive paradigm, and it allows one to construct theories that seem impressive enough. There are certain other extreme cases where it can be used, but any attempt to give it general currency runs up against the most flagrant of contradictions at the empirical level. The multiplicity of roles and the juxtaposition of *non-linked* behaviours engenders a number of complex effects, and because of this social change is ordinarily neither unintelligible nor amenable to straightforward deductive reasoning.

The most serious objection to these remarks stems from the fact that statistical regularities do occur. But, as I demonstrated above, their existence can in many cases be accounted for quite simply in terms of interactionist models. There is therefore no point in appealing to models derived from totalitarian realism to *explain* the steady increase in the demand for education. Individualist models of the Marxian type provide, as I have tried to show, a more illuminating explanation of this phenomenon.[58]

The three types of determinist paradigm that I have just described are so widespread that it is difficult to present illustrative examples. Sociologism (by which I mean the set constituted by hyperfunctionalism, hyperculturalism and totalitarian realism) has arguably been successful for much the same reasons as historicism. The historicist sets out to discover the necessary laws that preside over the future and takes it as axiomatic that the real is *necessary*. The *historian*, on the other hand, sets out to show why it makes sense that possibility P_1 should ensue rather than $P_2 \ldots P_n$ (for an illustration of this difference see François Furet's remarkable article, 'Le Catéchisme de la Révolution Française', *Annales*, XXVI, 2, Mar–Apr 1971, 255–89). In the same way, the sociologist is someone for whom the real is posited as necessary: it is as it is (in every case) because it cannot be otherwise; give or take a few statistical aberrations, the future of individuals and social systems is at every moment contained in their present. Sociologism's charm works in much the same way as historicism's, and both of them provide simplistic schema that make it possible with very little effort to master the complexity of societies and of their history.

D. METHODOLOGICAL DETERMINISM

This last incarnation of the determinist paradigm is the only acceptable one. It is of some importance in sociology and deserves a far more extended treatment than the one given here. Methodological determinism may be defined as a paradigm in which the only propositions used are those that both obey a determinist syntax (propositions of the type '*A* (prior to *B*) *explains B*') and yet remain compatible with interactionist interpretation. I will suppose, for the sake of a simple example, that I have calculated the coefficient of regression between socio-professional level and educational level. Assuming the coefficient of regression is positive and that its value passes a particular threshold, there is nothing to stop me from asserting that educational level (interior to socio-professional level) *explains* socio-professional level. But this raises a problem of semantics. Either I interpret the observed relation in *realist* terms, in which case I will have to superimpose an hyperculturalist, hyperfunctionalist and/or totalitarian realist interpretation on to the statistical relation, or I will interpret the relation as a synopsis of actions whose logical structure I will seek to understand at a later stage. In the latter situation I will take the statistical relation to be a descriptive fact that needs explaining and I will construct a generative model of the interactionist type to make such an explanation feasible.

A very simple example will illustrate my meaning here: demographers have observed an inverse relation between good dietary habits and birth-rates. Disregarding all other factors, a better dietary regime will automatically produce a fall in the birth-rate. A proposition of the sort '*A* (prior to *B*) explains *B*' sums up this result. But it is a *descriptive* proposition in the sense that the reason for the existence of the relation that it formulates remains obscure. This proposition can only be *explained* by applying a generative interactionist model and would interpret the result as an effect of composition. One can therefore postulate that, if a more hygienic diet does reduce infant mortality, a family unit that wishes, however obscurely, for a particular family size, may, with advances in dietary hygiene and if all else is equal, bring fewer children into the world.

These remarks would also apply to statistical analyses in which there were more complex models than those where there is merely a drop in one variable *vis-à-vis* another. In every single case it is worth taking models of causal analysis as providing a set of descriptive propositions that generative models of an interactionist kind help to explain.

To conclude this section on determinist paradigms I want to make some historical remarks that, in this context, will have to be kept fairly brief. Why is it that determinist paradigms are so much favoured in traditional sociology? I offer the following points as possible answers to this question.

1. As Leon Brunschvig[59] and Robert Nisbet[60] have both demonstrated, the birth of sociology as a separate branch of the social sciences is closely linked to the Romantic reaction against Enlightenment philosophy. The latter had fostered the notion of a Utopia founded on reason, contract, consensus and equality. After the upheavals of the French Revolution the Romantic reaction proposed an inverted Utopia in which society was based on tradition

and social distinctions, and was capable of recovering the warmth of the *Gemeinschaft*. Once sociology is institutionalised sociologists never stop referring to these themes, themes that appeared first with Bonald and Maistre. The mere fact of a link between sociology and the Romantic reaction against Enlightenment philosophy would not of itself lead me to argue for an unconditional rejection of the image of *homo sociologicus* that the latter had conveyed. But the existence of such a link does account for the suspicion that the sociologist feels for a *homo sociologicus* conceived as an intentional individual.

2. The institutionalisation of sociology coincided with a period of spectacular growth in the natural sciences, in physics and in chemistry. It is therefore not surprising that the paradigms in use in these disciplines should have been considered by the sociologists, more or less consciously, as worth imitating. This imitation was especially marked in the so-called *moral statistics* movement.

3. The phenomena with which sociology has been traditionally concerned (crime, suicide) would seem at first to be almost inaccessible to interpretations reliant on the definition of *homo sociologicus* that Enlightenment philosophy had espoused.[61]

4. Some of the sociological tradition's central concepts seem also to rule out this image. The minute one stresses the notion of *tradition* in the analysis of social behaviours, one is bound to stress *Weil-Motive* over *Wozu-Motive* (the terms derive from Schutz).[62] The reader should bear in mind here my remarks on ritual behaviours. It is only when *Weil-Motive* occur in stable structures that they provide an explanation for ritual behaviours: the walker who, obeying a *Weil-Motiv*, persists in carrying papers that he actually wants to get rid of, will naturally ask himself: *Wozu?* Why? (in that sense of *to what purpose?*)

Conclusion

I do not intend to set out yet again the typology of sociological paradigms: it is complex enough in itself and the above analysis shows it to good effect.

This analysis points to a serious imbalance between *interactionist* and *determinist* paradigms. Only the former would seem to provide an adequate basis for sociological analysis. Whenever sociologists have successfully deciphered obscure social phenomena, they have used *interactionist* analyses: the phenomena is accounted for in terms of the composite effect of individual *actions* whose logic is irreducible to schema of the stimulus-response or cause-effect kind. Even with ritual behaviours, an extreme case, the notion of intentionality can never be entirely ruled out. In any other circumstances the actors' intentions and preferences play a vital role in analysis.

More generally I would argue that sociological analysis cannot depend on a model in which individual behaviours are considered in one way or another to be the *product* of social structures. In looking to eliminate the subject's *freedom* the sociologist risks falling for reductionist paradigms.

The difficulty of adequately defining the notion of freedom is proverbial. I strove to give it a more precise meaning in the previous analysis. One should first of all insist on an ideal separation between the set of behaviours which can be adopted without consulting anyone or without gaining anyone's approval, and the set of behaviours that presuppose agreement. I can go for a walk whenever I want to and have no need to consult anyone; I can (if I am the right age and have the right qualifications) decide for or against going to university; I can buy an object today rather than tomorrow. On the other hand if I am a chemistry teacher I cannot take up geography teaching. One would naturally run into practical problems if one were to try and classify all imaginable behaviours in terms of the two categories. But the distinction is nevertheless a vital one. It was to make it more arresting that I linked it to the concepts of 'state of nature' and 'contract' as borrowed from eighteenth-century political philosophy. But these concepts have their modern equivalents: a behaviour classified as belonging to the 'state-of-nature' category belongs to the individual's private sphere or, as one can still say, to his inalienable *property rights* (the notion of property here clearly approximating to that of the ownership of objects). Ideally the *list* of these behaviours thus defines the private sphere (rights over property) or, in another idiom, the *freedoms* of the individual. Freedoms are in fact, in common usage, the behaviours that the individual may, without consulting others, assume. The social effects of these *freedoms* may not be excluded from the sociologist's domain, and their significance is well illustrated in the work of Marx and Tocqueville. In *The Ancien Régime* Tocqueville shows quite brilliantly how the choices made by French eighteenth-century merchants and landowners tended to converge and thus to produce all sorts of different social phenomena. Conversely there are all sorts of macro-social phenomena (including those which, like the distribution of towns according to their size, refer to the morphological stage) which may well be the result of an effect of composition due to the convergence of individual actions that the domain of freedoms comprises.

I want now to consider the other class of behaviours. I mean those that, because they are ordered by a 'contract', lie outside the private sphere. In another idiom these behaviours would be defined as the constituent elements of social 'roles'. They cannot, any more than the others, be reduced to stimulus-response or cause-effect schemes. In its essence a behaviour included in a role corresponds to (positive and negative) social sanctions of various types. But the notion of sanction implies that of responsibility, expectation and choice. Traffic lights and the threat of motorway police *encourage* me to stop my car, they do not *determine* my act of stopping it. On the other hand a role's contractual aspect is rarely defined with the precision one observes in the case of traffic lights or motorway infractions. My role as teacher entails a system of obligations, norms and sanctions. But these elements are extremely complex and some of them very loosely defined. There is a lot of room for interpretations, some of them mutually contradictory.

The sociologist has to take these different manifestations of individual *freedom* into account. If no attempt is made to grasp analytically the part that these different manifestations play, the fact of 'deviant' behaviours, effects of composition and social change become totally incomprehensible.

Although many have tried, the sociologist cannot *deny* the freedom that the subject enjoys. The sociological vulgate has it that it is advertising, purely and simply, that bludgeons consumers into buying things. If it really worked like that one would be quite at a loss to explain why, as Lindbeck[63] points out, advertising men have to carry out surveys into people's motivations and that, as commercial statistics show, a significant proportion of the products launched fail pitifully. The same vulgate has it that 'socio-professional' status or the educational level reached by a particular individual are the result of social determinisms. But the usually weak statistical correlations upon which this interpretation is based do not in any way imply an elimination of the notions of choice and freedom. Two individuals, one with £100 and another with £1 to his name, can hardly be said to be in an identical situation when offered the chance to participate in a fixed-structure lottery at £1 a throw. Given the structure of the lottery, the first will probably be less hesitant than the second. But this blatant correlation between financial status and readiness to participate in the lottery does not imply a determinist type of interpretation. Such an interpretation tends to have the unfortunate effect of rendering another fact totally opaque, i.e., the fact that the correlation between financial status and lottery structure may vary. To account for these variations, the individuals' situations must be treated as situations of *choice*. There are naturally enough situations in which choice is *forced*. This occurs when among all the options that are in theory available there is one that overrides the others because of the weight of the sanctions (positive or negative) associated with it. There is nothing in theory to stop me assaulting the police officer who has just fined me, but the consequences of this action will in all likelihood dissuade me. Similarly inequality has certain undeniable effects on freedom. As consumers the poor clearly have fewer options available to them than the rich do. In extreme cases it may happen that there is only one independent variable and therefore a maximum closure of options. Up to a certain threshold, I find myself *forced* to concentrate all my resources on winning my daily crust. But that is an extreme case and whilst such cases do correspond to universally observable situations, the use of determinist paradigms in their analysis would present few problems. But to treat these extreme cases as typical is to condemn oneself straight away to *simplistic* theories of the sort featured in much of the sociology of education, the sociology of consumption, and even in contemporary political sociology.

I will conclude this discussion by reminding the reader of a proposition that I have dwelt on for far too long, namely that the *effects of composition* so significant in sociological analysis may only be meaningfully analysed within interactionist-type paradigms. Only actors whose behaviour is *intentional* may produce an effect of composition like that of the *prisoner's dilemma*. Conversely, when a social phenomenon betrays the presence of an effect of the prisoner's-dilemma kind, only a language that has notions of intention, anticipation, choice and preference can do justice to it. A language not formed out of this core vocabulary has no chance of rendering intelligible the queue in front of the baker's after Mass. If one starts off with an impoverished language how can one possibly hope to understand the infinitely more complex phenomena that the sociology of education or political sociology traditionally deal with? In order to point out the importance of these *effects of composition* in sociological analysis, Marx spoke of dialectic. It is unfortunate that he also used the word in several other senses.

I want to broach another important question here. The above analysis showed that it was possible to identify many different interactionist paradigms in sociology. This tends to separate sociology off from economic theory which, by and large, depends on a paradigm known traditionally as *methodological individualism*. This instantly raised an epistemological problem: if a discipline uses several types of paradigm at once, what logical coherence can it have?

The answer to this question is, as a matter of fact, simpler than it seems. Take an elementary behaviour and try to analyse it *exhaustively*; for instance Mrs Jones's behaviour in filling her shopping basket. Suppose that she has finally opted for a series of products bought at particular prices and in particular quantities. Let the vector Q represent her basket. How do we explain Q? The following aspects would have to feature in the explanation:

1. Evidence concerning Mrs Jones' socialisation (she knows how to prepare one dish rather than another; she is used to 'saving' or to spending freely; she has a prejudice against jam);

2. Evidence concerning her resources (both financial and cognitive: a product may, for example, not be on her shopping list because she doesn't know of it);

3. Some representation of her ultimate purpose (to get all the foodstuffs necessary to feed a family for a given period);

4. Evidence concerning her underlying values (the importance of a good diet, meal structures, balance between different meals; ideal period for the purchases to cover);

5. Evidence concerning the structural constraints at work in the environment (family size, individuals' appetites, refrigerator size);

6. Evidence concerning the constraints imposed by the social system as a whole (the price of product *A*, substitute for product *B*, is twice that of product *B*);

7. Evidence concerning the way these constraints alter over time and the way in which Mrs Jones comes to perceive them (the price of product *A* has increased by 20 per cent since last month but Mrs Jones's memory is a little hazy here and she *believes* that it increased by 30 per cent);

8. Evidence concerning Mrs Jones's possible misapprehensions as to the various options (there are cherries on the market but she has not seen them).

This list is by no means exhaustive but it does give a fair idea of the sort of schema that the attempt to understand a particular action almost invariably demands.

But the analysis of particular actions was never my main concern here, and is seldom of interest to the sociologist. I am concerned rather to convey the logic of particular actions by explaining social phenomena presumed to be the consequence of these actions. The complex schema that exhaustive description of a particular action requires may, and in most cases must, take on a much simpler form. To analyse a particular person's decision to invest one would have to have recourse to a complex schema of the kind just described. Similarly if one wanted to explain why a particular landowner acquired a royal office at Romorantin in 1775, on would need to know in some detail where his property was, what his resources were, what sort of life he led, who the town's notables were, what his social network was, and so on. But if one simply wants to explain why French landowners tended to neglect their land more than the English did, a much simpler schema will do: one only has to note the structural facts that differed in each case and the different systems of options and values that this difference produced. A simple schema presuming a rational decision-maker, will work well enough here, and one can conclude that since option O^1 is offered more often than O^2 in France and is more prestigious (compared with England), that people will also tend to choose it more often. Tocqueville adopts an elementary schema for this example: action is presumed to be intentional, rational and utilitarian. This does not mean that Tocqueville considers every action to be reducible to this schema but merely that it provides a satisfactory explanation of the phenomenon with which he is concerned. In other words the *utilitarian* representation of the action in this analysis is meant to imply for it a methodological and not an ontological status: a utilitarian schema is all that this analysis needs, even if this schema seems unrealistic the minute a real example is considered. One could say the same of Marx's example (to which I alluded earlier): a particular person's decision to invest invariably implies a complex schema. But a far simpler schema will show quite clearly the kind of logic that drives everyone in a capitalist system to raise their productivity just because other people are raising theirs.

This example was meant to highlight the following proposition: whilst I hold that interactionist models are the only ones that are of any use in explaining social phenomena, I also maintain that such models may differ in their complexity and may alter with the phenomena to be explained. One can see from the work of Tocqueville, Marx and Merton, to cite only them, that a simple schema will often account quite effectively for complex social phenomena. This goes for the representation of structural constraints as well. There are circumstances in which it is possible to do as Marx does and classify agents in terms of a small number of social groups differentiated by their resources. Merton does this too in his analysis of the vicious circle of unemployment in which blacks were caught after the First World War. There are other circumstances in which a more complex description of structural constraints is necessary. There are also analyses in which the introduction of cognitive elements is implied (in the preceding example, whites believe that the blacks are actually not able to demonstrate their solidarity with the unions). There are other analyses in which there seems little point in introducing them: Olson's theory shows that this aspect can safely be ignored, if one wants to understand why someone who provides *collective* goods will be considerably more successful if he is in a position to offer his potential clientele individual goods and services. If a phenomenon is generated by a set of independent actions in a state of nature or by actions occurring in a contractual context, different sorts of paradigm will then be needed. The concept of role is useless in the first case and vital in the second. More or less irrelevant in the analysis of the increase in the demand for education, it becomes indispensable if one wants to explain why, in the case of American students in the sixties, the better the university the more unhappy they were with their teachers.

I hold, in other words, that a paradigm may not be judged on an ontological level but only on a methodological one. Rational psychology is clearly inadequate for explaining neurosis, but it is clearly up to explaining many daily behaviours, and those that concern the sociologist in particular. Whilst structural constraints may be very complex there are many circumstances in which simple descriptions will suffice (social classes in Marx, blacks and whites in Merton). It would be unrealistic to suppose that individuals always have a precise idea of the options available to them and of their respective advantages and disadvantages. But one can *often* argue that on *average* if option O_1 is preferable to option O_2 this will be perceived. A paradigm cannot in short be called true or false, realistic or unrealistic. It may however be better or worse adapted to the phenomenon one seeks to analyse.

With regard to the coherence of sociological paradigms I would in the end argue as follows: first I would propose that a paradigm's pertinence is crucially dependent on the research context and above all on the structure of the phenomenon being studied. Secondly I would argue that the different types of interactionist paradigm be distinguished one from another, not because of syntactical differences but because of differences in the sort of *evidence* considered. In some but not in all cases it is pertinent to introduce evidence concerning the effect of socialisation processes; in other cases evidence of this kind is bracketed out, excluded from the explanatory schema. In some but not in all cases it is pertinent to introduce evidence concerning the sanctions that a subject will run up against in opting for O_1 or O_2. This sub-division may on the other hand be usefully disregarded when the phenomena studied encourage one to consider the actions of which it is composed as deriving from a *state of nature*.

The different types of interactionist paradigm are in short produced by in each case bracketing out the different sorts of evidence in turn. But these different types share a *syntactical unity* which may be attributed to the logical atom of which they are composed, the notion of individual action or of intentional behaviour.

On the other hand determinist and interactionist paradigms have a radically different syntax, since the first only allows propositions that take the form '*A* (prior to *B*) explains (in the different senses of the word 'explain') *B*'.

Notes

CHAPTER 1

1. The Unanticipated Consequences of Purposive Social Action', *American Sociological Review* I (1936) 894–904. Merton also quotes Vico and Bossuet and could clearly have cited Spinoza too.
2. (Paris: Colin, 1973).
3. 'Note on the Appearance of Wisdom in Large Bureaucratic Organisations', *Behavioural Science* (Jan. 1961) 62–78.
4. 'The Unanticipated Consequences . . .', op. cit.
5. My interpretation of Goethe's text is confirmed by that of George Lukacs in his *Goethe und seine Zeit*.
6. Cf., for example, A. Etzioni, *The Active Society* (London: Macmillan, 1968).

CHAPTER 2

1. Karl Popper, *Misère de l'Historicisme* (Paris: Plon, 1956).
2. Gabriel Tarde, *Les Lois de l'Imitation* (Paris: Alcan, 1890).
3. Lynn White, *Mediaeval Technology and Social Change* (New York: Macmillan, 1930).
4. Henri Mendras, *The Vanishing Peasant: Innovation and Change in French Agriculture*, transl. J. Lerner (Cambridge, Mass.: MIT Studies in Comparative Politics, 1970).
5. Alain Touraine, *Production de la Société* (Paris: Seuil, 1973).
6. Ralf Dahrendorf, *Class and Class Conflict in Industrial Society* (Stanford: Stanford University Press, 1959).
7. 'Discourse on the origins of inequality', in Jean-Jacques Rousseau, *The Social Contract and Discourses*, transl. and introd. G. D. H. Cole (London: Everyman's University Library, 1973). The widespread refusal in France to undertake an individualist and utilitarian reading of Rousseau's political work may perhaps be attributed to Michelet (cf. *History of the French Revolution*, transl. C. Cocks, ed. and introd. G. Wright, Chicago, Ill.: Classic European Histories, 1967) who, in opposing what we would today call the intuitionism of *La Profession de foi du vicaire savoyard* to the utilitarianism of the *Contract*, accuses Rousseau of 'inconsistency'.

8. Lester C. Thurow, 'Education and Economic Equality', in *The Public Interest* (Summer 1972) 66–81.
9. It is not feasible to present here a bibliography of the works dealing with the economics of education. The reader is advised to consult the very useful collection of texts assembled by UNESCO: *Textes choisis sur l'économie de l'éducation* (Paris: UNESCO, 1968).
10. Thurow shows that there is not only a correlation between these phenomena, there is also a relationship of cause and effect. I come back to this text later in order to demonstrate this.
11. *Conférence sur les politiques de développement de l'enseignement* (Paris: OECD, 1972).
12. Raymond Boudon, *Education, Opportunity and Social Inequality: Changing Prospects in Western Society* (New York: Wiley Series in Urban Research, Wiley, 1974).
13. Because the model refers to an ideal type rather than to a particular industrial society, it is difficult to synchronise the model's time with real time. It may help to understand it better if I point out that the time-interval separating the two successive periods of the model is approximately equal to five years. One can then deduce from the model a set of growth curves that are close to those observable at the level of educational accounting.
14. Thomas Farraro and Kenji Koseka have produced a mathematical formalisation of parts of the models used in 'Educational Opportunity and Social Inequality: Changing Prospects in Western Society : A Mathematical Analysis of Boudon's IEO Model, *Information sur les sciences sociales*, XV (1976) 2–3. This is a part of the symposium devoted to *Educational Opportunity and Social Inequality* and published in the same journal.
15. S. M. Lipset and R. Bendix, *Social Mobility in Industrial Societies* (Berkeley, Calif.: University of California Press, 1958).
16. S. M. Lipset, 'Social Mobility and Educational Opportunity', *The Public Interest*, XXIX (Autumn 1972) 90–108.
17. Mancur Olson, *The Logic of Collective Action* (Cambridge, Mass.: Harvard University Press, 1965).
18. Thus in France, the overall rate of unionisation is 20 per cent but is as much as 75 per cent in educational institutions, cf. *Le Monde*, 13 Oct. 1976. There do of course exist various obstacles to participation in Unions (intimidation, lack of the relevant information etc.). But Olson's theory shows that even when such factors are not operative participation is normally reduced when the union produces only collective benefits and is not able to force people to participate.
19. See Robert Michels, *Political Parties*, (New York: Dover, 1959).
20. Besides, the form of the consultation generally escapes the consultants. I think it is fair to say that there are specific sets of conditions that have to be operative if the constituents are to use a consultation effectively in order to correct the line followed by the oligarchy.
21. Michels is only cited once by Olson and then merely in passing.
22. In other situations the dialectical notion of *contradiction* should be compared with the *defective equilibrium* structures of game theory.

23. Albert O. Hirschman, *Exit, Voice and Loyalty*, (Cambridge, Mass.: Harvard University Press, 1970).

24. 'Defection' et 'prise de parole' dans la traduction française.

25. Harold Hotelling, 'Stability in Competition', *Economic Journal*, XXXIX (1929) 41–57. It would be simple enough to imagine other variants of Hotelling's model besides the ones that Hirschman presents. Take a multi-party system that a change in the form of voting had caused to veer drastically towards bipolarisation. To work out the position of each of the original formations one would certainly need to take into account the *cost* of the ideological displacement brought about by the institutional change.

26. Anthony Downs, *An Economic Theory of Democracy* (New York: Harper & Brothers, 1956).

27. Buchanan and Tullock, *The Calculus of Consent* (Ann Arbor, Mich.: University of Michigan Press, 1965).

28. Op. cit.

29. Thomas Schelling, 'On the Ecology of Micromotives', *The Public Interest* XXV (Autumn 1971) 61–98, and 'Dynamic Models of Segregation', *Journal of Mathematical Sociology* (1971) 143–85.

30. Cf. *Social and Cultural Dynamic*, (New York: Bedminster Press, 1962).

CHAPTER 3

1. Raymond Boudon, 'La Crise Universitaire Française: essai de diagnostic', *Annales*, XXIV (May–June 1969) 738–64; idem., 'Sources of Student Protest in France', *Annals of the American Academy of Political Science*, CCCXCV (May 1971) 139–49. (Reprinted in Philip G. Altbach and Robert S. Laufer (eds), *The New Pilgrims: Youth Protest in Transition* (New York: D. McKay, 1972).

2. There are several exceptions. For example the *baccalauréat* is not required for admission to the University of Vincennes which was created in 1968.

3. These random factors may include the creation of either new institutions like the *Instituts Universitaires de Technologie* (IUT) or new channels within old institutions, such as the masters programmes in science and technology.

4. Edward F. Denison, *The Sources of Economic Growth in the United States and the Alternatives Before Us* (New York: Committee for Economic Development, 1962).

5. On the history of the French educational system in the nineteenth and twentieth centuries see Antoine Prost, *L'Enseignement en France, 1800–1967* (Paris: Armand Colin, 1968).

6. Study by the *Centre d'Études et de Recherches sur les Qualifications* (CEREQ), *L'Accès à la vie professionelle à la sortie des universités*, document no. 26 (Paris, 1975).

7. For basic data on the feminisation of the French university system see *Ministère de l'Éducation/Secretariat d'État aux Universités, Études et Documents,*

no. 31 (Paris, 1975); and *Service des Études Informatiques et Statistiques/Service Central des Statistiques et Sondages*, document no. 4.614 (Paris, 1975).

8. It is ironic to note that at the time when the French university system seems, to say the least, not optimally adapted to the 'needs' of the economic system, a fairly large part of French sociology of education attempts to show that the sole objective of this teaching system is to produce adequate manpower at different levels of socio-professional categories. See, for example, Pierre Bourdieu and Jean Claude Passeron, *La Reproduction* (Paris, 1970); Claude Baudelot and Roger Establet, *L'École capitaliste en France* (Paris: Maspéro, 1971); and Viviane Isambert, 'L'École adaptée à la division du travail', *Le Monde de l'Éducation*, no. 4 (Mar. 1975). Interestingly enough, these theses were put forth and received a great deal of publicity at a time when it was becoming evident that a large proportion of the students of the old 'faculties' (colleges of letters and sciences), representing about 50 per cent of all students, were facing considerable difficulty in finding employment. For many years these students had been absorbed by the teaching profession itself, but thereafter a combination of various factors (demographic factors and changes in the demand for education, etc.) changed the situation, thereby causing a gap between the university system and the economy.

   Research data confirm the traditional importance of the auto-reproductive function of the educational system. See for example the monograph by Boudon and François Bourricaud, 'Le choix professionel des lycéens'. (DGRST convention, 1968), which draws on a sample of 12 to 13 year old students and shows that a very large percentage of them plan to go into teaching.

9. These factors stem in part from fairly well-known demographic phenomena, and in part from long-term and short-term changes in the demand for education which are unfortunately not well understood. The rapid rise in the demand for education since 1960 might reveal a tendency toward saturation – a phenomenon which remains to be studied, social category by social category. Conversely it is plausible that the social devaluation of school and university degrees resulting from the inflationary process we have witnessed in recent years could bring about a backlash effect that would tend to readjust downward the individual demand for education. These problems, although fascinating from the point of view of the sociology of education and for an analysis of the social system and the relationship between the individual level and the macro-sociological level, have not been explored thoroughly to date, at least not in the French case. A useful reference on the evolution of the 'needs' of the French social system for teaching personnel over the period of the last two decades is to be found in Alain Norvez, 'Les Enseignants du second degré en France: effectifs actuels et besoins futurs', Doctoral diss., Third Cycle, Sorbonne/Université de Paris.

10. It must be noted that on the average these students are absorbed at a relatively low professional level. A research study by Philippe Vrain, *Les Débouchés professionnels des étudiants* (Paris, 1973), shows that a sample of teachers with a *licence* who graduated in 1966 earned an average of

F. 1502 (for men) and F. 1391 (for women). These figures are computed in 1970 francs.

11. This *arrêté* of 16 Jan. 1976 was published on 20 Jan. 1976 in the *Journal Officiel*. It was completed by a *circulaire* urging the universities to create new channels leading to professional degrees. These decisions provoked a heterogeneous opposition movement; 'traditional' teachers sometimes perceived it as a threat against certain university disciplines which were considered intellectually noble but which had no practical application (i.e. Latin and Greek); leftist teachers saw in them an objectionable attempt to integrate the university system into the economic system. See the editorials in *Le Monde*, 22 Jan. 1976.

12. The following discussion draws on Boudon, Philippe Cibois and Janina Lagneau, 'L'Enseignement supérieur court et pièges de l'action collective', *Revue Française de Sociologie*, XVI (Apr.–June 1975); 'Short-Cycle Higher Education and the Pitfalls of Collective Action', *Minerva*, XIV (Spring 1976). See also Lagneau, 'L'Enseignement supérieur court en France', *La Documentation Française*, no. 4001 (29 June 1973).

13. The '*propédeutique*' (university preparatory class), created in 1947 for the sciences and in 1948 for liberal arts, consisted of one year of general studies at the end of which students selected a narrow field of specialisation.

14. In 1968 the IUTs were one of the targets of the academicians' 'movement'. Petitions were signed stressing that the IUTs were a threat to the traditional university system because of their professional objectives. These petitions revived the classic theme that the IUTs had been essentially designed to dissuade poorer students from enrolling in long university studies and to force them to take the less desirable positions in the socio-professional hierarchy. In short the IUTs were presented as a manoeuvre to strengthen those forces that ensured the perpetuation of existing social classes. Again it is interesting to note that these charges were subsequently contradicted by the facts. The income level of IUT graduates is *not* lower than that of university graduates. On the other hand the slowness with which the IUTs developed does not enable them to play the essential role which was assigned to them. On the topic of the IUTs consult the article by John H. van de Graaff, 'Politics of Innovation in French Higher Education: the University Institutes of Technology', *Higher Education*, no. 2 (1976). The article is well documented, but I would hesitate to agree with the author in his claim that IUTs are 'a modestly successful innovation'. The disappointment of the government in the 'modesty' of this success was considerable, as I have tried to show. Even if it is true that IUT students are on the average from lower social backgrounds than those of other institutions, I do not think that this difference should be overrated. The 'democratization' of the student body is primarily due to the traditional universities. The IUTs' contribution to this is only marginal.

15. Ministry of Education, *Direction Générale de la Programmation et de la Coordination, Bilan d'exécution du VIe Plan dans le Domaine de l'Éducation* (Paris, Sep. 1975).

16. The last figure (17 per cent) overestimates the percentage of scholarship

recipients among Second-Cycle students. In fact it relates to *all* students (short and long cycles). Moreover the percentage of scholarship holders among short-programme students is far higher than the percentage of recipients among long-cycle students. On the other hand the students in the long programme represent only a small portion of the entire student population. All of this suggests that the percentage of scholarship holders among long-cycle students should be realistically closer to 13 per cent. Thus the IUT students have about three times more chance of getting a scholarship than the long-cycle students. Despite the differences in the composition of the two sub-populations, it is undeniable that in the distribution of scholarships the IUTs were clearly favoured. Recent studies dealing with student resources show that there is a fairly high uniformity of resources across all different social categories. The combination of family resources, public aid and income from employment brings all students to a comparable level of resources. Besides, the differences between social categories in relation to paid employment as a source of income have decreased considerably between 1963 and 1973.

17. A research study by the CEREQ, 'L'Accès à la vie professionnelle à la sortie des Instituts Universitaires de Technologie', *La Documentation Française*, dossier no. 7 (Paris, June 1973), shows that in 1971 10.2 per cent of male students who left the IUTs in 1969 were earning less than 1200 francs. This percentage was 14.4 per cent in 1970 for a sampling of teachers who received their licence in 1966. (See Vrain, *Les Débouchés professionnels* . . ., op. cit.) On the other hand the same two studies stress that 17.3 per cent of certified teachers have an income of 2000 francs or more, as opposed to 10.2 per cent of IUT graduates.

18. It is useful to note that the economic reasoning I am using in this article, as well as in several of my previous publications in the area of the sociology of education, is not well received and sometimes considered a kind of heresy by many French sociologists, especially by those who have worked in the area of the sociology of education themselves. Individual demand for education is generally interpreted by these sociologists not as a result of the individuals' effort to make a reasonable investment in line with their resources, but rather as an automatic result of their social origins. This prevailing interpretation may have had an impact on French politics in the area of education. In-depth studies would be essential to the further exploration of this problem but it does seem that the failure of certain political measures comes from the fact that there was a failure to analyse changes in the behaviour of the participants, perhaps explaining why the failure of the IUTs surprised many observers. For my own approach to the sociology of education, see my *Education, Opportunity and Social Inequality* (New York, 1974).

19. Medical schools are an exception in that enrolment is not open. The 1968 law contained certain optional provisions which allowed the universities to regulate enrolments, but these provisions have remained a dead letter. Article 21 of the general 1968 law stipulates that 'the universities are to provide organisation by way of units of teaching and

research, by orientation workshops for newly admitted students when they deem it necessary to test the students' aptitude for the field the students are undertaking.' This provision was the target of student protests.

20. On the history of French university reforms from 1950 to the 1968 law, see Bourricaud, 'La réforme universitaire en France après 1945 et ses déboires', monograph (GEMAS, Maison des Sciences de l'Homme, 1976).

21. Louis Lévy-Garboua, 'Les Demandes de l'étudiant ou les contradictions de l'université de masse', *Revue Française de Sociologie*, XVII (Jan.–Mar. 1976) 53–80.

22. It is evident that discussions about the drop in student quality are as frequent as they are useless. It seems certain however that an average decrease in the time devoted to studying must be accompanied by a lowering in the quality of education.

23. See Cibois and Lagneau, *Les étudiants dans l'enseignement supérieur court: France, Grande-Bretagne et Yugoslavie* (OECD: Paris, 1976). This book presents the results of a study of IUT students, demonstrating that students consider the IUTs to be superior to the universities with respect to career possibilities, quality of teaching, the level of interest of course content and general atmosphere.

24. Pierre Oléron, 'Opinions d'étudiants en psychologie, sur leurs études et leur future profession', *Bulletin de Psychologie*, XX, no. 222 (Jan. 1967) 329–45; Oléron and M. Moulinou, 'Données statistiques sur un échatillon d'étudiants en psychologie', *Bulletin de Psychologie*, XXI, no. 263 (Oct. 1967) 1–4; Raymond Poignant, *L'Enseignement dans les Pays du Marché Commun* (Paris: Institut Pedagogique National, 1965). Poignant estimated that the French universities would double in size before 1968. A 1974 CREDOC study, quoted by Lévy-Garboua, shows the low rate of success in various levels of university programmes. Michel Amiot, *et al.*, *L'appareil universitaire et le marché de l'emploi urbain* (Paris: Centre d'Étude des Mouvements Sociaux, Maison des Sciences de l'Homme 1974–6), show (in five booklets of research on the academic future of a group of students at Lille and Nice) the prevalence of the pattern of change in orientation by students in the middle of their course of study.

25. *Le Monde*, 23–24 Dec. 1975, entitled an article '52 per cent Voter Turnout in 1969, 25 per cent in 1972, the Indifference of the Students toward University Elections is Confirmed'. In fact we are dealing not with a continual decline, but a sudden one which appears with the second elections. During the 1970–1 elections overall voter participation was 23 per cent. Since 1972 the rate has stabilised near 25 per cent. The rates of participation are much higher in the IUTs and the institutions organised as a *school* rather than as a *university* (more class hours, stricter attendance and workload obligations, more channelled curriculum, etc.). During the same elections, while the University of Rennes had an average voting rate of 30 per cent the Rennes IUT had a 62 per cent participation rate; the Lannion IUT, attached to Rennes but located in a smaller town, had an 87 per cent turnout. At Toulouse III, the average rate was 43 per cent. The UERs in 'fundamental scientific fields' have voter

participation lower than this average (organic chemistry, 13 per cent; mathematics, 20 per cent; experimental physical sciences, 20 per cent). The UERs in applied fields and leading to a specific professional degree have rates higher than this average (odontology, 78 per cent; medical sciences, 54 and 57 per cent; physical education, 71 per cent; IUTs, 61 per cent).

26. We observe fairly important social protest movements by certain groups of physicists, for example. See Jean-Marc Lévy-Leblond and Alain Jaubert, *(Auto)critique de la science* (Paris: Editions de Seuil, 1973.)

27. We find 'guides' of this type in *Le Point*, no. 193, 31 May 1976; *Le Nouvel Observateur*, no. 591, 8–14 Mar. 1976; *Le 'Monde' de l'Éducation*, no. 19 (July–Aug. 1976).

28. Mancur Olson, *The Logic of Collective Action* (Cambridge, Mass.: Harvard University Press, 1965.)

29. Before 1968 appointments were made by the entire faculty, including professors from all fields. This process has been maintained only in a few institutions, such as the *Collège de France*. In all others appointments are made at the department.level.

30. Julien Benda, *La France Byzantine* (Paris: Grasset, 1945).

31. See on this point Michel Crozier and Joseph L. Bower, *The Changing Role of the Intellectual in Modern Society* (Paris: *Centre de Sociologie des Organisations*, 1971); Alfred Grosser, 'Une Nouvelle Trahison des clercs?' *Contrepoint*, no. 10 (1973), 37–51; Bernard Cazes, 'Experts et prophètes?,' *Contrepoint*, no. 10 (1973); Crozier, 'The Cultural Revolution', *Daedalus* (Dec. 1963).

32. Lewis Coser, 'The Intellectual as Celebrity', *Dissent*, XX (1973) 45–56.

33. The intellectual '*tout-Paris*' as an institution has also played an important role in the past. Consult on this topic the essay by Terry N. Clark, *Prophets and Patrons: The French University and the Emergence of the Social Sciences* (Cambridge, Mass.: Harvard University Press, 1973). This study shows how nineteenth-century university and professional institutions, together with what I call the '*tout-Paris*' of the intellectuals and which he calls the Latin Quarter culture, constitutes a mutually complementary system.

34. This over-investment is in reality not 'required' by anyone. The 'requirement' comes simply from institutions and the rationalisation of individuals functioning within these institutions.

35. See references in note 1.

36. Albert Hirschmann, *Exit, Voice and Loyalty* (Cambridge, Mass.: Harvard University Press, 1970).

CHAPTER 4

1. More precisely, in cases where access to long-cycle higher education is 'free', i.e., subject only to completion of secondary school.

2. In fact the invention of this example is attributed to Tucker. In this respect see Martin Shubick, *Game Theory and Related Approaches to Social Behaviour* (New York: Wiley, 1964). On the importance of the prisoner's dilemma in the political writings of Rousseau, see W. G. Runciman, and

A. K. Sen, 'Games, Justice, and the General Will', *Mind*, LXXIV, 296 (Oct. 1965), pp. 554–62. See also R. Boudon, 'Justice sociale et intérêt général, à propos de la théorie de la justice de Rawls', *Revue française de science politique*, XXV, 2 (Apr. 1975), pp. 193–221. In fact this type of structure and other unbalanced structures can readily be found in all those authors – Thucydides, Rousseau, Tocqueville, Marx, etc. – who have paid particular attention to what we now call aggregations of individual action.

3. See J. Lagneau, 'L'Enseignement supérieur court en France', *Documentation française: notes et études documentaires*, no. 4001 (June 1973); P. Cibois, and J. Lagneau, *Bilan de l'enseignement supérieur court: Grande-Bretagne, France, Yougoslavie* (Paris: OECD, 1975).

4. In social science unit of one of the Parisian universities for example, in 1971–2, only 104 out of 297 students in the final year of the first cycle of sociological studies had not studied any subject previously in the course of their work at university. The remaining two-thirds included: 53 graduates in arts and sciences; 30 graduates in economics and political science; 14 graduates in law; 24 who had graduated from either a school of higher commercial studies or the science faculties; 10 graduates of the *Institut des Sciences Politiques*; 5 graduates in law and political science; and 8 graduates in medicine.

5. This theme has been dealt with in detail in R. Boudon, *L'Inégalité des chances* (Paris: Colin, 1973). On the relationship between average income over the life-cycle and level of instruction, see R. Pohl, C. Thelot and M. P. Jousset, 'L'Énquête formation-qualification professionelle de 1970', INSEE, no. 129 (*INSEE Collections*, series D, no. 32, May 1974): 'Ancienneté, niveau d'instruction et salaires', *Population et Sociétés, Institut National d'Études Démographiques*, newsletter, no. 76 (Jan. 1975).

6. See, in this respect, J. C. Eicher, and A. Mingat, *Éducation et égalité en France*, Proceedings of Seminar on Education, Inequality, Life Chances, Paris, 6–9 Jan. 1975 (Paris: OECD, 1975). See also, A. Mingat, J. Perrot, *Transferts sociaux et éducation* (Dijon: *Institut de recherche sur l'economie de l'education, Université de Dijon, Faculté de science économique et de gestion*, Sept. 1974) mimeographed.

7. Readers interested in details relating to the establishment of the IUTs will find a wealth of information in Y. Bernard, *Les Instituts universitaires de technologie* (Paris: Dunod, 1970); and J. L. Cremieux-Brilhac, *L'Éducation nationale* (Paris: Presses Universitaires de France, 1965).

8. Report to the Prime Minister recommending the establishment of IUTs, quoted from J. I. Boursin, *Les instituts universitaires de technologie* (Paris and Montreal: Bordas, 1970) p. 14.

9. Ibid, p. 10.

10. Ibid, p. 29.

11. The so-called 'Article 35' Committee on various ministerial decrees governing access to opportunities for study; cited by J. L. Boursin, op. cit. p. 151.

12. At the time of writing – 9 Mar. 1975.

13. See two studies carried out by the *Ministère de l'Éducation Nationale: Centre d'Études et de Recherches sur les Qualifications* (CEREQ), *Insertion professionnelle*

des anciens étudiants des IUT, no. 10 Aug. 1972; and *Direction Chargée de la Prévision, Groupe de Travail IUT-STS, note intermédiaire,* 15 Jan. 1973 (mimeographed).

14. *Ministère de l'Éducation Nationale, Direction des Objectifs, Groupe de Travail IUT-STS, dossier de travail,* Sept. 1973, preliminary note, p. 8.

15. Level III refers to persons occupying posts normally requiring two years' education following the *baccalauréat.* See, *Bulletin officiel de l'education nationale,* no. 29 (20 July 1967).

16. *Ministère de l'Éducation Nationale, Direction Chargée de la Prévision,* op. cit.

17. The differences between table 4.4 and table 4.5 regarding France result from the fact that the OECD study included in its definition of short-cycle higher education the candidates for the legal practitioners' qualification and students' preparatory classes for the *Grandes Écoles.*

18. Although the proportion of scholarship-holders declined in both the universities and the IUTs in 1972–3, the difference between the two remained similar; the corresponding percentages were 36 per cent and 11 per cent respectively (*Ministère de l'Éducation Nationale, Statistiques et sondages,* document 4414, Oct. 1973).

19. *Centre d'études et de recherches sur les qualifications.* op. cit.

20. Of course this is only a very rough comparison. Median earnings shown in table 4.8 are slightly lower than the corresponding average earnings not shown in the table. By and large the difference amounts to about F. 100. This difference arises from the tendency of income distributions to take the form of a log-normal curve.

21. CEREQ, 'L'Accès à la vie professionnelle à la sortie des Instituts Universitaires de Technologie', *Documentation française,* dossier no. 7, June 1973.

22. P. Cibois and J. Lagneau, op. cit., p. 91.

23. Of course we are aware of the possibility that these attitudes of IUT students derive to some extent from a 'rationalisation effect'. Unfortunately no data are available on the way the IUTs are perceived by non-IUT students i.e., long-cycle students or secondary school students.

24. The survey from which these results were taken formed the French section of an international study undertaken on behalf of the OECD, which also included a survey of short-cycle higher education in Great Britain and Yugoslavia. In Great Britain, the percentages were 12 per cent 'satisfied', 50 per cent 'opponents', 11 per cent 'converts' and 22 per cent 'disappointed'. Yugoslavia occupied an intermediate position between those of France and Great Britain.

25. This is the estimate given by IUT directors and expert education authorities.

26. See, for example, C. Baudelot and R. Establet, *L'École capitaliste en France* (Paris: Maspero, 1971); P. Bourdieu and J. C. Passeron, *La Reproduction* (Paris: Éditions de Minuit, 1970); and V. Isambert, 'L'École ajustée à la division du travail', *Le monde de l'éducation,* 4 (Mar. 1975).

27. We would recall that this model applies to the countries of Western Europe but not to the United Kingdom and the United States for example, both of which are characterised by different institutional

combinations, e.g., general selectiveness of access to long-cycle higher education. Concerning short-cycle higher education in the United States, see Jerome Karabel, 'Community Colleges and Social Stratification', *Harvard Educational Review*, XLII, 4 (Nov. 1972) 521–62.

28. Of course the comparative evaluation of costs is difficult, since long-cycle students spend more years at school but are subjected to less intensive work, so that they can more easily obtain additional income from part-time employment.

29. See, for example, Gary Becker, *Human Capital* (New York: National Bureau of Economic Research, 1964); Mark Blaug (ed.), *Economics of Education* (Harmondsworth: Penguin Books, 1968); Lloyd Reynolds, *Labor Economics and Labor Relations* (Englewood Cliffs, N.J.: Prentice Hall, 1974), 6th ed.; and L. Lévy-Garboua, 'Les Inégalités intergénérationnelles dans la société française' (Paris: *Centre de Recherches et de Documentation sur la Consommation* [CREDOC], 1974).

30. J. Lagneau, 'L'enseignement supérieur court en France', *Documentation française: Notes et études documentaires*, 4001 (June 1973) 25.

31. The *licence* is equivalent to the bachelor of arts or other first degree. The proportion of entrants who successfully completed the course for the IUT diploma were 90 per cent, 80 per cent, 70 per cent, 76 per cent and 75 per cent, respectively, for the five classes entering between 1966 and 1971.

32. Our strategy in this analysis has been to use a model as simple as possible. It is known that $\Sigma px = y$ does not necessarily imply that the *utility* of Σpx is equal to the *utility* of y. I can very well not be indifferent to the following event, for example: earn one franc with probability one, and the event: earn two francs with the probability of one-half, and 0 with the probability of one half. Given the general nature of the model, we have chosen to neglect this point.

33. In fact this hypothesis would be totally unrealistic if we were concerned here to analyse the alternatives of the university and the *Grandes Écoles*. Only those students who, judging from their results at the end of their secondary education, consider themselves better than the others, decide to enter the preparatory classes for the *Grandes Écoles*. The hypothesis is less unrealistic in the comparison of the alternatives of IUT and university. This is so because the *baccalauréat* is both the sufficient and nearly always necessary condition for entrance to the university. It is not unreasonable to suppose that in the group which does not seek admission to the *Grandes Écoles* each student considers himself more or less as good as the others. As a result of gaps in our knowledge concerning candidates for entrance to the IUT, we cannot compare the distribution of distinctions in the *baccalauréat* in this group with that of the students in the long-cycle stream.

34. Even in certain severe competitions, like the *agrégation*, one encounters students for whom confidence in their success is part of a long tradition. They see it as a vital factor in their success: 'confidence breeds success'.

35. *Agrégation* and *CAPES* (*Certificat d'aptitude à l'enseignement secondaire*) are degrees which automatically give access to a permanent post as a secondary school teacher. The former has more prestige and provides a

higher income than the latter.

36. In reality most students probably do not worry about the numbers likely to choose long-cycle higher education. They probably make the assumption which is the most realistic assumption for France: namely that a large proportion of potential students will choose long-cycle higher education.

37. B. Girod de l'Ain, 'Trois exemples d'accès à l'enseignement supérieur', *Le monde de l'éducation*, 4 (Mar. 1975) 20–1, provides an excellent treatment of this subject.

38. Unlike many classical sociologists from Rousseau to Marx and Pareto, contemporary sociologists are reluctant to employ the paradigm of *homo economicus* in their analysis. No doubt this is partly due to the influence of Durkheim on modern sociology and to the fact that Durkheim's sociology was developed in opposition to the utilitarian tradition, which has been the permanent central feature of economics and which played an important role in sociology until Durkheim's time. The present essay in no way wishes to propose an unconditional return to the utilitarian paradigm. It merely shows that in certain cases, depending upon the nature of the problem being dealt with and the analytical level, this paradigm may turn out more effective than others. Needless to say, a return to a utilitarian sociology would be just as sterile as anti-utilitarian sociology.

39. It is interesting to note that even such authors as Runciman and Sen ('Games, Justice, and the General Will', loc. cit.), who base their interpretation of the *Contrat social* on Rousseau's discovery of the existence of 'deficient' collective patterns of decision, refuse to recognise the possibility of the case, obsessively reiterated by Rousseau, in which the will of all is opposed to the general will.

The model which has been put forward in this paper results in an outcome in which no one chooses the short-cycle stream. In reality however a minority of roughly one student in seven does choose it, according to maximum estimates for France. This is not incompatible with the model, since the latter seeks merely to demonstrate the logic of a collective pattern of decision while leaving aside the problem of adjusting the model to particular data. If we were to modify the model slightly, by assuring, for example, a rise in the numbers of subsequent cohorts, unaccompanied by a corresponding shift in the structure of available outcomes, we would be able to construct a situation in which the short-cycle stream is dominated by the 'long-cycle stream' strategy – not for every hypothesis which each player is capable of devising concerning the behaviour of others, but for a substantial proportion of hypotheses. In this case, allowing for the addition of a few complementary hypotheses, we can construct a model in which some students choose the short-cycle stream. The chief conclusion arising from this variant is that the aggregation of individual decisions can only reduce the disadvantageous outcomes if one introduces a number of very particular hypotheses.

CHAPTER 5

1. W. G. Runciman, *Relative Deprivation and Social Justice* (Berkeley: University of California Press, 1966).

2. A. de Tocqueville, *L'Ancien Régime*, trans. M. W. Patterson (Oxford: Basil Blackwell, 1933) pp. 185–6.
   See also James C. Davis, 'Toward a Theory of Revolution', *American Sociological Review*, 1962, pp. 5–19.

3. E. Durkheim, *Suicide*, trans. John A. Spaulding and George Simpson, Edited with an introduction by George Simpson (London: Routledge and Kegan Paul, 1970) p. 287.

4. Samuel A. Stouffer, *The American Soldier*, vol. I (New York: Wiley, 1965); R. K. Merton, A. S. Rossi, 'Contributions to the theory of reference group behaviour', in R. K. Merton (ed.), *Social Theory and Social Structure* (Glencoe, Illinois: The Free Press, 1957). Along with Durkheim, Tocqueville and Stouffer, one could cite the Danish sociologist, Kaare Svalastoga, who, in *Prestige, Class and Society* (Copenhagen: Gyldendal, 1959), defends the notion of a curvilinear relation between social mobility and individual satisfaction.

5. E. Durkheim, *The Division of Labour in Society*, trans. George Simpson, (London: Collier-Macmillan, 1964) p. 235.

6. The hypothesis implicitly adopted here, according to which an expectation of a gain of a given value is seen as equivalent to an assured gain of the same value, is clearly a simplification, which is meant to place my argument in terms of the simplest examples. In fact, it is generally admitted (cf. Arrow, *Essays in the Theory of Risk-Bearing* (Amsterdam: North Holland, 1971) that a lottery where there is an expectation of gain X offers the individual an assured gain to the value of $X - h$ (where h is positive). It is obvious that, by supposing individuals to be indifferent to the risk involved ($h = 0$), one maximises the rate of frustration.

7. One thus supposes that the objective opportunities offered to individuals are weaker than in the previous case. Another way of simulating the deterioration in objective opportunities would consist in reducing the amount of gains offered by the society or by the organiser of the game.

8. There is a considerable difference between the two structures corresponding to my first two examples. In the first case, each player has a dominant strategy, and therefore has no need for any information about the behaviour of the other. In the second case, on the contrary, Ego's interest in each of his strategies depends on the number of others adopting the same strategy as him. If the group in question was a face to face one, the emergence of a structure of this sort would give rise to *negotiations* between the actors. In the case I am considering here, although, in order to simplify the analysis, I took it that $N = 20$, I presume that individuals cannot negotiate with each other. This is a characteristic situation, for instance, in educational behaviour or in behaviour affecting mobility.

9. One could well contest the 'solution' of the game in this example. The

maximin strategy could be defended. The 'solution' employed here relies on the following observation: if each player employs the strategy that consists in giving himself x chances out of N of participating in the game, in the case where a number of players greater than x entails a negative expectation for each, this combination of strategies results in an *equilibrium*. In fact, a player who would unilaterally abandon this strategy, in order to give himself a greater chance than x/N of participating in the game, would be punishing himself. What would happen if $x = 10$? Suppose that all the players decide to allow themselves $x/N = 1/2$ chances of participating in the game. Each person's expectation is then $1/2 [(2/10)4 + (8/10)(-1)] = 0$. In choosing unilaterally to participate in the game when he is certain, the player lowers his own expectations, since the sum between brackets becomes negative. On the other hand, if all the players allow themselves a probability p lower than $x/10$ of participating in the game, it is in the interests of each to choose a value higher than p. The solution here is naturally far more difficult to determine than in the previous example. But the important thing to note is that the difference in structure, with respect to the preceding example, must entail a corresponding fall in participation. If, like Rapoport, one admits that, when no dominant strategy exists for anyone, and multiple Pareto equilibria exist, 'rationality' consist necessarily in minimising risks, participation is zero. The 'solution' envisaged here corresponds to a less marked fall in participation.

10. I have applied this type of formalisation to problems in the politics of education (cf. Chapter VI below), thus giving rise to an interesting reaction on the part of Jon Elster, in 'Boudon, education and game theory', *Social Sciences Information*, 1976, XV, 4–5, pp. 733–40. Jon Elster asks if one may realistically apply game theory to situations of competition in which hundreds of thousands of students in a country like France are, *volens nolens*, placed. This strikes me as being a thoroughly interesting question, and one that calls for comments that I cannot give in full here. The value of N does, naturally, play a vital role here. Consider, for instance, the second of the examples analysed above. If N is large, a player who unilaterally allows himself a probability higher than x/N of participating in the game hardly affects his expectation of gain. Thus, the strategy of eliminating oneself is only justifiable when N is not too large. It is also the case when N is large but one is dealing with a latent group of the federative type (in Olson's sense). The overall number of pupils who finish is, for example, a group of this type. I have the impression that out of the 20 pupils involved, only 2 will have anything to gain from 'investing' in (for instance) a class preparing them for a *Grande École*, self-eliminating strategies will probably be seen to emerge. The fact that there are a significant number of last-stage classes does not alter this situation in any way. In other words, the conclusions that may be drawn from the preceding examples may, in certain circumstances, be taken also to refer to cases in which N is large.

11. Cf. Arrow, op. cit.

12. If we still presume that the players wish to maximise their expectation

of gain, and that they are indifferent to the structure of the lottery proposed.

13. In what follows I have only considered what I termed above *quarrelsome* frustration.

14. George C. Homans, 'Social behaviour as exchange', *The American Journal of Sociology*, 62, 1958, pp. 697–706. See also W. G. Runciman, 'Justice, Congruence and Professor Homans', *Archives Européennes de Sociologie*, VIII, 1, pp. 115–28, and Lucien Karpik, 'Trois concepts sociologiques: le projet de reference, le statut social et le bilan individuel', ibid., VI, 2.

15. Where the hypothesis is that the members of each of the two categories reckon that those of the other will behave as they do.

16. As regards this notion, see François Bourricaud, 'Contre le sociologisme une critique et des propositions', *Revue Française de Sociologie*, 1975, XVI, supplement, pp. 583–603.

17. Christopher Jencks, *Inequality, a Reassessment of the Effect of Family and Schooling in America* (New York: Basic Books, 1972); Richard A. Easterlin, 'Does Money buy Happiness?', *The Public Interest*, 30, pp. 3–10. See also Victor R. Fuchs, 'Redefining poverty and redistribution of income', *The Public Interest*, 8, pp. 88–95. This article perhaps dispenses once and for all with the doctrine according to which there exists a maximum tolerable dispersion of the distribution of goods.

18. David Easton, *A Systems Analysis of Political Life*, (New York and Amsterdam: Wiley, 1965).

CHAPTER 6

* J. Rawls, *A Theory of Justice* (Cambridge, Mass.: Harvard University Press, 1971). Article prepared for the one-day study session organised by the *Société Française de Science Politique* on recent trends in political theory, October 1974.

1. '... pondering upon the first and simplest operations of the human mind, I believe that I discern therein two principles anterior to reason, one of which makes us fervently concerned for our well-being and for the preservation of ourselves and the other inspires in us a natural repugnance towards seeing any sentient being, and principally our fellows, perish or suffer. From the converging and combining of these two principles, performed by our minds insofar as they possess this faculty, and without it being necessary to bring the principle of sociability into it, all the rules of natural law seem to me to proceed.'(*Discours sur l'origine et les fondements de l'inégalité parmi les hommes*, from Jean-Jacques Rousseau, *Œuvres complètes*, vol. 2 [Paris: Seuil, 1971] p. 210). The lexicographical ordering of the two principles clearly emerges from the following passage: '... so long as he [man] does not withstand the inner impulse of commiseration, he shall never do harm to another man, nor even to any sentient being except in the legitimate case when, his own preservation being at stake, he is bound to give preference to himself.' Ibid.

2. Ibid., p. 229.

3. While Rousseau was the first to see the importance of the illustrative

case which was subsequently to be called the 'prisoner's dilemma', he was not the first to identify it: in the *Peloponnesian War* Pericles endeavours to convince the Athenians to wage war again against the powerful Lacedemonian confederation by pointing out to them that, in the absence of an executive board, since each of the confederates feels chiefly concerned by his own particular interests, he will count on the others to serve the common interests (*Historiens grecs: Hérodote-Thucydide* [Paris: Gallimard, 1964] p. 783, coll. *La Pléiade*).

4. *Discours* . . ., op. cit., pp. 223–4.

5. B. Barry in *The Liberal Theory of Justice: A Critical Examination of the Principal Doctrines in 'A Theory of Justice' by John Rawls* (Oxford: Clarendon Press, 1973) has made a detailed analysis of Rawls's theory in which he reveals a series of contradictions which I shall naturally not take up again here.

See also, among the many commentaries to which Rawls's book has given rise: D. Rae, *Rawls' Indifference Principle and an Alternative* (Yale University, Department of Political Science) mimeograph; R. Nisbet, 'The Pursuit of Equality', *The Public Interest*, (Spring 1974) 102–20.

6. The definition of 'primary goods' within the framework of Rawls's theory raises considerable problems which are dealt with extremely well by B. Barry, op. cit.

7. Cf., for instance, A. Rapoport and M. Guyer, 'A Taxonomy of 2×2 Games', *General Systems*, 11, (1966) 203–14.

8. Some passages in *A Theory of Justice* are however concerned with the socialist societies. See in particular section 42 (Some remarks about economic systems).

9. Rawls does not explicitly state that industrial societies tend towards the ideal model described by *A Theory of Justice*. If my interpretation on this point is correct, the remarks which follow demonstrate that industrial societies are not in conformity with the model put forward by Rawls, whose effect is one of simplification. If it is false, and if Rawls' purpose was to offer industrial societies a plan for moral reform, my remarks take on another sense: they show that Rawls's model is Utopian, and, at all events, that industrial societies are incapable of approaching it without imposing virtue at the expense of liberties, thus contradicting the first principle of justice.

10. K. Davis and W. Moore, 'Some Principles of Stratification', *American Sociological Review*, 10 (Ap. 1945) 242–9; see also M. Tumin, *Social Stratification* (Englewood Cliffs, NJ: Prentice-Hall, 1967).

11. R. Boudon, *L'Inégalité des Chances* (Paris: Colin, 1973) Trans., *Education, Opportunity and Social Inequality* (New York: Wiley, 1974).

12. M. Olson, *The Logic of Collective Action* (Cambridge, Mass.: Harvard University Press, 1965).

13. R. Hardin, 'Collective Action as an Agreeable *n*-Prisoner's Dilemma', *Behavioral Science*, 16 (1971) 472–81.

14. J. L. Nicholson, 'The Distribution and Redistributions of Income in the United Kingdom' in D. Wedderburn (ed.), *Poverty, Inequality and Class Structure* (Cambridge: Cambridge University Press, 1974) pp. 71–91.

15. Refer for the case of the United States to L. Thurow, 'Education and Economic Inequality', *The Public Interest* (Summer 1972) 66–81.

16. This is Thurow's interpretation (ibid.) See also my article 'Educational Growth and Economic Equality', *Quality and Quantity*, 8 (1974) 1–10, which reaches the same conclusion by a different approach.
17. Cf. *L'Inégalité des Chances*, op. cit.
18. Of course the reader will once again have recognised the familiar figure of the prisoner's dilemma.

CHAPTER 7

1. Robert K. Merton, *Social Theory and Social Structure* (Glencoe, Ill.: Free Press, 1949; new ed, 1957) pp. 50–5.
2. Thomas Kuhn, *The Structure of Scientific Revolution* (Chicago, Ill.: Chicago University Press, 1962).
3. Thomas Kuhn, ibid. p. 10.
4. This definition, which becomes clearer as the text proceeds, is more exact than the one that I used in 'Théories, théorie et Théorie' in *La crise de la sociologie* (Paris and Geneva: Droz, 1971) pp. 159–204. Further on I do, for instance, define a paradigm as *determinist* when the *language* is one that uses only propositions of the type 'if *A* (prior to *B*) then *B*'. Similarly I call a paradigm *interactionist* when the *language* includes statements made concerning the subject's representation of states of affairs considered by him to be the possible result of his acts. In this sense the notion of paradigm recapitulates the more classic notion of *metalanguage*.
5. I take attitudes to be included within the concept of behaviour.
6. Andrew Henry and James Short, *Suicide and Homicide* (Glencoe, Ill.: Free Press, 1954).
7. There are, in other words, four possibilities: '*A* is the necessary condition for *B*', '*A* is the sufficient condition for *B*', '*A* is the necessary and sufficient condition for *B*' – these are the three formulations possible within strict determinism. Where it is a question of probabilistic determinism it is impossible to associate any of the three preceding senses with the proposition 'if *A* then more frequently *B*'. *Prior* is to be understood in the temporal or logical sense.
8. Cf., for example, R. G. Allen, *Mathematical Economics* (London: Macmillan, 1956).
9. Talcott Parsons, 'Social Structure and Dynamic Process: The Case of Modern Medical Practice', in *The Social System* (Glencoe, Ill.: Free Press, [1951] 428–79).
10 Each of these terms has its disadvantages. The term 'composition' is not in general use and, as employed here, the term 'aggregation' represents a divergence from the term as it tends to be used in normative economy.
11. Gordon Tullock, 'Does Punishment Deter Crime?', *The Public Interest* (Summer 1974) 103–11. Cf. also Gary Becker and William Landes, *Essays in Economics of Crime and Punishment* (New York: Columbia University Press, 1975); Frederic Jenny, *La théorie économique du crime: une revue de la littérature*, roneo, Apr. 1976.
12. With regard to these appellations the reader should note that the

paradigms used by the eponymous authors cannot properly be contained within just one of my categories. It is clearly easy enough to find in Marx's historical writings paradigms quite close to those of Tocqueville.

13. Sir Karl Popper would seem to have inadvertently omitted this interpretation from what was, in other respects, an extremely illuminating article, 'What is Dialectic?', in *Conjectures and Refutations: The Growth of Scientific Knowledge*, 3rd edn (London: Routledge & Kegan Paul, 1969).

14. I do of course interpret 'utilitarian' objectives in Bentham's terms (an axiomatic in which the calculating individual seeks to realise his own preferences as best he can) rather than in Sidgwick's (the quest for the maximisation of collective well-being). On Marx's utilitarianism cf. Talcott Parsons, 'Social Classes and Class Conflict in the Light of Recent Sociological Theory', in *Essays in Sociological Theory* (New York: Free Press 1949; revised edn 1964) pp. 323–35. See also Michel Henry, *Marx* (Paris: Gallimard, 1976) chapt. 1; Jon Elster, *The Logic of the Social Sciences* (forthcoming); and Joachim Israel, 'The Principle of Methodological Individualism and Marxian Epistemology', *Acta Sociologica*, XIV, 3, (1971) 145–50.

15. Bernard de Mandeville, *The Fable of the Bees*, edited, with an introduction, P. Harth (London, 1976); Karl Marx *Capital*, I, chapt. 14, sect. 4, note 33 (the reference is to Mandeville, [1976] p. 475).

16. It is a simple matter to demonstrate that the hunting party described by Rousseau at the beginning of the second part of the *Discourse on Inequality*, just at a critical stage in his argument, can be considered a classic game-theory configuration, i.e., a defective-equilibrium structure.

17. Kingsley Davis and Wilbert Moore, 'Some Principles of Stratification', *American Sociological Review*, X, 2, (1945) 242–9; Melvin Tumin, 'Some Principles of Stratification: Critical Analysis', *American Sociological Review*, XVIII (Aug. 1953) 387–93.

18. These rewards would on occasion include symbolic elements.

19. Thomas Schelling, 'On the Ecology of Micro-Motives', *The Public Interest*, XXV (Autumn 1971) 61–98; Thomas Schelling, 'Dynamic Models of Segregation', *Journal of Mathematical Sociology*, I, 2 (July 1971) 143–86; Jacques Lautman, *Essai sur les fortunes quelconques, le logement et la spéculation immobilière, Doctorat d'État* thesis (forthcoming).

20. Mancur Olson, *The Logic of Collective Action* (Cambridge, Mass.: Harvard University Press, 1965).

21. Cf. Daniel Bell, *The Coming of the Post-Industrial Society* (New York: Basic Books, 1973), who gives the following global unionisation rates: United States, 22.9 per cent in 1947, 25.2 per cent in 1956, 23 per cent in 1968, 22.6 per cent in 1970; France, 20 per cent in 1971; Holland, 40 per cent; Germany, 40 per cent; United Kingdom, 45 per cent; Belgium, Luxembourg, 65 per cent. The historical importance of the 'closed shop' in Great Britain, the existence of the 'pillars' in Holland, the political distances that prevail in Germany, and the plethora of individual goods that the unions are able to provide are all factors that account for the relatively high unionisation rates in these countries.

22. I am talking in the first example of collective goods, pure and simple.
23. Ralf Dahrendorf, *Class and Class Conflict in Industrial Society* (London: Routledge & Kegan Paul, 1963).
24. Using a modified version of the kind of models employed in Raymond Bouden, Philippe Cibois, Janina Lagneau, 'L'Enseignement supérieur court et pièges de l'action collective', in *Revue Française de Sociologie*, XVI, 2, 159–88, or here also, chapt. 4.
25. It would, incidentally, be of interest to incorporate in the model a feedback system analogous to that found, for example, in the spider's-web theorem, and then to consider the effects of the non-fulfilment of expectations.
26. Cf. for instance (amongst many others), Alain· Gras (ed.), *Sociologie de l'éducation* (Paris: Larousse, 1974).
27. Alexis de Tocqueville, *The Ancien Régime and the French Revolution*, transl. S. Gilbert, introd. H. Brogan (London: Fontana, 1971).
28. Ibid.
29. In raising objections against utilitarianism (in the wide sense), Parsons emphasises the not-altogether clear or proven notion of a *randomness of ends*. The two configurations that are distinguished do not correspond to the couple random ends/non-random ends but to the couple ends = independent variables/ends = dependent variables. In *Human Action* (New Haven, Conn.: Yale University Press 1966) p. 124, Ludwig von Mise stresses that classical economics treats preferences as given *a priori*: the convexity of indifference curves is not derived from observation but is deduced analytically from the notion of preference. It is hard to understand why Parsons applies the concept of *randomness* to situations in which preferences, since they can be determined analytically, assume the status of independent variables. It is still harder to understand why the sociological domain should be restricted, as it is in *The Structure of Social Action*, to situations in which preferences have the status of independent variables.
30. Robert K. Merton, 'The Unanticipated Consequences of Purposive Social Action', *American Sociological Review*, (1936) I, 894–904; and *Social Theory . . .*, op. cit., pp. 421–36.
31. Just as it is with Bossuet. It seems to me that Bossuet's case is nevertheless to be distinguished from that of Mandeville and Marx, for whilst the Mertonian notion of unexpected consequences is clearly present in Bossuet, that of effects of composition is not to be found.
32. I am using here the excellent translation of Mendras, op. cit.
33. Robert K. Merton, *Social Theory and Social Structure*, op. cit. (1957) p. 424.
34. Ibid.,p. 435.
35. Louis Lévy-Garboua, 'Les Demandes de l'étudiant ou les contradictions de l'université de masse', in *Revue Française de Sociologie*, XVII, 1, Jan.–Mar. 1976, 53–80.
36. Raymond Boudon and François Bourricaud, *La position sociale des intellectuels en France* (provisional title, in preparation).
37. Lewis Coser, 'The Intellectual as Celebrity', *Dissent*, 1 (1973) 45–6.
38. Edward Shils, 'The Intellectual and the Powers', in P. Rieff (ed.), *On Intellectuals* (New York: Doubleday, 1969).

39. James Buchanan, *The Limits of Liberty*, (Chicago, Ill.: University of Chicago Press, 1975).

40. It is nevertheless worth noting that a system of interaction characterised by a state-of-nature context does not imply the absence of roles. They are merely irrelevant for the purposes of the analysis. Thus a simple commercial exchange presupposes a distinction between the roles of seller and buyer, a definition of norms and expectations corresponding to these roles etc. But when the functioning of the market as a whole is analysed, this role structure is normally ignored.

41. With respect to these notions, see Robert K. Merton, *A Social Theory* . . ., op. cit., and Lewis Coser (ed.), *The Idea of Social Structure* (New York: Harcourt, Brace, 1975). Among the articles included in this volume Arthurt Stinchcombe's 'Merton's Theory of Social Structure' is particularly worth consulting. See also the very interesting collection edited by Peter Blau, *Approaches to the Study of Social Structure* (London: Open Books, 1976).

42. Peter Blau, *Structural Constraints of Status Complements*, and Lewis Coser, *The Idea of Social Structure*, op. cit.

43. Seymour Martin Lipset, 'Academia and Politics in America' in T. Nossiter (ed.), *Imagination and Precision in the Social Sciences* (London: Faber, 1972).

44. Cf. the above, chapt. 3.

45. Ezra Suleiman, *Politics, Power and Bureaucracy in France*, (Princeton, N.J.: Princeton University Press, 1974).

46. As is apparent, this kind of paradigm is close to the sort of analyses that one may find in novels. See, for instance, the work of Proust.

47. There is a helpful presentation and criticism of Bernstein's writings in an article by Mohamed Cherkaoui, 'Structures de classes, performances linguistique et types de socialisation', in *Revue Française de Sociologie*, XV, 4, 1974, 585–99.

48. *Education, Opportunity and Social Inequality: Changing Prospects in Western Society* (New York: Wiley Series in Social Research, Wiley, 1974).

49. See Alain Girard's articles in *Population et L'Enseignement* (Paris: PUF, 1970).

50. We say that there is interaction in the statistical sense when the effect of one variable on another depends on a third variable.

51. The distinction between interest and preference is not always explicitly drawn. In this text, unless I state otherwise, interest is always taken to mean preference. Jean Izoulet, in a text that has, unjustly, been forgotten (*La Cité Moderne*, Paris, Alcan, 1895) puts the problem of the relation between interest and preference very well. A significant case of a discordance occurring between the two notions would be that in which the subject acted according to his own preferences through ignorance of the objective relations between means and ends. The amateur mountaineer who acts against his own interest by ignoring the old adage ('it takes six hours to get to the top if you walk fast and four hours if you go slowly') fits into this category. The ambiguous relation between interest and preference that crops up in the case of collective benefits is another important example of this: scientific research may

well be in each person's interest but there are few persons who would willingly agree to finance it. Izoulet perceives quite clearly that there are circumstances in which individuals act against their own interests, not because of a false representation of the means-ends relation but in, so to speak, a rational and reasonable manner. In modern terms one could say that defective equilibrium structures explain why in some cases individuals, in following their preferences, act against their own interests.

52. See, in relation to this subject, Herbert Simon, 'On the Definition of the Causal Relation', in *Models of Man* (New York: Wiley, 1957).

53. See, in relation to this, Lewis Coser's analysis, 'Violence as a Mechanism for Conflict Resolution', in *Continuities in the Study of Social Conflict* (New York: Free Press, 1967) pp. 96–100, on machine-breaking in the anarcho-syndicalist era. This phenomenon is often interpreted, in a Culturalist manner, as a reaction on the part of the workers to the advance of mechanisation and its supposed effects on the work situation. Coser advances a hypothesis that is, in my opinion, far more interesting: the breaking up of the machines was in fact a strategic manoeuvre intended to strengthen the workers' bargaining power.

54. Ezra Suleiman, op. cit.

55. See, in relation to this, the critique that François Bourricaud, in his article 'Contre le sociologisme, une critique et des propositions', *Revue Française de Sociologie*, XVI, supplement (1975) 583–603, makes of hyperculturalist and hyperfunctionalist tendencies in contemporary French sociology. It is from François Bourricaud that I borrow the expression 'hyperfunctionalism'. It is worth comparing this article with a classical critique of functionalism's excesses: Dennis Wrong, 'The Oversocialised Conception of Man in Modern Society', *American Sociological Review*, XXVI, 2 Apr. 1961, 183–93. Bourricaud's critiques may also be compared with those that Alain Touraine directs at what I here call totalitarian realism (cf. *La Société Invisible*, Paris, on 'Lunaires appareils idéologiques d'État', pp. 217–21) and hyperfunctionalism (ibid., p. 160).

56. Jean Piaget, *Études sociologiques* (Geneva: Droz, 1955) p. 145.

57. The reader will note that the fact that sanctions are never carried out immediately but are always deferred for *shorter or longer periods*, allows the capitalist a margin of freedom. This makes the notion of forced choice seem a little excessive, even in this case. On the other hand the capitalist has many different ways of boosting his productivity.

58. Raymond Boudon, 'Les limites des schémas déterministes dans l'explication sociologique', in Giovanni Busino (ed.), *Les Sciences sociales avec et après Jean Piaget* (Geneva: Droz, 1976) pp. 417–35).

59. Leon Brunschvicg, *Les progrès de la conscience dans la philosophie occidentale* (Paris: PUF, 1927; 2nd edn., 1953).

60. Robert Nisbet, *The Sociological Tradition* (New York: Basic Books, 1966).

61. I would want to refer here to the interesting analyses of Jack Douglas (in *The Social Meanings of Suicide*, Princeton, N.J.: Princeton University Press, 1967) and Jean Baechler, *Les Suicides*, (Paris: Calmann-Levy, 1975) on the phenomenon of suicide. Baechler tries to explain it within the limited

theoretical compass of a rationalist psychology. Although his project raises problems, it does represent an undeniable innovation. With respect to the influence of physics as a scientific model it is worth citing the bearing that Henry Adams's works have on this: at the beginning of the twentieth Century he sought to apply what he called 'the rule of Phases' to history (the duration of each intellectual period is the square root of the duration of the previous phase). One could also cite *La Mécanique Sociale* (Paris: Haret, 1910). The influence of the physicist paradigm is visible, of course, and much less extreme, in Durkheim and in Quetelet also.

62. Alfred Schutz, *Collected Papers: II. Studies in Social Theory*, A. Brodersen (ed.) (The Hague: Martinus Nijhoff, 1964). See also Georg Henrik von Wright, *Explanation and Understanding* (London: Routledge & Kegan Paul, 1971). Schutz's *Weil-Motive* raise, implicitly, the problem of the use in sociology of concepts drawn from psychoanalysis. The *unconscious* is a useful concept when there is a discordance between the *Wozu* and the *Weil*. I think that dogmatism would, at this point, be inopportune. One can however say that sociology, and still more macro-sociology, are generally concerned with phenomena that are the result of the composition of *banal* social behaviours, that is, behaviours in which *Weil* and *Wozu* coincide. On the other hand when the sociologist's interests more closely concern the individual, psychoanalytic schema will naturally occur. Those sociologists who have been most concerned with social psychology (for instance Lazarsfeld in his studies in political sociology, Zeisel in his works on consumption patterns) have been deeply committed to exploiting the resources of psychoanalysis. See Paul Lazarsfeld, 'An Episode in the History of Social Research: A Memoir', in *Perspectives in American History*, II, 1868, pp. 270–337; and Hans Zeisel 'L'École viennoise des recherches de motivations', *Revue Francaise de Sociologie*, IX, 1, (1968) 3–12. It would perhaps be apt to say that a book like Lazarsfeld's *Voting* is a sociology of the *Weil* that hesitates between explaining the *Weil-motive* in terms of the *Id* and in terms of the *Wozu*. I cannot do more than raise the problem in the context of this article.

63. Assar Lindbeck, *The Political Economy of the New Left: An Outsider's View*, foreword by P. A. Samuelson, 2nd. edn. (New York: Harper and Row, 1971).

Index